Computer Skills and Concepts: A Mastery Approach

Sixth Edition

By

Robert V. Price, Ph.D.

Steven M. Crooks, Ph.D.

Jongpil Cheon, Ed.D.

ISBN 978-1-60904-108-3

Published by

Stipes Publishing L.L.C.
www.stipes.com

Information for Users

To complete the exercises included in this book you will need a personal computer and the following software:

- *Microsoft Windows 7*
- *Microsoft Word 2010*
- *Microsoft Excel 2010*
- *Microsoft PowerPoint 2010*
- *Microsoft Publisher 2010 (optional)*
- *Adobe Photoshop CS 5* (trial version available for free download)
- A web browser such as *Internet Explorer 9*
- Access to tool and educational software (for software reviews)

Do not purchase used copies of this book. This book is revised annually.

Information for Instructors

This book is available from Stipes Publishing L.L.C. at the address below. Examination copies are available to instructors at no charge. Practice files that accompany some of the application assignments and a test bank are available to adopters from the publisher's web site at no charge. For more information on this book or to order review copies, contact Stipes Publishing L.L.C.

Stipes Publishing L.L.C.
202-204 W. University Ave.
Champaign, IL 61820

Phone: 217/356-8391
E-mail: stipes01@sbcglobal.net
Web site: www.stipes.com/price

Notes on Software Covered In This Book

The instructions, practice exercises, and application assignments which deal with *Microsoft Office* applications for this edition are written for *Office 2010*. Earlier versions of *Office*, such as *Office 2003* and *Office 2007* are quite different from *Office 2010* and users of these earlier versions of *Office* will be unable to follow the step by step instructions provided in this book. The *Windows 7* operating system is covered in detail.

Adobe Photoshop CS 5 or later is needed to complete Module 8. Users should not attempt to substitute another image editing program to use for the Module 10 exercises. Users who do not have *Adobe Photoshop* may obtain a 30 trial version of *Photoshop* as a free download.

Instructions for use of *Microsoft Publisher* are included in Module 5. However, it's use is optional. Users may use another desktop publishing program, including *MS Word,* to complete the exercises dealing with desktop publishing.

Introduction

For many college students, the computer age has always existed. However, for those who are over the age of thirty, the computer age seems to have advanced so suddenly that many have been caught unaware.

The earliest computers were introduced in the 1940s, but computers did not become generally available until the introduction of the personal computer in 1976. Advances in computing technology since then have been staggering. Consider this analogy: If automobile transportation had advanced at the same rate as the computer industry for the past 40 years, cars would now travel at a speed of four billion miles per hour, and a person could travel round trip from San Francisco to New York in 7 seconds, at a cost of less than 25 cents.

As a society, we have entered a technological era where information is the primary power source. The key to accessing this information is the computer. Computer education programs have been incorporated into the curriculum of most educational programs. Each year, more people become comfortable with using computers, while those who are not computer literate are "left in the dust." Those who are technologically literate achieve higher personal productivity and move ahead in their careers because of their technical skills.

This book is designed for those with limited computer experience. The material covered in this book has been designed to help you become more familiar with the world of computers and related technology. You will learn about computers, their history, and applications. More importantly, you will learn how to use computers. Specific applications include word processing, database management, electronic spreadsheets, desktop publishing, computer graphics, tool software, digital imaging, and use of the World Wide Web. After completing this material, you should have a working knowledge of each of these applications.

About This Book

The approach employed in this book is best suited for a mastery approach to learning. The book is organized into modules (or units of instruction). Each module is designed to be independent of the others and is self-guided for individualized instruction. Assignments are not always quick and easy. If learners are to master the use of the computer, they must read each module carefully and work through each hands-on exercise with the computer. Application and practice are essential to the development of any skill. Learning to use computers comes only through practice, and continued practice will bring increased confidence in, and mastery of, using the technology of the personal computer.

Each module involves both a reading assignment, practice exercises, and several hands-on computer application assignments. The focus of the book is on practical skills.

The **mastery approach** applied in this book is different from what students commonly experience in traditional classes. In many classes, the learner attends lectures, participates in discussions, and completes course projects and exams based on material presented in a textbook and in lectures. Grades are determined by percentage grades earned on exams and assignments. The mastery approach is different. No grades are given on assignments and exams. Instead, these assignments are judged by the instructor to determine whether the student has mastered the content. To master each module, the student must do two things: complete the application assignments correctly, and complete a module exam with at least 80% accuracy.

The 11 modules covered in this book are:

Module 1	Introduction to Computers & Technology
Module 2	Windows7 and Microsoft Office 2010
Module 3	Word Processing
Module 4	Advanced Word Processing & Desktop Publishing
Module 5	Spreadsheets
Module 6	Presentation Graphics
Module 7	Database Management
Module 8	Computer Graphics
Module 9	The Internet
Module 10	Productivity Software
Module 11	Computer Application Skills

This book includes forms and software questionnaires that may be completed by students and removed from this book to submit to instructors as application exercises are completed. Therefore, this book should not be resold or purchased used.

Module Format

The format for each of the nine modules is described below.

Introduction. The module introduction is intended to provide a general overview of the subject of the module and the material and assignments presented in it.

Module Objectives. Objectives are stated in terms of measurable student outcomes. Learners can use the objectives to determine their mastery of the module. Instructors can see clearly what learners are expected to know or to be able to do after completing each module. Use the module objectives in the following ways:

- As a preview, to guide you in your learning; and
- As a review, to verify that you understand the material before submitting completed assignments and taking the module exams.

Materials Needed. This is an explanation of the specific materials including hardware, software, and other materials needed in order to properly complete the module.

How to Proceed. Step-by-step instructions are provided to explain exactly what learners are to do. Taking shortcuts is not recommended. Reading material has been designed to build an understanding of content and prepare you to master the module objectives by completing the application exercises and mastering the module test. Some of the material is technical. Speed reading and skimming is not recommended. Attempting to "shortcut the process" will most likely result in an incomplete understanding of the material and may hinder completion of the assignments and mastery of the module tests.

Reading Material. Each module includes both conceptual information and specific instructions on using software to complete tasks. Key terms are included and appear in boldface type. Illustrations have been included to help clarify instructions. Read this material carefully.

Key Terms. Key terms are listed near the end of each module. These terms are printed in boldface print within the module and are defined and described in context. Users should review these carefully after reading the module. Review any terms that are not clearly understood.

Review Questions. Each module includes a set of *Module Review Questions*. These are short multiple choice quizzes which review the important concepts covered in the module. A set of exam questions covering each module is also available from the publisher for instructors. These exam questions are different from the *Module Review Questions* although some review questions may be included in the module exam.

Computer Application Assignments. These assignments are hands-on exercises designed to help students apply the skills covered in the module. Describing computer skills is of little value if these skills are not put to immediate, practical use. Learners should complete each of these assignments carefully, paying close attention to the requirements of each assignment. Each assignment will result in documents that are to be submitted in to the course instructor.

Typographic Conventions Used

This book uses several different typefaces and symbols as follows:

Italic: Titles - Such as titles of software programs, menus, books, etc.

Boldface: Key terms

Underlining: Important points or instructions

These conventions may be used in combination.

Menu commands are written using the following style: **File>Save As**

The first menu name indicates the main menu title (in the example "File" on the menu bar at the top of the screen). The ">" symbol is a separator between subsequent menu items. The sequence above means to choose the *Save As* menu item from the *File* menu.

Table of Contents

MODULE 1

Introduction to Computers and Technology

Introduction to Computers

This first module provides an introduction to the world of computers and acquaints the user with **Personal Computers (PCs)**.

This module will help you learn some basic computing concepts and skills. By working through Module 1 step by step, you will gain new knowledge that will give you the confidence needed to complete the assignments that lie ahead in later modules.

Module Objectives

When you have completed this module, you should be able to:

- Describe, in general terms, society's attitudes toward computers and technology;
- Identify major developments and personalities in the history of computers;
- Describe the major uses of computers;
- Identify the components of a computer system and their functions.

Materials Needed to Complete This Module

- This book
- A Personal Computer, preferably with *Windows 7* Operating System

How to Proceed

1. Read this module. Read carefully as parts of this module are detailed and somewhat technical.
2. Review the *Key Terms* at the end of the module.
3. Complete the *Module 1 Review Questions* at the end of the module. Check your answers at the end of the book.
4. Complete the *Module 1 Applications Assignment.* This is a 3-part assignment which involves answering 3 short essay questions. Specific instructions for the assignments are provided later in this module.
5. Submit your answers to the *Module 1 Review Questions* and the Module 1 assignments to your instructor. Assignments may be submitted either electronically or by removing the exercises from this book to hand in. Your instructor will tell you how to submit your assignments.
6. Take the Module 1 Test.

Introduction to Computers & Technology

1.1 Introduction to Computers & Technology

Computers are machines that can expand and facilitate human abilities. The complexity of computers, their potential to transform society, and their ability to model human intelligence (**AI or artificial intelligence**) are part of our contemporary mythologies. Computers are sometimes portrayed in movies as overpowering and evil machines. The theme of the computer as a dangerous machine has had an impact on our attitudes. Though less true today, there is a significant segment of society that still fears the computer. The trend for computers to become increasingly "user friendly" has done much to reduce computer anxiety. HAL, the huge, unpredictable, and ultimately hostile computer in the movies *2001* and *2010*, has been largely replaced in the movies with images like *R2D2* and *Commander Data* of the *Starship Enterprise*. Now children grow up with computer-based video games that serve as a natural bridge to using computers. Children generally regard computers and robots as friendly and fun. It is no wonder that children approach computers with less apprehension and hesitation than do many adults.

The popularity of Lara Croft, the animated persona of the computer and Playstation game Tomb Raider, became a cinematic character played by Angelina Jolie. Tomb Raider © and ™ 1996 Core Design Limited. © and published 1996 Edios Interactive Limited. Tomb Raider movie © and ™ 2001 Paramount Studio. All Rights Reserved.

In addition to the anxiety that computers create in some people, another problem is how society views those who understand computers from the "inside out." In primitive societies, ordinary tribal members were not permitted to deal directly with the gods, as that was the role of the shaman or holy man (or woman). Similarly, prior to the 1970s only the "experts" could communicate with the giant computers. Behind locked doors in glass-walled rooms, computers were considered mysterious and complicated by most of the population. People were told that computers were like high-voltage power lines and radioactive materials, and were not to be tampered with by everyday "tribal" members. It would appear that aspects of the "shaman" model are still with us today. Those who do not understand computers remain at the mercy of the technologists, those who have the education and experience to understand how to use and to maintain computers and computer networks. This social segregation can be seen in advertisements directed toward information technology (IT) professionals: Your boss says, "I approved some great new software." Translation: "I approved software that's incompatible with our systems." (From an advertisement in *PC World*, July 2001). Several decades ago it was a company's accountants who would convey the security and importance of their work by saying, "If the company closes its doors for good, we will be the ones to turn the key." Today, it is the company's information technology professionals who can make that claim.

1.2 Computer Literacy Is Essential

The computer revolution has brought about a demand for computer education. Early computer literacy classes often dealt with programming, operating systems, and technical terms. Such courses did little to help the average person to understand and to use computers productively. Computer programming and computer systems architecture are still important areas of development in computer technology; however, educators today agree that it is more important to teach users to use computers as tools that can improve their personal productivity.

1.3 Computers in Everyday Life

Computers affect almost every aspect of modern society. Today, computers do much more than simply compute. A computer interface is used when we access **ATMs (Automated Teller Machines),** make phone calls (with a smartphone), and read books (e-readers). Automobiles are designed, manufactured, and even operated with the aid of computers. Computer-aided design and **computer-aided manufacturing (CAD-CAM)** have revolutionized the way most things are designed and made. Computer-controlled simulations are used to train pilots to fly modern jetliners. You can go to movie theaters to see computer-generated, digitally animated feature films portraying computer game heroines and heroes.

You can access your bank's computers to inquire about an account from anywhere in the world. You can purchase merchandise using a credit card over the Internet from a store in Dallas, Texas or Beirut, Lebanon. Computers complete transactions quickly and accurately, and with more security than sending credit card information to sellers by phone or in the mail. In reality, the computer has become such a necessity in many businesses that loss of electrical power for the computers can cause business operations to shut down temporarily, resulting in the loss of millions of dollars. Schools, businesses, and all levels of government use computers to record, store, and process data. **Computer-aided instruction** (**CAI**) and **Web-based instruction (WBI)** help provide an alternative to brick-and- mortar classrooms and face-to-face teaching.

Medical science is another example of a field that is increasingly reliant on computers and computer-controlled equipment. Examples include the delivery and computer-assisted interpretations of x-rays, **computed tomography (CT scans)**, and heart monitors as well as other diagnostic and life saving systems. Physicians have been experimenting with computer-controlled robotic surgeries in which the physician is in one part of the United States and the patient is in another. Medical students practice surgical techniques on **virtual** or computer-generated patients. The use of computers in tumor excisions, facial reconstruction, and brain surgery has revolutionized the medical field and created many new and exciting employment opportunities for individuals involved with computer use.

Meteorologists use computers to record daily statistics and track storm systems for weather prediction. The combination of computers and Doppler radar systems have allowed the use of a computer-generated model of a cloud system on TV to enhance warning capabilities for viewers. This use of computers can be credited with saving hundreds of lives by warning people about approaching severe weather in time to take shelter. Long range weather predictions have been more accurate and understandable by weather models routinely run on computers.

Artists use computers to create music, video special effects, and animation. The movie industry has become a notable user of **computer-generated graphics**. Movies such as *Avatar, Ice Age, Toy Story,* and *Shrek* are a few examples.

Newspapers, magazines, and books use computers to compose and publish their products. This text was created using a **desktop publishing** computer application known as *Adobe InDesign*®. Book publishers are moving to print-on-demand where you select a title and it is printed and bound in a few minutes. Other publishers and authors use **e-books** that can be read with **e-book readers** (i.e., portable electronic devices that display digital text). We are now at the point where lifelong learners can access just about any book, or view just about any multimedia presentation, without setting foot in a brick-and-mortar bookstore or library.

Home computers have been transformed into multimedia centers. Home computers are now used for e-mail, Internet access, MP3 audio files, MPEG, and streaming video. They have also been transformed into home entertainment centers that run our digital TVs, and stream music and movies from the Internet or store them to be played later. The same computer can also oversee such household duties as restocking groceries, controlling thermostats, and monitoring home security. Virtually every appliance in the home can now be connected and customized to the individual family's need. Customized programming of these computers entails little more than telling the computer (by means of voice recognition software) what you want and when you need it done.

The rapid exponential expansion of information creates a need to separate useful information from the volumes of information available, some of the information being good and some erroneous (for example, intentionally false or uninformed). The principle of separating the vital few from the trivial many is known as the **Pareto Principle**. Advances in artificial intelligence (AI) have already produced **intelligent agent (IA)** software and expert system software that is used to help physicians make diagnoses. Autonomous intelligent agents can act as financial portfolio managers that operate independently, making buy-and-sell decisions without human intervention. Futurists such as **Peter Cochran** have predicted that people will some day wear computers to help augment memory. Cochran in his book *Tips for Time Travelers* questions, "Why do people resist the idea of silicon (chip) augmentation, but place their names on waiting lists to get silicone (implant) augmentation?"

It is clear that computer technology is advancing faster than people ever dreamed possible only a few years ago. Based on the accomplishments seen in the last two decades, the future uses of computers in our lives are nearly unimaginable.

1.4 How Computers Work

All computers, large and small, have the same basic components and operate using the same basic principles. The term computer system is used throughout this book and the tests. The five **components of a computer system** are:

1. People
2. Data (or information)
3. Hardware
4. Software
5. Procedures (or protocols)

- *People.* A business professor at a leading university once made the observation that the computer-controlled, automated factory of the future will have two employees, a dog and a man. The man's job is to feed the dog. The dog's job is to keep the man from touching the machinery. In reality, computers exist for people. Ideally, computers should release people from mundane tasks as well as expand the human experience so that people can become more creative stewards of the environment and caregivers for each other.
- *Data.* Data are the raw facts that computers process into understandable information. At least that is the way it is supposed to work. In reality, the human operator has to be vigilant about the quality of data. The "old" saying, "Garbage in, garbage out," is as true today as it was when coined several decades ago.
- *Hardware.* **Hardware** is the physical equipment that consists of the computer and its attachments or peripherals such as monitor, printer, keyboard, and other I/O (input/output) devices.
- *Software.* **Software** is the collective name given to computer programs. **Programs** are the instructional codes that tell the hardware what to do. These can be written in a variety of programming languages such as machine language, assembly language, high level languages such as COBOL, or object-oriented languages like C++ or Java. Data is the raw material acted upon by the program. Data may be names and addresses; sales figures; experimental results; scientific formulas; or graphic, video, and audio files.

  Application software are programs containing instructions that direct computer hardware to do something that helps the users. Examples of application software are *Microsoft Word* and *Microsoft Excel.*

  Another software category is **operating systems (OS) software**. These software programs function between computer hardware and application programs running on the computer. An operating system is the software that controls the computer from startup, and controls the computer's operation while it is running. Examples are *Linux; Microsoft Windows*, and *Apple Mac OS* (See Figure 1.1 and 1.2).
- *Procedures.* Procedures or **protocols** are the instructions that tell computer users what to do and how to do it. This includes which programs need to be run, what data should be entered, and what to do with the output.

Computer hardware components include **input devices** that receive data and instructions, and transform them into a form the computer can understand. **Output devices** transform electronic signals from the computer into a form that people can understand. The **CPU** or **central processing unit** is the center of computing activity.

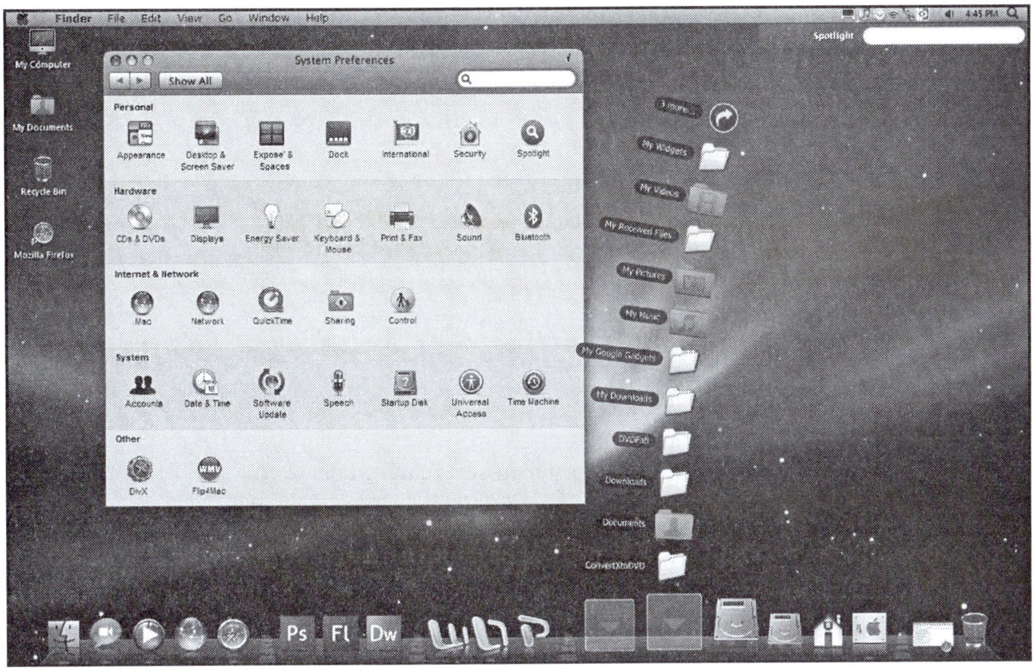

Figure 1.1: Mac OS X

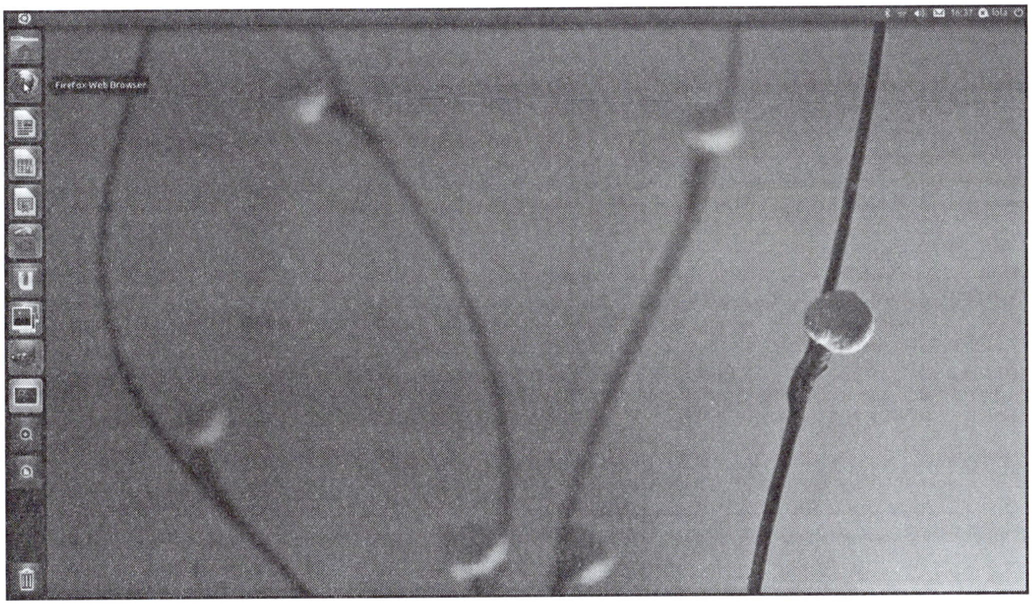

Figure 1.2: Ubuntu Linux

The CPU is where data is manipulated, arithmetic calculations are done, and comparisons are made. The CPU interacts with the main memory or **primary storage**. **Secondary storage** is external to the CPU and stores data and programs that are not in use. Communication devices provide for data flow to and from computer networks external to the computer. Computer components are connected by buses or channels (shared data paths) that move data and instructions in electronic form.

1.5 More About the CPU

Because of its size, another name for the CPU is the microprocessor. Processor functions of the CPU are carried out by the control unit and arithmetic-logic unit (ALU).

The **control unit** coordinates the action of the other hardware components, and it interprets instructions contained in computer programs and carries them out. It also controls input and output devices as well as data transfer to and from memory. The control unit does not manipulate data, it simply controls the data flow, processing only one instruction at a time (but at a speed of millions of instructions per second).

The **arithmetic-logic unit** (ALU) contains the circuits that execute or implement each math or logic instruction, causing data in the form of electrical signals to flow through the computer's electronic circuitry. Math instructions processed by the ALU include addition, subtraction, multiplication, and division, and logic instructions, including equal to, greater than, or less than comparisons.

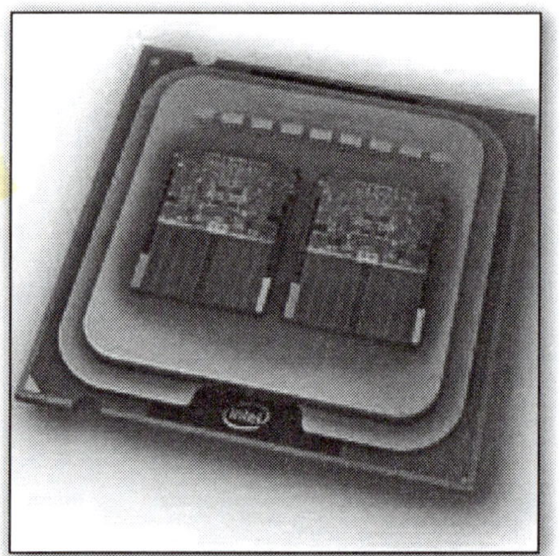

The CPU or microprocessor is small, but it is the center of computing activity. Pictured is a dual core processor that has two separate cores on the same die. Each core handles incoming data string simultaneously to improve efficiency.

1.6 Microprocessors and Moore's Law

Gordon Moore is one of the founders of *Intel Corporation*, a leading manufacturer of microprocessors. Early in the development of microprocessors, Moore "predicted" that computer processing power (indicated by the number of transistors that a silicon chip can hold) will double approximately every 2 years. This has become known as **Moore's Law** and has been surprisingly accurate. The progress in microprocessor development is shown in the graph, Figure 1.3. There are, however, limits to technology based on silicon, and an upper limit to Moore's Law appears to be in sight. Even so, some futurist believe that Moore's Law will hold true until long after the year 2020.

1.7 Storage

Computers need a place to store data and instructions while data is being processed. Similar to our own "memory" we can talk about "computer memory" as the place where computer-generated data is stored. Primary storage or main memory has three functions:

1. Storing input data until transferred to the ALU for processing;
2. Holding processed data until transferred to an output device; and
3. Holding program instructions received from input devices or Secondary storage.

There are two main types of primary memory available in our computers: (1) the registers, which are high-speed memory areas storing temporary data from ALU operations and are part of the CPU (very fast), and (2) the internal memory chips, which are of two types: **Random-access memory (RAM)** and **read-only memory (ROM)**.

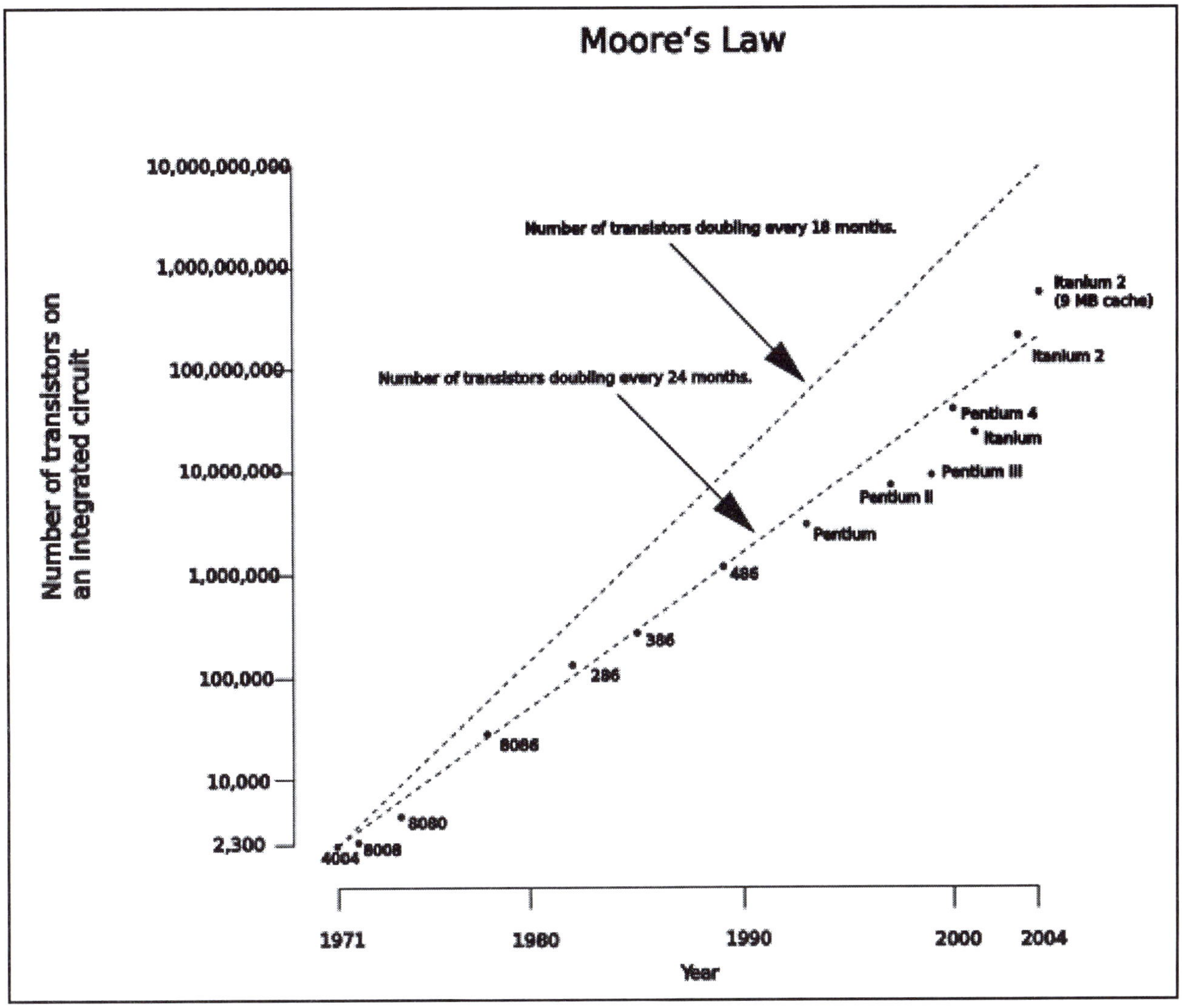

Figure 1.3: Moore's Law

- **RAM (random-access memory)** is the portion of the main memory where the CPU stores instructions and the data it is processing. The larger the area (more RAM), the larger the programs that can be run (executed). Typically multimedia programs need at least 2-4 gigabytes of RAM to run applications that combine animation, video, graphics, and sound. RAM is very fast at storing and retrieving data (textual or animation). When you open a computer application (word processor or spreadsheet), a copy of that program is moved into RAM to be more quickly accessible by the computer. A problem with RAM is its volatility. **Volatility** means that all data and instructions stored in RAM are lost when the power is turned off. For this reason, it is prudent to routinely save your work every 10-15 minutes. Professors now categorize "My computer crashed and I didn't back up (and lost) my homework" with the excuse from an earlier era, "My dog ate my homework." Neither excuse works.
- **ROM (read-only memory)** is a part of primary storage that cannot be changed or erased. It is permanently programmed and is non-volatile; that is, ROM retains program instructions even when the power is off. An example of a program stored in ROM is the instructions needed to start the computer.

1.8 Secondary Storage

Secondary storage is not part of the CPU or primary storage. As mentioned previously, primary storage (RAM) is volatile, being contained in memory chips. It can store and retrieve data very fast. In contrast, secondary storage is non-volatile, which means that it does not disappear when power is turned off. Secondary storage devices are less expensive than RAM but are slower than primary storage. Some of the more common secondary storage options include:

- **Hard drive**. Today, there are two general types of hard drives: **hard disk drives** and **solid state drives**. Either type can be mounted inside the computer or attached to the computer by cable. Although solid state drives are becoming more popular, most computers sold today include 1 or 2 hard disk drives. The hard disk functions something like an old record player containing a stack of metal-coated records (called platters) that rotate rapidly. Data is assigned and stored on the disk at specific addresses that can be directly accessed. Magnetic read/write heads locate the appropriate addresses for storing and retrieving data. This operation can be performed in 5-thousandths to 10-thousandths of a second. The hard disk drives of personal computers commonly have up to several hundred gigabytes of data storage. This storage capacity makes hard disks ideal for permanent storage of programs and software. Solid state drives sold today are more expensive and smaller than hard disk drives, but they have no moving parts which allows almost instantaneous data access.
- **Online storage services.** There are several third-party storage providers that allow you to upload and store your data on servers connected to the Internet. These servers can be located at the providers' home office or at a remote location. This is often a convenient secondary storage solution because it enables you to access your data from any location as long as you have an Internet connection. In addition, online storage with a reputable company provides a safe way for you to back up your files at a remote location in case of fire, theft, or a natural disaster. Online storage services often provide both free and paid options, depending on your storage needs.
- **Compact disks.** A **CD** stores about 650-700 megabytes of information. CDs are typically more durable and portable than hard disk drives, but they have the disadvantage of relatively limited storage capacity.
- **Digital video disk (DVD)** is another medium for secondary storage that is entering the SOHO market (Small Office/Home Office). DVDs offer higher quality and much denser storage capacities than CD-ROMs. The storage on commercially available DVDs is approximately 17 gigabytes, which is sufficient capacity to store approximately 5 movies with 6-track stereo audio.

Floppy disks are becoming obsolete. They can be easily damaged by heat or magnets. Flash drives plug into the USB port of the computer. They use a computer chip instead of a magnetic disk to store information.

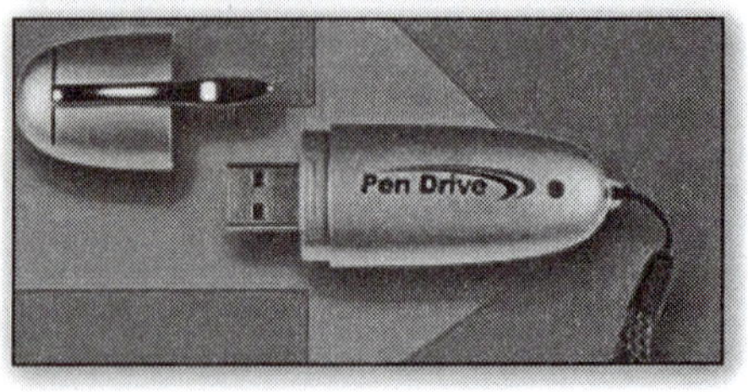

- **Flash Drives** are another popular form of secondary storage. The pen drive is so called because it looks similar to a regular writing pen. Some pen drives are actually a writing pen with the memory storage located inside the cap. Flash drives are plugged into the USB port of the computer. Information is stored on a chip located inside the pen drive. The pen drive can be removed and transported as necessary. It easily fits in a purse or pocket. Pen drives come in various storage capacities.

1.9 Input Devices

The flow of data through a computer system is called the **input-processing output (or IPO) cycle**. On the input side, users need to communicate with computers by generating data and commands using one or more input devices.

Each input device generates a different form of data that the CPU must process. There are a great variety of input devices meeting the needs of many different users and many different applications such as developing interactive Web pages, composing digital music, and making movie animations. Several common input devices are listed in Table 1.1.

Table 1.1 – Examples of Input Devices

Keyboard	*Mouse, touch screen, light pen, and joystick*	*Other input devices*
The most common input device, the keyboard, retains the typewriter key positions from the 19th century. Some computer keyboard models are ergonomically designed (i.e., made to fit human physiology).	The mouse is a hand-held device or a "glide-and-tap" device that signals a cursor (an arrow symbol) on the computer screen. The mouse is faster than using the "arrow " keys on the keyboard, especially if you have not learned keyboard shortcuts.	Microphones (voice recognition), bar code scanners, wand readers, digital cameras, optical scanners, and video cameras, etc., are other input devices.

1.10 Output Devices

Just as input devices are necessary for the user who wants to communicate instructions and data to a computer, output devices are necessary for the computer to communicate information back to the user. The most common output devices are monitors, printers, and sound systems. The trend in monitors is that they are becoming thinner with better resolution and larger screen size.

Printers have moved from the impact printer that functioned similarly to a typewriter to non-impact printers such as laser printers and ink jet printers. In a laser printer, information is "written" on a photosensitive drum by a laser beam, one page (instead of one line) at a time. Print (book) quality text and graphics are the result. Ink jet printers actually spray ink onto the paper in the shapes of letters, one line at a time.

Most home computers today come with sound and video cards. Many users play music CDs and DVD movies making the computer system an expensive CD and

DVD player. Multimedia refers to this combination of media such as video and audio that allows the user to more realistically interact with software programs (simulations) such as computer games and interactive tutorials.

1.11 Representing Data

Computer memory is measured in units called **bytes**. A byte is composed of 8 **bits.** Each bit may have a value of 1 (one) or 0 (zero) and is known as **binary data**. The relationship of bits and bytes to other measures of size are:

1 byte = 8 bits
1 kilobyte (KB) = 1,024 bytes
1 megabyte (MB) = 1,024 kilobytes
1 gigabyte = 1,024 megabytes
1 terabyte = 1,024 gigabytes

An **integrated circuit** (also called a computer chip) is composed of millions or billions of transistors that function in either the "on" or "off" position. This "on-off" state of a transistor is the basis of the binary digit or bit. As noted above, a byte is 8 bits. The arrangement of bits in a byte could take several forms where 0 (zero) represents the "off" position and 1 (one) represents the "on" position. The 8 bits that make up the byte can be arranged in 2^8 different ways, or 256 unique combinations. Bytes are used to make the characters recognized by the computer. For example, in **ASCII code** the character "A" is represented by the byte 10100001, while the number "1" is represented by the byte 01010001. Coding schemes have been devised so that all computer programs use the same combination of bits to make a specific character. One of the most common coding schemes is ASCII (pronounced *ask ee*), or the American Standard Code for Information Interchange.

> A *bit* of trivia: If one bit were the size of a dot made by a sharp pencil on a piece of paper (and it is much smaller), one gigabyte could represent the distance between the mid U.S. and Paris, France.

The 256 characters possible with ASCII code are sufficient to represent languages such as English, German, or Spanish, but 256 characters are not enough to represent the alphabets of other languages such as Chinese, Hebrew, or Cyrillic. A 16-bit code was devised that would provide for 2^{16} or 65,000 characters. Unicode is an example of a 16-bit code.

A convenient way of thinking about bytes and computer memory storage is to compare it to pages of printed text. If we assume that the average word is 5 letters long, and one byte of memory can represent one text character, then about 204 words can be held in 1 KB (kilobyte) of memory storage (1,024 divided by 5). Since the average double-spaced, typewritten page contains approximately 285 words then about 1.4 KB of computer memory would be required to store a page of typewritten material. By comparison, a floppy disk (1.4 MB) can contain approximately 1,000 similar typewritten pages. A computer file composed of pictures or more ornate font styles requires much more memory for storage.

1.12 A Brief History of Computing Technology

The history of processing data began centuries ago when primitive peoples first used their fingers and toes as counting devices. As commerce developed, a need arose for a device that could count higher than 20 (or less depending on one's skill as a hunter or gatherer). One of the earliest forms of calculation was the abacus, which is still used today in many areas of the world.

Now fast forward to the eighteenth century. Several mathematicians sought to develop machines that would make calculations faster and more accurate than hand methods such as the abacus. **Blaise Pascal**, for whom the Pascal programming language is named, was a French mathematician who developed such a mechanical calculating machine. This device, known as a Pascaline, employed gears and wheels to allow the user to perform addition and subtraction calculations. The Pascaline was fast and accurate, and could have been put to practical use in many banks and businesses of the day; however, it was so far ahead of its time that few people saw an application for it.

An idea borrowed from Pascal's work that did gain widespread acceptance was **Jacquard's loom**. The Frenchman, Joseph Marie Jacquard, was a weaver. In the seventeenth and eighteenth centuries, rugs and other textiles of great intricacy in design were popular. Weaving these by hand was time consuming and tedious, and one mistake could ruin an entire piece. Jacquard solved this problem by applying "music box technology" (paper with holes representing a specific music notation) to the weaving process. He designed looms in which punched cards controlled the pattern of woven material. In Jacquard's looms, needles fell through holes in punched cards. The needles lifted the threads in a way that produced a pattern.

In the nineteenth century, **Charles Babbage** developed the essential idea for a computer over 100 years before the first computer was constructed, and he is known today as the "father of computing." The son of a wealthy banker, Babbage devoted his time to the pursuit of science. In 1822, he conceived the idea for the **Difference Engine**, which was to be composed of gears and wheels and powered by steam. Its purpose was to automatically perform elaborate computations. The British government provided money for Babbage to build the Difference Engine. For 10 years, he worked on this machine. As he worked, Babbage conceived the idea for another device that he called the **Analytical Engine**. It was to have a memory unit called "the store" and an arithmetic/logic unit that would drive a typesetter. Programs for the device were to be written on punched cards. Although the device was not completed within his lifetime, a working version of the analytical engine was eventually completed.

Babbage traveled widely in Europe and the United States and gave many lively dinner parties attended by personalities such as Charles Darwin and Lord Byron, the poet. He became close to Lord Byron's daughter, Ada, the Countess of Lovelace, a beautiful and wealthy aristocrat. **Ada Lovelace** was an excellent mathematician. The Countess loved horse racing, and it may have been inevitable that she would use Babbage's Difference Engine and her own algorithm or "program" to calculate the "odds" of winning.

Her plan did not work out so well. She lost the family jewels at the track, and her mother had to buy them back. When Ada died of cancer at the age of 36, her death was a great loss to Babbage, and perhaps to the rest of the world as well. Ada is considered the "first programmer", and the ADA programming language is named for her.

Many of the mistakes that Babbage made have been, and continue to be, repeated in the computer industry of today. The classic list below appears in many computer science texts and on the walls of many computer centers and offices.

Babbage's Mistakes

1. Vague problem definition and requirements
2. Implementation started before design was complete
3. Requirements added during implementation
4. Working documentation not complete
5. Dependency on one person
6. System used for unintended purposes
7. Elaborate plans that exceed technology

Babbage contributed more to computing technology than mistakes. Many of his ideas and designs were incorporated into later devices. His analytical engine could be programmed using punched cards. The idea of using punched cards was later used to tabulate all sorts of mathematical data and continued to be used to program computers and enter data into the 1970s.

The analytical engine machine also employed several features subsequently used in modern computers, including sequential control, branching, and looping.

In 1824, Babbage won the Gold Medal of the Royal Astronomical Society "for his invention of an engine for calculating mathematical and astronomical tables." From 1828 to 1839 Babbage was a Professor of Mathematics at Cambridge. He contributed largely to several scientific periodicals, and was instrumental in founding the Astronomical Society in 1820.

In the late eighteenth century, the U.S. Census Bureau had a problem. The census of 1880 took 7 1/2 years to complete, clearly too long for a 10-year census! By the time the census data was processed, the information was no longer useful. With a growing population and the need for accurate and timely information, it looked as though the 1890 census could not be completed before the 1900 census was to begin. **Herman Hollerith**, a census bureau employee, conceived the idea of using punched cards, much like those used in the textile industries, to process information. He designed and constructed a punched-card processing machine that came to be known as the Hollerith Tabulating Machine. Data, in the form of numbers, letters, and special characters, was stored using the punched cards. Each card could store 80 different characters that were represented by a unique combination of holes in the card's 12 rows and 80 columns. Punched cards were fed into the tabulator, which moved them under a group of pins. If a hole occurred in the card at a given location, a pin would fall through and touch a pan of mercury. This closed a circuit and registered on a meter.

The Hollerith Tabulator used punched cards to process information.

Using Hollerith's system, the census of 1890 took only 6 weeks to complete. Hollerith decided that he had a marketable idea. He quit his job with the census bureau and sold his machines to the railroads and other large businesses. His punched card company was the beginning of automated data processing. Hollerith eventually sold his company, which later became *International Business Machines,* or ***IBM.***

The first true electronic digital computer was the *Colossus*, which was developed by the British during World War II. The *Colossus* was a huge collection of vacuum tubes and electronic registers controlled by an old style telephone switchboard. It had a single purpose—to decode captured Nazi communications. The Allies had captured a German coding machine, called the *Enigma*, early in the war. However, deciphering messages by conventional means was still almost impossible due to the large number of settings that the *Enigma* possessed. *Colossus* was designed and built to calculate all the combinations of settings and messages, quickly and efficiently. The ability to intercept and decode secret German military communications contributed significantly to the victory by Allied Forces.

1.13 Evolution of Computers

The **first-generation computers** (1945-1956) used vacuum tubes to store and process information. In 1944, *IBM* completed work on a mechanical calculator called the *Mark I.* At the same time, the U.S. government signed a contract with the University of Pennsylvania to build a computer, which was to be entirely electronic, that would aid the military efforts during World War II. The result was the *ENIAC*. The *ENIAC* was the first entirely electronic computer. It had 19,000 vacuum tubes, 70,000 resistors (short term data storage), and 5 million soldered joints. *ENIAC* could perform 5,000 additions per second but used so much electrical power that when it was turned on, the lights of Philadelphia dimmed! One example of how far computer technology has come is that the *ENIAC* had less computer power than a contemporary, throwaway birthday card that plays "Happy Birthday."

In 1946, a company was formed that became known as *Remington-Rand Corporation*. Their first product was the *Univac I,* which was the first commercial computer. The census bureau bought one that was used continuously from 1951 through 1963. It can now be seen in the *Smithsonian Institution* in Washington, D.C.

These first-generation computers were huge. They generated tremendous amounts of heat, were expensive to run, and often failed. A staff of dozens was required to maintain and operate these monsters. First-generation computers were programmed in machine language, (1s and 0s), the native language of computers. Only a few large corporations, government agencies, and universities with large research grants were able to afford these earliest computers.

The **second-generation computers** (1957-1963) used transistors for storing and processing information. Transistors had several advantages over vacuum tube technology. They were less costly, more stable, and more reliable. Transistors were smaller and used less power than vacuum tubes, which meant that they also generated less heat.

In 1954, *Texas Instruments* started commercial production of silicon transistors that replaced vacuum tubes in radios, TVs, and computers. A new memory system called core memory was developed. Cores were little donut-shaped magnets. A positive charge on one of these magnets represented 1 (one) and negative charge was read as 0 (zero). Through use of the cores, computers could store programs and data indefinitely, and instructions could be easily changed. Today some people still use the term *core memory* to refer to the computer's main or primary memory capacity.

The first "people-oriented," or high-level languages, were developed during this time. Among these were FORTRAN and COBOL. High-level languages enabled programmers to use English terms (sort of) instead of machine language to instruct the computer. Higher-level languages used the power of the computer to translate commands into machine code so that human programmers did not have to do the translation.

Another major development of these second-generation computers was off-line memory storage. Magnetic drums and tapes were used to store programs and data "external" to the computer. Saved information could be read back into the computer's memory whenever necessary. This secondary storage capability vastly expanded the usefulness of computers.

Third-generation computers (1964-1979) used integrated circuits for storing and processing information. Integrated circuits are made by imprinting large numbers of transistors on silicon chips. Early chips contained circuitry that could be compared to the street map of a small town. Large-Scale Integrated Circuits or LSI chips contained circuitry comparable to a major city.

The use of chips meant that third-generation computers were smaller, faster, and cheaper than second-generation computers. Vast improvements were subsequently made in memory systems, off-line storage, and computer languages. Soon the *minicomputer* was introduced. These minis were smaller, less expensive, and could do most of the work of their larger cousins, the *mainframes*. Although both minicomputers and mainframe computers continue in widespread use today, the silicon chip produced an even more profound development, the microcomputer. The **microcomputer** is a small desktop computer that has all of the characteristics, and operates on the same principles, as the minicomputer and mainframe computer.

In 1975 the microcomputer made its debut when *Altair Corporation* announced a computer kit in *Popular Electronics* magazine. The kit was a big hit with hobbyists. At that time no one thought there might be a mass market potential for small computers. When Steve Jobs and Steve Wozniak approached their employer, *Hewlett-Packard* that same year about developing a **Personal Computer (PC)**, they were turned away. Their bosses did not think that "regular" people had any use for computers. Working in a garage, Jobs and Wozniak founded their company, *Apple Computer*. Their first product was the *Apple I,* which was only a circuit board with a few processor and memory chips. It had no case, no disk drive, and no keyboard. Nonetheless, it was a big hit with the hobbyists.

In 1977, *Apple* announced the improved *Apple II* computer, a self-contained personal computer designed to use a cassette tape recorder to store programs. *Commodore Business Machines* also introduced the *PET* computer, and *Radio Shack* brought out the

The Apple II self-contained personal computer became available in 1977.

TRS-80 Model I. Each of these were smashing successes in spite of a general lack of software, hastily written programming languages, and numerous technical flaws. The personal computer revolution had begun.

Fourth-generation computers (1980-present) resulted from an increase in the size of circuits used to store and process information. Terms such as *very large-scale integrated* (VLSI) circuits and *ultra large-scale integration* (ULSI) came into use. With ULSI, 10 million transistors could now be placed on a single chip.

IBM entered the PC market with the introduction of its own PC in 1981 but concentrated its products in the business sector of the personal computer market. *IBM* contracted with Bill Gates' *Microsoft Corporation* to develop an operating system for its PC, which was called the *Microsoft Disk Operating System* or ***MS-DOS*** (DOS for short). The operating system organizes all of the background tasks of the computer system, places programs in RAM, and finds information necessary for the computer to function. Soon *IBM* compatibles, computers that looked like and operated like *IBM* PCs, appeared. They used *MS-DOS* and ran programs written for the *IBM* PC. They were targeted at the home user or consumer PC market. The *IBM* compatible "clones" sold for less than the *IBM* personal computers, and often included additional features as well.

More recent computers use *grand-scale integrated (GSI)* circuits where over 1,000 million transistors can be placed on one chip. Contemporary operating systems can use more RAM memory and support multi-tasking, a technical term which means that the computer appears to do several things simultaneously. The availability of more powerful (faster) microcomputers and cheaper memory, the mass appeal of the Internet and WWW, combined with computer multimedia capabilities have led to an explosion in consumer software development, which in turn has fueled more sales of computer hardware.

A recent trend in information processing is the use of massively parallel processing (neural computing) to process multiple instructions at one time. Conventional computer systems are based on what is known as *von Neumann architecture* where computer hardware processes information sequentially, one instruction at a time. Massively parallel computers are networks consisting of thousands of inexpensive chips (interconnected CPUs) that together are able to handle large computing operations. Networks of microcomputers have been constructed that achieve supercomputer speeds capable of performing more than a trillion operations per second.

Fifth-generation computers are the computers of tomorrow. It is hard to predict if massively parallel processing will usher in a fifth generation of computers. There are other innovations in experimental stages that may result in technology breakthroughs. One area of experimentation is with *DNA computers*. DNA is the information molecule that is fundamental to all life. DNA is based on only four molecules, designated by the symbols *A*, *T*, *G*, and *C*. The *A* molecule is always paired with a *T* molecule, and *G* is always paired with *C* in what is called a double helix. In other words, the blueprint that makes every cell in your body, and which also makes every other creature on earth unique, is encoded in only four molecules. It is estimated that DNA computers could easily process information twice as fast as the fastest supercomputers and have storage densities that require a trillion times less space.

1.14 Computer Operating Systems

An **operating system** (OS) is an essential software program that manages the hardware and software resources of a computer.. The OS performs basic tasks, such as controlling and allocating memory, prioritizing the processing of instructions, controlling input and output devices, facilitating networking and managing files. The first computers did not have operating systems. However, software tools for managing the system and simplifying the use of hardware appeared very quickly afterwards, and gradually expanded in scope. By the early 1960s, commercial computer vendors were supplying quite extensive tools for streamlining the development, scheduling, and execution of computer operations.

We can use the analogy of a building manager to describe how a computer operating system works. A building manager preforms routine management duties such as checking tenants in and out, moving them from one location to another, and keeping records of available space. A building manager would also be available to deal with users and prospective tenants to answer their questions. The manager would serve as a gate keeper to keep out unwanted intruders and would call for help in an emergency. An operating system is to a computer as a manager is to a building. The OS keeps track of disk space available and allocates programs and files to specific locations on disk storage. It also provides an interface to the computer user with menus and icons.

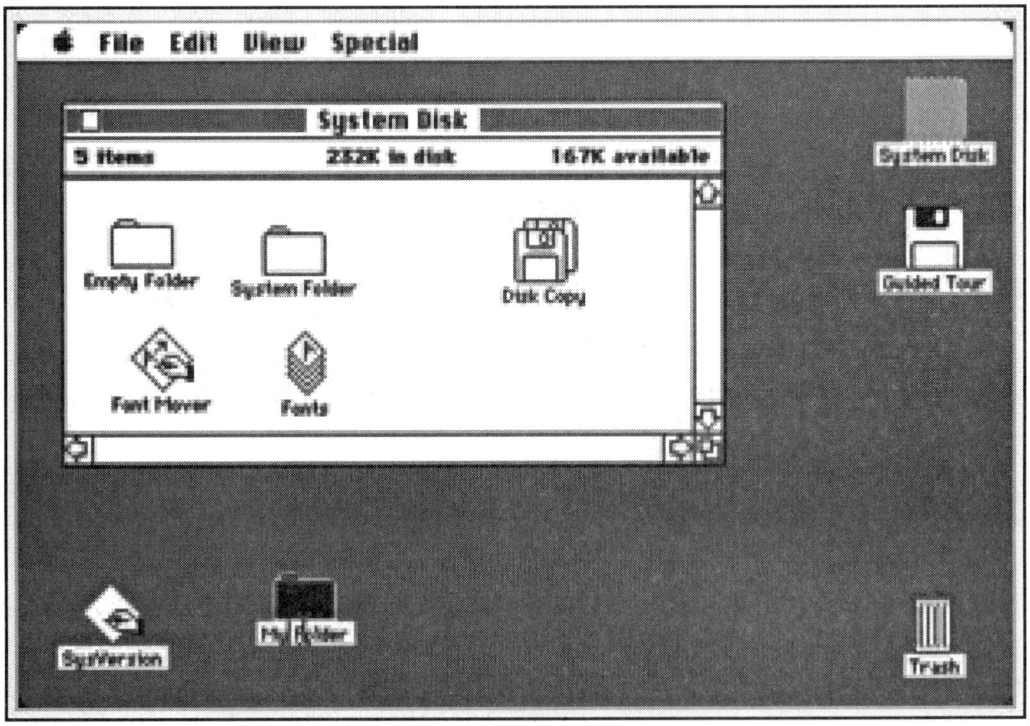

Figure 1.3: Original 1984 *Mac OS* Desktop

One notable early operating system was **CP/M,** which was supported on many early microcomputers and was largely cloned in creating **MS-DOS**. MS-DOS became wildly popular as the operating system chosen for the **IBM PC.** MS-DOS was published by **Microsoft Corporation**, making Microsoft one of the world's most profitable companies. The major alternative throughout the 1980s in the microcomputer market was **Mac OS**, tied intimately to the **Apple Macintosh** computer.

By the 1990s, the microcomputer had evolved to the point where extensive **GUI** facilities became increasingly desirable. The Apple Macintosh OS lead the way in pioneering the GUI interface for personal computers. Microsoft's response to this was the development of the **Windows OS**, which has served as the basis for Microsoft's entire operating system line since 1999.

Since the early 1990s the choice of operating systems for personal computers has been largely limited to the *Microsoft Windows* family and the **Unix**-like family, of which **Linux** and **Mac OS X** are the major choices. Mainframe computers use a variety of different operating systems, many with no direct connection to *Windows* or *Unix*, but they are typically more similar to *Unix* than to *Windows*.

Today, *Windows OS* holds a near monopoly of around 90% of the worldwide desktop computing market. *Windows OS* is also used on low and mid-range servers, supporting applications such as web servers and database servers.

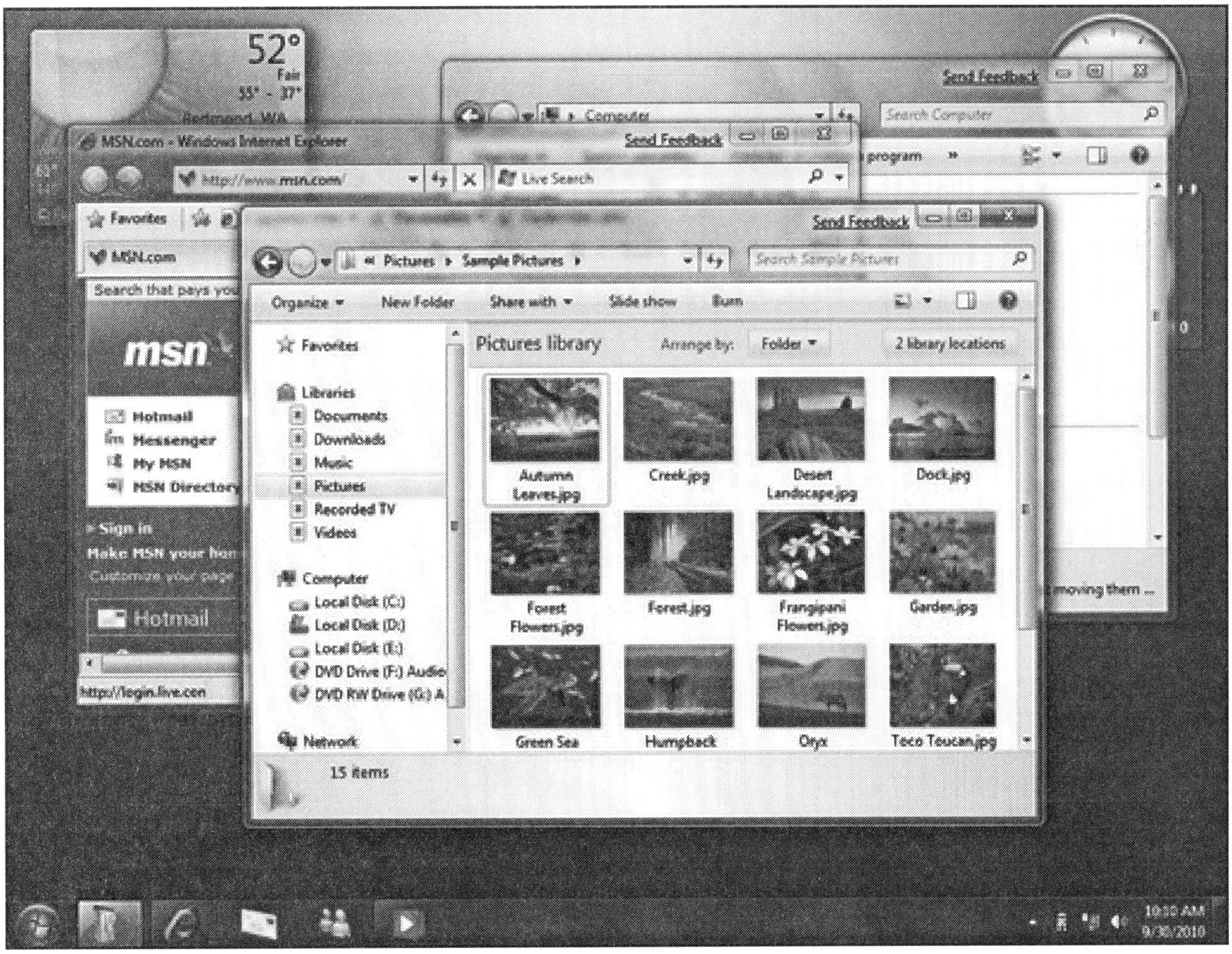

Figure 1.4: A Modern *Windows Desktop*

1.15 What's New With Windows?

The latest version of the *Windows* Operating System is *Windows 7*. *Windows 7* will be discussed in detail in the next chapter. *Windows 7* was introduced in 2009 and the computer using public is now making the change from older versions of the *Windows* OS, primarily *Windows XP* and *Vista*. At the current time, *Windows XP* is still the most commonly used OS for personal computers but this is rapidly changing.

1.16 Computer Networking

Computer networking is concerned with communication between computer systems. Such networks involves at least two computers, which can be separated by a few inches or thousands of miles. Computer networking is sometimes considered a sub-discipline of telecommunications.

Networks, and the technologies needed to connect and communicate through and between them, continue to drive computer hardware, software, and peripherals industries. The numbers and types of users of networks varies from researchers and businesses to families and individuals in everyday use.

Computer **networking** evolved from computer technology advances that have been discussed in this Module. In the 1960s, technology was invented (packet- switching technology) that greatly facilitated the development of **ARPAnet.** Initiated in 1969 by the Advanced Research Project Agency of the U.S. Department of Defense, the ARPA-net was the predecessor of the Internet. The first electronic mail (e-mail) message was sent in the early 1970s. Another notable invention that furthered computer networking was the development of the **TCP/IP** (Transmission Control Protocol/Internet Protocol) in 1974. A **protocol** is a set of rules and procedures that govern transmission of data across a network. The TCP/IP protocol can send large files of information across networks of varying reliability without being corrupted.

Most computers today are connected to some type of network. In an office, individual workstations may be connected to facilitate communication and to share a common core of data and peripherals such as hard drives, commonly used files, and printers. In school computer labs, computers are networked to facilitate teaching; the teacher may use the network to distribute practice files to a class and to collect homework electronically. A computer network generally consists of a group of connected computers. Connected computers in a single building or geographical location are examples of local-area networks or **LANs**. Computers that are connected across separate geographical locations are called wide-area networks or **WANs**. The operating systems and hardware systems used on networks of today vary. Networks can be complicated to install and are more costly than stand-alone computers. Networks eliminate the handling of floppy disks and can provide access to hundreds of programs continuously and to many users at once.

> Contrary to some common usage, the Internet and the World Wide Web are not synonymous. The Internet is a collection of interconnected *computer networks*, linked by copper wires, fiber optic cables, and wireless connections. The Web is a collection of interconnected *documents*, linked by hyperlinks and URLs that are accessible using the Internet. The Internet also provides other services including email and file sharing.

Most schools, large and small businesses, government agencies, military installations, and other organizations have some type of network. If the network at your office can communicate with other networks, your network may be part of the Internet. Current LANs are most likely to be based on switched **Ethernet** or **Wi-Fi** (wireless) technology running at 10, 100, or 1,000 Megabits (also known as 1 Gigabit) per second.

1.17 Internet

The **Internet** is a worldwide system of computer networks. Initially known as the **ARPAnet**, the original purpose of the Internet was to allow research computers at universities to communicate with each other in case of an emergency. Because messages could be routed and rerouted, the ARPAnet would continue to function even if parts of it were destroyed. This was part of the U.S. cold war strategy of the 1960s and 1970s. In 1973, the first international connections to the ARPAnet were made. This began the Internet on a global basis.

By June of 2010, almost 2 billion people were users of the Internet world wide according to *Internet World Stats*. Today, the Internet is a public, cooperative, and self-sustaining entity that is accessible to hundreds of millions of people across the world. The Internet uses a portion of the total resources of currently existing public telecommunication networks using the previously mentioned TCP/IP protocols. Other well-known products of the Internet are e-mail and the **World Wide Web** ("**WWW**" or "the Web"). The Web allows users access to billions of pages of information. The Internet and World Wide Web will be covered in more depth in later modules.

1.18 Conclusion

This first module has provided you with important information about how computers evolved and how they operate. In later modules, you will build on this foundation to learn to use computers to improve your personal productivity.

Key Terms

ARPAnet
ASCII
Application software
Babbage, Charles
Binary data
Bit
Bytes
CAI
CD-ROM
CPU
Components of a computer system
DVD
Difference engine
Fifth-generation computer
First-generation computer
Fourth-generation computer
Hard disk drive
Hardware
Hollerith, Herman
IBM
Input devices
Integrated circuit (IC)
Internet
Jacquard's loom
LAN
Lovelace, Ada
Microcomputer
MS-DOS
Mac
Moore's Law
Networking
Office 2010
Operating system (OS)
Output devices
PC
Pascal, Blaise
Primary storage
Programs
Protocol
RAM
ROM
Secondary storage
Second-generation computer
Software
TCP/IP
Third-generation computer
Windows Vista
WAN
WBI
WWW

Computer Application Assignments

The computer application assignment for this module consists of the 3 short essay questions given below. Type your answers using *MS Word* and submit them to your instructor.

If you are submitting the assignments in print form, staple the completed questionnaires together with your short essay question answers, and turn them in to your instructor. If you are submitting your assignments electronically, follow your instructors directions.

Assignment: *Short Essay Questions*

1. Reflect on a typical day in your life. Knowing what you do about the presence of computers in the world today, what encounters do you have with them during your daily routine? In one page or less, describe some of the main ways that computers effect you in day-to-day life. Were you aware of the extent of computers in your life before completing this module? How do you expect computers to impact you in the future?
2. In one or two paragraphs, describe the computer **input-processing-output cycle.** Try to avoid using the same words given in this module. Use your own words. Pretend that you are explaining it to a friend who knows nothing about computers. You may use analogies or other examples to clarify your explanation.
3. Describe the primary computer system that you plan to use to complete the exercises in this book. If you do not own a computer, describe the primary computer that you plan to use. Give the following information about your computer system:
    1. Computer brand and model
    2. Monitor size, brand, and model
    3. Printer brand and model
    4. Other perpipherals (eg. video camera, speakers, scanner, etc)
    5. CPU type and speed
    6. Amount of RAM Memory
    7. Operating System
    8. Number and size of hard disks

MODULE 2

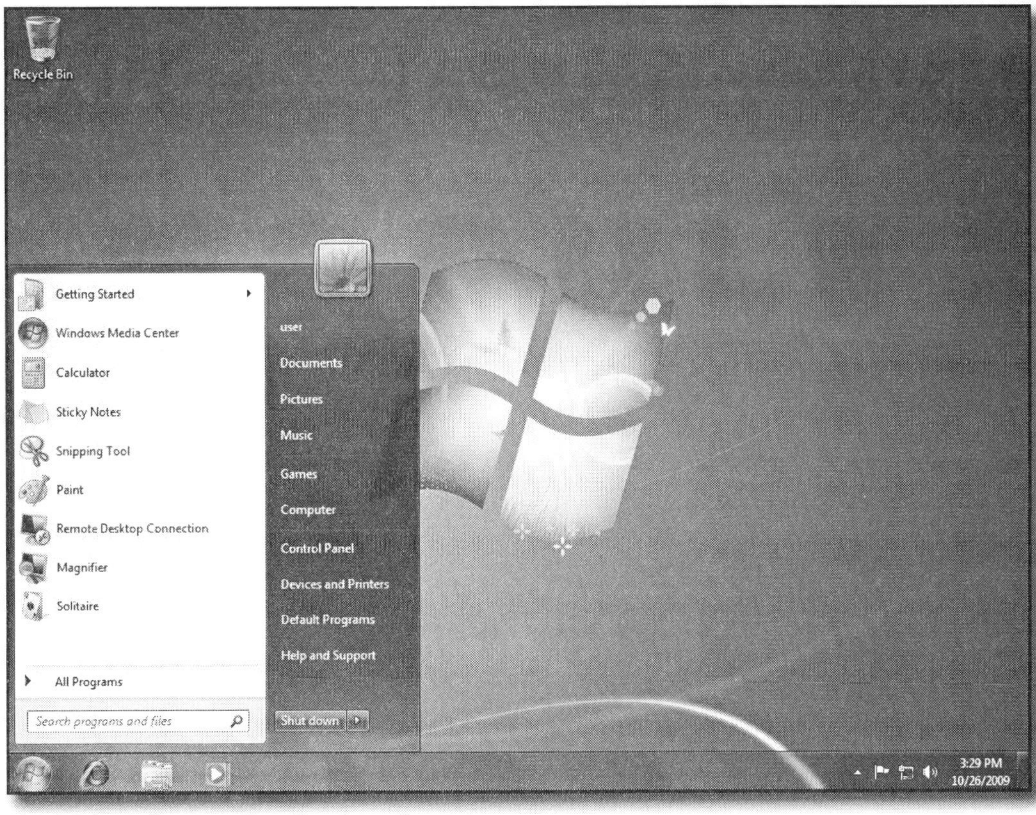

Windows 7 & Microsoft Office 2010

Introduction to Windows 7 and MS Office 2010

Windows 7 was introduced in 2009 and *Office 2010* was introduced in early 2010. Since then, the computer using public has been making the transition from *Windows Vista* and *Office 2003* to the newer Microsoft software. Many users continue to prefer the older versions. However, *Windows 7* and *Office 2010* offer many improvements over the older versions of the software. Therefore, this edition of *Computer Skills and Concepts: A Mastery Approach* uses *Windows 7* and *Microsoft Office 2010* for all instructions and assignments. In this module, a detailed review of *Windows 7* and *Office 2010* are provided. You will build on this knowledge as you complete projects and assignments in later modules.

Module Objectives

When you have completed this module, you should be able to:

- Describe several new features of *Windows 7*
- Describe several new features of *Office 2010*
- Explain the major differences between *Windows 7* and *Windows Vista*
- Describe the major differences between *Office 2010* and *Office 2003*
- List and describe the software applications included in *Windows 7*
- List and describe the software applications in *Office 2010*

Materials Needed to Complete This Module

- This book
- Storage media such as a flash drive
- *Microsoft Word 2010*

How to Proceed

Read this module. From your reading you will learn about the *Windows 7* Operating system and *Microsoft Office 2010.*

1. Review the key terms at the end of this module.
2. Complete the Module 2 Review Questions at the end of the module
3. Check your answers at the end of the book.
4. Complete the Module 2 Application Assignments. These assignments include answering several short essay questions about *Windows 7* and *Microsoft Office 2010.* Turn in your assignments to your instructor.
5. Take the Module 2 Test.

2.1 Windows 7

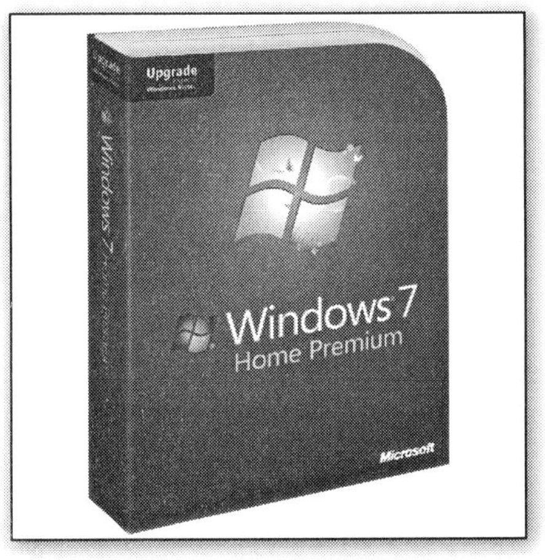

In 2009, Microsoft announced the release of the latest version of its *Windows* Operating System, *Windows 7. Windows 7* is the successor to *Windows Vista. Windows 7* was under development at least since 2007 when it was first announced by Microsoft. *Windows 7* was released 2 years after the introduction of *Windows Vista.*

Windows 7 contains many new features; some of the most significant include an updated and faster graphical user interface, improved searching features, better user account control, and improved networking, audio, and overall performance. *Windows 7* also aims to increase the speed of communication between computers on a home network, making it easier to share files and digital media between computers and devices. For developers, *Windows 7* aims to make it significantly easier for developers to write high-quality applications.

In spite of the many new features offered by *Windows 7*, Microsoft's primary objective with *Windows 7* was to make the lives of PC users easier by increasing usability and functionality. They sought to make an operating system that is both easy to use and that works well with other hardware and software applications. *Microsoft* appears to have succeeded in winning over the hearts of PC users with their release of *Windows 7*. By mid 2010, 150 million copies of *Windows 7* had been sold, making it the fastest selling operating system in history, selling an average of 7 copies every second.

The main criticism of *Windows 7* is related to concerns about pricing and upgrade options. It's more expensive to upgrade from *Vista* to *Windows 7* than it was to upgrade from previous versions of *Windows*.

2.2 New Features of Windows 7

The major new features of *Windows 7* are summarized in this section.

- **Windows Aero Enhancements.** *Windows* Aero was a new hardware-based graphical user interface first introduced with *Windows Vista*. Aero is an acronym for **Au**thentic, **E**nergetic, **R**eflective, and **O**pen. The new interface was designed to be cleaner and more aesthetically pleasing than those of previous *Windows* operating systems, including new transparencies, live thumbnails, live icons, and animations. *Windows 7* retains the basic *Windows* Aero interface but adds some notable improvements. Some of these improvements include more desktop themes, a desktop slideshow option, and improved Gadget functionality. Gadgets are lightweight single-purpose applications (e.g., clock, weather info, sports scores) that can sit anywhere on the Windows desktop.

Figure 2.1 Windows Aero

- **Window Explorer.** The look of *Windows 7* is also different from *Windows Vista* offering a new range of organization, navigation, and search capabilities. Windows Explorer, the Windows file management application, now includes **Libraries**, or virtual folders that combine content from different folders, including shared folders on networked drives. In Libraries, you can also arrange your photos and other files in various ways. For example, you can select "By Month" and view all photos organized in folders by the month they were taken; or, you can select "By Artist" and view your music files in folders organized by artist.

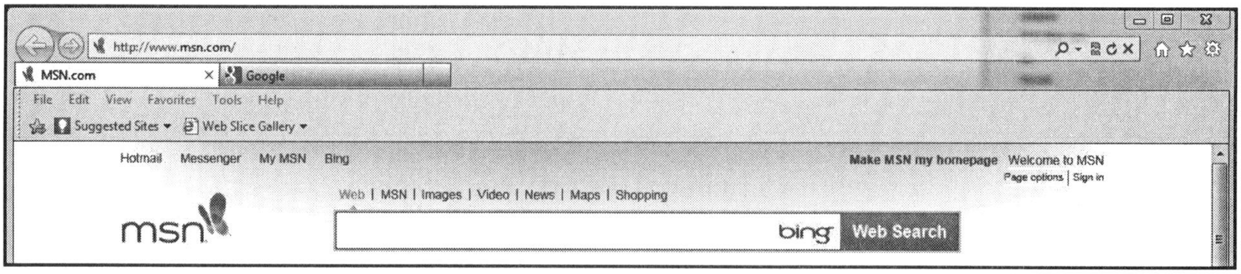

Figure 2.2 Windows Internet Explorer

- **Windows Search.** The search capabilities of *Windows 7* have also been enhanced from *Windows Vista*: You can now search for Control Panel items and even corporate Intranets. Searching for programs and files is also easier. For example, if you want to find a particular program you don't have to scan through a long list of programs in the start menu. You can simply type the name of the program you want (e.g., calculator) in the **Start menu search box,** and you'll instantly see the program you want. If you want to find a particular document, photo, or e-mail, you can type in the file name to instantly access it. If you can't remember the file name you can type something you remember about it, like a key word or

the day you created it, and you'll get a list of relevant results. You can also refine your searches in a folder or library with filters (e.g., date or file type). To search a particular library (e.g., Documents, Music, or Videos), go to the library and type a search term in the search box (upper right corner) and you'll see your results instantly, highlighted in yellow.

- **The Taskbar.** The *Windows 7* taskbar (long horizontal bar at the bottom of the desktop screen) is larger than the *Windows Vista* taskbar, making touch input easier. The larger task bar also allows greater compatibility with newer high-resolution monitors. A new *Windows 7* taskbar feature is **Pinning.** Pinning allows you to easily access items without having to search or browse for them. For example, you can pin your favorite applications anywhere on the taskbar by just clicking and dragging them to the taskbar. You can also pin individual documents, pictures, or music files.
- Another new feature is **Jump Lists**. Jump lists help you go right to your most frequently used documents, songs, pictures, or websites just by right-clicking an item on the taskbar. For example, right-clicking on the *Windows* Media Player icon on the taskbar displays a Jump List of your most frequently played music and movies. Just select an item on the list and it opens! If you right-click a web browser on your taskbar, you'll get a Jump List of your most frequently visited web sites. If you right click a Word document, you'll get a Jump List of other recently opened documents.
- **Live taskbar previews** is another new feature to the *Windows 7* taskbar. Just move your mouse over an item on the taskbar to see a thumbnail view of its open windows. Slide your mouse over the thumbnail to see a full screen view and click it to open the window. In short, the new taskbar features are designed to make accessing the content you want easier than ever.

Figure 2.3 Windows Taskbar

- **Snap.** You've probably viewed 2 windows side-by-side on the same screen before, but it probably took you some time to resize and move things around to get it just right. Now you can use **Snap** to do it in an instant. For example, if you want to view 2 documents on the same screen, simply drag one document to the right edge of the screen, let up on the mouse, and it snaps into place, filling the right side of the screen. Then do the same with the other document on the opposite side, and it fills the left side of the screen. Better yet, if you drag a window back away from the edge, it returns to its previous size. Snap makes reading, comparing, and organizing windows easy, and kind of fun too.

> Windows 7 contains hundreds of new features and it can back up your entire computer.

- **Shake and Peek. Shake** is a great feature to use if your desktop is cluttered with open windows and you want to zero in on just one of them for awhile. All you have to do is select the title bar of the window you want to keep open and drag it back and forth (i.e., shake it), and everything else is minimized. To put things back the way they were, just shake the open window again. Another feature, **Peek**, can be used to quickly minimize all open windows to check something on your desktop (e.g., weather or calendar gadget). To use Peek, just slide your mouse over the **Show desktop** button (right edge of the taskbar) and all open windows will fade away, revealing your desktop. Just slide your mouse off the Show desktop button and everything will be back the way it was.
- **HomeGroup.** If you have more than one computer on the same network, HomeGroup makes it easy to share files. With HomeGroup, you no longer have to use a flash drive or send e-mail attachments to yourself to move files from one computer to another on your network. Once you set up a password-protected HomeGroup, sharing files on multiple computers is a easy as right-clicking on a document or folder, selecting Share With, and then selecting whatever share options you want.
- **Touch.** *Windows 7* now supports **multitouch** technology. Limited touch capability has been available with previous versions of *Windows*, but now you can zoom in, zoom out, or right-click on an object by using nothing but your fingers. As long as your computer has the appropriate hardware and software its possible to do away with your mouse!
- **Windows Internet Explorer 9 (IE9).** *IE9* is the current version of the *Internet Explorer* web browser from *Microsoft*. *IE9* contains several new features including a simplified design, **One Box** searching, **Pinned Sites**, and other performance improvements. One Box is *IE9*'s sole location for both searching the Web and for navigating to specific web sites. One Box also uses AutoComplete or word-wheeling to anticipate what you are looking for so you can find and access websites quickly. Simply start typing in One Box and search results will immediately appear as you type. Pinned Sites lets you get to your favorite web sites quickly without have to open IE9 first. As with Pinning in *Windows 7*, you can simply drag your favorite web sites to the taskbar for easy access. IE9 is also optimized to run faster, and to install faster, than previous versions of Internet Explorer.
- **Windows Media Player 12** is the latest version of *Microsoft's* program for playing and organizing music and video. Windows Media Player 12 plays more media formats that previous versions of Windows Media Player, including Flip Video (a digital video camcorder) files and unprotected songs from iTunes. There is also built-in support for a variety of audio and video file formats (including 3GP, MPEG-4, AVI, and DivX). You can also stream music and video to other computers on your network. With an Internet connection, you can even access all of the media files on your desktop computer from any location through Remote Media Streaming.

> *Windows Media Player* includes the ability to rip music from and copy music to compact discs, synchronize content with a digital audio player (MP3 player) or other mobile devices.

Figure 2.4: Windows Media Player

- **Windows Media Center**, Windows Media Center for *Windows 7* was designed to be a PC entertainment system. You can watch HDTV, play DVDs, show photos, and play music on your PC. You can also share all this material with any other PC on your network using HomeGroup. **Internet TV,** another new feature, enables you to watch a variety of shows (e.g., news, video podcasts) on your PC over a broadband Internet connection for free. You can also make professional looking slide shows, with music, using the new slide show maker**.**

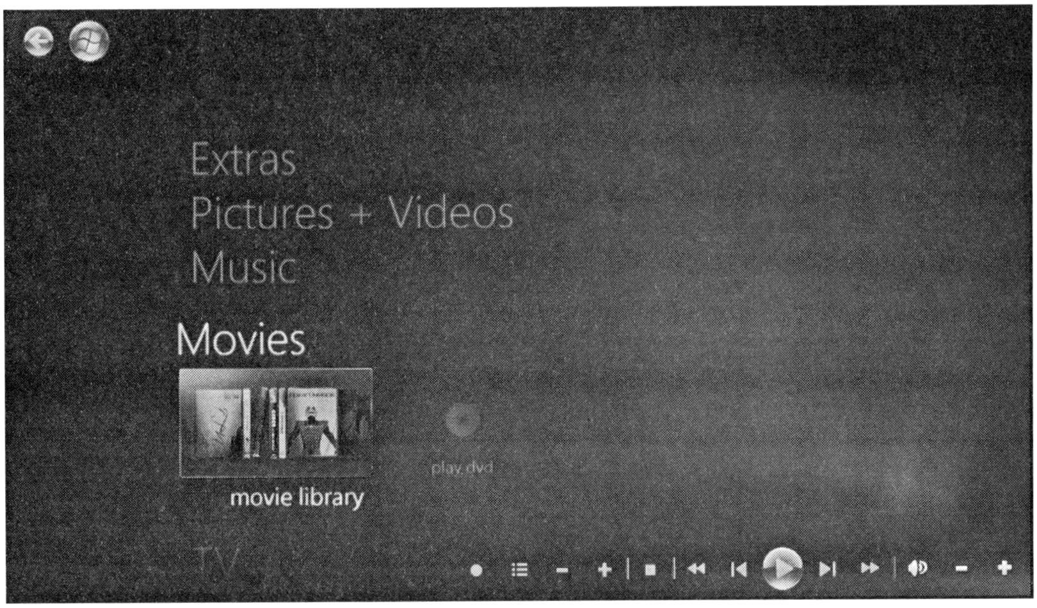

Figure 2.5: *Windows Media Center*

- **User Account Control (UAC).** UAC lets you know when your PC is threatened by any malicious software or when a program makes changes to your PC that requires administrator permission. UAC was made less intrusive with *Windows 7* by letting you adjust how often you want to receive UAC pop-up alerts. For example, if you don't want to receive alerts every time certain changes are made to your PC, you can adjust the UAC settings to prevent them. In *Windows 7*, UAC contains 4 settings that allow you to control the amount of notifications you receive. Also, UAC adjustments no longer require you to restart your computer to take effect.

2.3 Hardware Requirements for Windows 7

Computers capable of running *Windows 7* are classified as **Windows 7 Capable** and **Windows 7 Premium Ready**. A *Windows 7* Capable PC is capable of running all editions of *Windows 7* although some of the special features and high-end graphics options may require additional or more advanced hardware. A *Windows 7* Premium Ready PC can take advantage of *Windows 7's* high-end features.

Windows 7's **Basic** and **Classic** interfaces will work with virtually any graphics hardware that supports *Windows XP* or *Windows Vista*; accordingly, most discussion around *Windows 7's* graphics requirements centers on those for the Windows Aero interface. Microsoft offers a tool called the *Windows 7 Upgrade Advisor* to assist users in determining what versions of Windows their machine is capable of running. *Windows 7* hardware requirements are summarized as follows:

- 1 gigahertz (GHz) or faster 32-bit (x86) or 64-bit (x64) processor
- 1 gigabyte (GB) RAM (32-bit) or 2 GB RAM (64-bit)
- 16 GB available hard disk space (32-bit) or 20 GB (64-bit)
- DirectX 9 graphics device with WDDM 1.0 or higher driver

2.4 Compatibility Issues

A problem with upgrading to any new operating system is compatibility. Some application programs written for *XP* are not directly compatible with all editions of *Windows 7*. In some cases, software publishers provide a downloadable software patch so that a user who upgrades to *Windows 7* can use their old application programs with *Windows 7*. However, in some cases, it will be necessary to purchase a newer version of the programs that are compatible with *Windows 7*.

To Upgrade or Not to Upgrade? Because of the more restrictive licensing, compatibility issues, and the fact that many users have just grown comfortable with *Windows Vista* or *XP*, many computer users have been reluctant to upgrade to a new operating system.

While *Windows 7* is definitely superior to *Vista* and *XP*, for most users, it may not be worth the expense and hassle to switch to the new operating system in the short run. However, in the long run, changing to the new operating system is inevitable. New application programs are being written which will work only with *Windows 7* and publishers will eventually stop supporting older versions of their programs which were written for *Vista* or *XP*.

There are 4 versions of Windows 7. They are the **Starter** edition, the **Home Premium** edition, the **Professional** edition, and the **Ultimate** edition. Here's an overview of each version:

1. Starter

The *Windows 7* Starter edition is designed exclusively for use on **netbook computers.** A netbook computer is a new type of laptop computer that is defined by size, price, and speed; they are small, cheap, and relatively underpowered. The Starter edition is basically a stripped-down version of one of the regular editions of *Windows 7*. The Starter edition does not support some of the features discussed earlier such as Taskbar Previews or Peek. You also can't change desktop backgrounds and window colors. There is also no support for using multiple monitors, DVD playback, remote streaming, or Windows Media Center.

If you can live with the limitations discussed above, and you want the stability of *Windows 7*, the Starter edition may be a viable option for your netbook. You may also be able to install one of the regular editions of *Windows 7* on your netbook if your computer meets the system requirements.

While the Starter edition of *Windows 7* is quite limited, many users will find it more than adequate for the main uses of a netbook, which typically include surfing the Internet, checking email and light word processing. If you need your netbook to do more, consider upgrading to a regular edition of *Windows 7* or consider moving up to a non-netbook laptop.

The suggested retail price for the *Windows 7* Starter edition is $199.

2. Home Premium Edition

Home Premium is the preferred edition of *Windows 7* for home desktop and laptop PCs. It includes Windows Media Center, which lets you easily use digital photos, Internet TV, movies, and music. Also, like the other editions of *Windows 7*, it provides a better level of security and reliability. *Windows 7* Home Premium is the version that should appeal to most home users. Most of the features that Microsoft wants home users to know about are included. Peek, for previewing and clearing the desktop, Snap, for resizing windows, and the *Windows 7* Taskbar, for jumping and pinning, are all in effect. Multitouch is also enabled, along with HomeGroup, for sharing music, video and other files among computers on your network. A 64-bit version of Home Premium is available, but it only supports 16GB of RAM.

While *Windows 7* Home Premium may sound like it has it all, it's definitely lacking some features found in the Professional and Ultimate editions. For example, location aware printing, presentation mode, and *XP* mode are not supported. Some security features such as BitLocker and Home Premium are also not included.

The suggested retail price for *Windows 7* Home Premium is $199. To upgrade from a licensed version of another version of Windows, the suggested upgrade retail price is $119. The actual cost may vary and prices are subject to change. It will pay to shop around. The *Windows 7* Home Premium edition can also be upgraded using the Anytime Upgrade to either Professional or Ultimate.

Office made its first appearance in 1989 on the Mac, with a version for *Windows* following it in 1990.

3. Professional Edition

The *Windows 7* Professional Edition is designed to meet the needs of power users and small businesses. The Professional Edition includes all the features of the Home Premium Edition plus some extra features for business users, making it flexible enough to be used at home or at the office. The Professional Edition supports up to 192GB of RAM in 64 bit mode, enables you to run *Windows XP* programs, and allows you to back up your data to a networked drive.

The Professional Edition also includes the presentation mode, which enables you to project your presentations in a professional setting without displaying the customized screensaver and wallpaper on your personal system. You can also disable pop-ups like instant messages and system notifications. The Professional Edition does not, however, support the BitLocker and the AppLocker features.

The *Windows 7* Professional Edition is for small businesses, serious gamers, high-quality media creators, and enthusiasts who demand the most from digital media. The suggested retail price for the full Professional Edition package product is $299. The suggested upgrade retail price is $199.

4. Ultimate Edition

The *Windows 7* Ultimate Edition offers an advanced, business-focused infrastructure, mobile productivity, and the home digital media features. The features that separate it from the *Windows 7* Professional edition pertain primarily to intensive international or network use. So, most home users will not need the extra features bundled with the Ultimate edition.

Specifically, The *Windows 7* Ultimate Edition offers all of the features found in *Windows 7* Professional plus virtual hard-disk booting, Windows Services for UNIX, and other security and network-related features. For example, BitLocker and Applocker are fully supported. BitLocker protects your data in the event that your computer is lost or stolen. BitLocker enables you to encrypt your data so that if someone has access to your physical computer, your protected drives are unreadable. Applocker allows centrally managed control of access to specific applications on individual systems.

The suggested retail price for full package product is $319. The suggested upgrade retail price is $219.

There are also other editions of *Windows 7* available. *Windows 7* Home Basic is between the Starter and Home Premium editions in terms of features offered. This edition is primarily for emerging markets like India and Mexico. *Windows 7* Enterprise is the same as *Windows 7* Ultimate, but it's only available through volume licensing.

2.5 A Comparison of the Editions of Windows 7

A comparison of the Starter, Home Premium, Professional, and Ultimate editions of *Windows 7* are shown in the following table.

Windows 7 Comparison Chart

Features	Home Basic	Home Professional	Professional	Ultimate
Make the things you do every day easier with improved desktop navigation.	✓	✓	✓	✓
Start programs faster and more easily, and quickly find the documents you use most often.	✓	✓	✓	✓
Make your web experience faster, easier and safer than ever with Internet Explorer 8.	✓	✓	✓	✓
Watch, pause, and record TV on your PC with Windows Media Center.		✓	✓	✓
Easily create a home network and connect your PCs to a printer with Home Group		✓	✓	✓
Run many Windows XP business programs in Windows XP Mode (separate download).			✓	✓
Connect to company networks easily and more securely with Domain Join			✓	✓
In addition to full-system Backup and Restore found in all editions, you can back up to a home or business network.			✓	✓
Help protect data on your PC and portable storage devices against loss or theft with BitLocker				✓
Work in the language of your choice and switch between any of 35 languages.				✓

2.6 Microsoft Office 2010

Microsoft's latest version of *Office* was launched together with the *Vista* operating system in early 2007. ***Office 2010*** has hundreds of new features. Here we take a look at some of the most important ones.

***Office 2010* New Features**

- **Ribbon**: The ribbon is the new graphical user interface that was included with some of the applications in Office 2007. In Office 2010, the ribbon is included with every application in the Office suite. The ribbon replaced the menus and toolbars that had been the cornerstone of Office since its inception. It has a sleek design and can be collapsed and hidden when necessary. The new ribbon can also be customized by users to suit their needs. To customize, simply right-click the ribbon and select **Customize the Ribbon**. From there you can use the dialogue box to add, remove, and rearrange tools any way you want.

Figure 2.6: Microsoft Word 2010 Task Menu

- **Backstage View.** While the Ribbons contain commands for doing something *in* a document, the Backstage view contains commands for doing something *to* a document (e.g., save it, print it, etc.). The new File button replaces the Office button included with Office 2007, the big round button in the upper-left corner of Office applications. Selecting File enables you to Save, Save As, Open, Close, and Print files. You can also change properties and manage versions of the file.
- **Paste Preview**. The new Paste Preview feature lets you preview the information copied to your clipboard before you actually paste it in your document. From the Home ribbon, select the Paste drop-down menu and slide your mouse over the options to see a preview of what your pasted content will look like. Because the preview disappears when you move your mouse away from the buttons, you can save time by not having to undo any paste results you don't like.
- **Web and Mobile Apps.** With Office 2010, *Microsoft* has included online versions of four Office applications: **Word**, **Excel**, **PowerPoint**, and **OneNote**. These online applications can be accessed through your Internet browser for free. Even though they are stripped down versions of the desktop counterparts, they still give users enough tools for basic editing and content creation. If you have a *Windows* Phone, you can even modify your documents on our smart phone.
- **Protected View.** In Protected View, you can open Office documents without worrying whether they pose a security threat (e.g., contain malicious code). The new Protected View opens documents as read only when they fail validation, have been downloaded from the Internet, are from a suspicious location, or contain attachments. You can edit the document, if you trust the file, by simply selecting Enable Editing on the Message Bar.

- **Themes.** With themes you can easily create professional looking documents in Word, Excel, and PowerPoint. Each theme includes a consistent color scheme to unify the look and feel of your documents. Office 2010 has twice as many builit-in themes (40) as Office 2007 had (20).

2.7 Office 2010 Application Suites

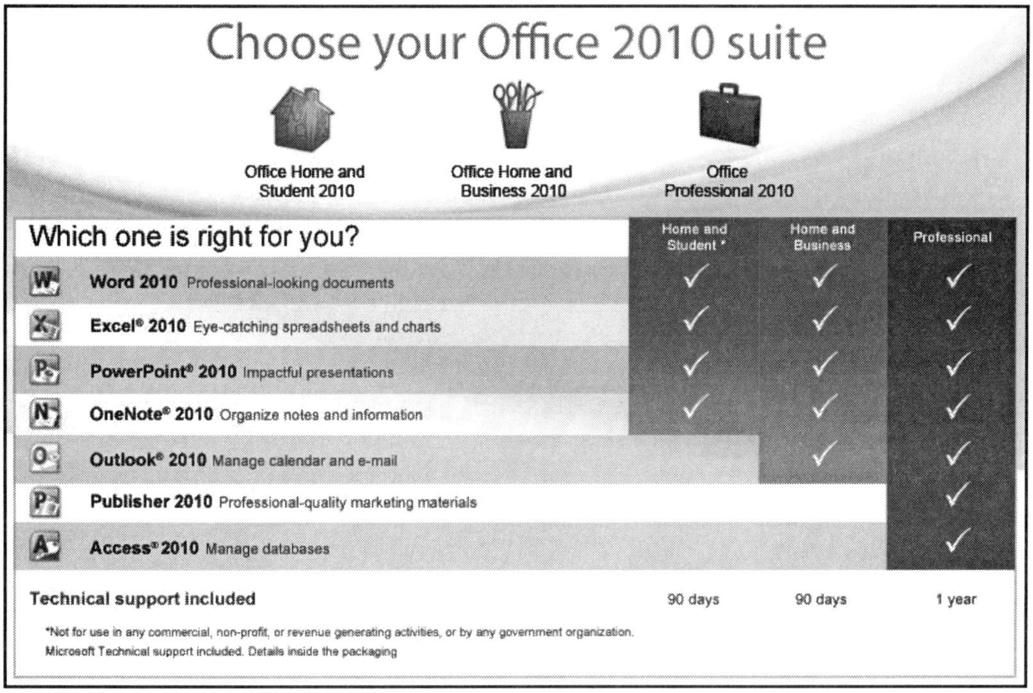

	Home and Student *	Home and Business	Professional
Word 2010 Professional-looking documents	✓	✓	✓
Excel® 2010 Eye-catching spreadsheets and charts	✓	✓	✓
PowerPoint® 2010 Impactful presentations	✓	✓	✓
OneNote® 2010 Organize notes and information	✓	✓	✓
Outlook® 2010 Manage calendar and e-mail		✓	✓
Publisher 2010 Professional-quality marketing materials			✓
Access® 2010 Manage databases			✓
Technical support included	90 days	90 days	1 year

Three basic editions of Office 2010 are available through traditional retail channels: 1) **Home and Student**, 2) **Home and Business**, and 3) **Office Professional**. You can purchase any edition as a download or as a Boxed Full version. Download editions are accessed through Product Key Cards that you can purchase. The Key Cards look like credit cards, but their plastic stripes contain activation codes that enable you to download a single install of Office 2010. The Boxed Full editions include full CD copies of the applications, printed manuals, and licences for two computers. Obviously, the Boxed Full edition licence is more expensive than Key Card licences.

The Home and Student edition is the least expensive of the three editions. It includes full versions of Word 2010, Excel 2010, PowerPoint 2010, and OneNote 2010. This edition is tailored to the needs of students and home users that want to create presentations, write documents, and manage finances. The Home and Student edition enables you to design professional presentations; manage household and small-business budgets; organize information; and create resumes, newsletters, and reports. The suggested retail price for the Home and Student edition is $149.99.

The Home and Business edition includes all of the applications contained in the Home and Student edition, plus Outlook 2010. This edition is tailored towards home-business users and active home users. This edition helps you stay connected with others whether you're at home, on the road, or at the office. The suggested retail price for the Home and Business edition is $279.99.

In *Word 2010,* you can choose a set of styles that are designed to work together. The style colors and formats in a single style set create an attractive and readable document.

The Office Professional edition includes all of the applications contained in Home and Business edition, plus Access 2010 and Publisher 2010. This edition is tailored toward business professionals. This edition also enables you to develop professional databases and marketing materials. The suggested retail price for the Office Professional edition is $499.99.

2.8 New Features in Office Applications

Microsoft Word 2010 New Features

Microsoft Word, or **Word** as it is commonly known, is a word processing program that was first released by Microsoft in 1983. Word allows you to create documents such as letters, brochures, resumes, flyers, and even books. Let's look at some of the new features included in the Word 2010.

- **Screenshots.** In Word 2010 you can easily capture and paste screenshots within your document. The Screenshot button is located on the Insert tab of the Ribbon. When you click the Screenshot button you will see a number of options to select depending on the number of windows that are currently open. Just select the option you want to insert into your document. You can then edit the screen shot using the picture tools.
- **SmartArt Graphics.** You can create professional looking visual representations of your information using SmartArt graphics in Word, Excel, PowerPoint, and Outlook. For those possessing minimal artistic skill, creating designer-quality graphics can be a very challenging and time-consuming process. But with SmartArt graphics, you can easily create professional charts, graphs, and diagrams by simply selecting from a variety of options and customizing the visual with familiar editing tools.

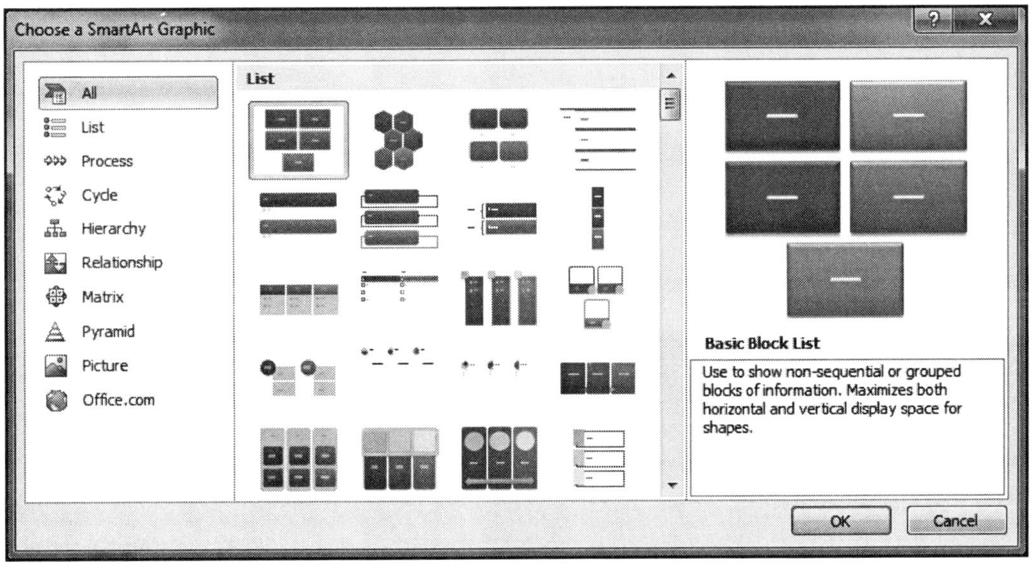

Figure 2.7: Smart Art

- **Artistic Effects.** With Artistic Effects you can easily add professional looking "artistic" effects to any picture in your document. This is an easy way to enhance your images without the need for expensive photo editing programs. Word 2010 has 20 new artistic effects including: Plastic Wrap, Photocopy, Pencil Sketch, Watercolor Sponge, and Paint Brush.

Figure 2.8: Artistic Effects

- **Background Removal Tool.** Another picture editing option in Word 2010 is the Background Removal Tool. This tool enables you to remove unwanted portions of a picture, such as the background, to highlight the subject of the picture.
- **Recover Unsaved Files**. In Word 2010, it's easier to recover an unsaved file, or to return to an earlier version of a file. You can use AutoRecover to automatically save a file at time intervals that you select. This allows you to easily recover files that have accidentally closed. You can also access a list of autosaved files from the Backstage view.
- **Translation Options.** Word 2010 enables you to translate an entire document, selected text, or just a word into another language. The document translation option lets you view your document in a Web browser. The selected text option lets you select any text in your document and see the translated text in the right side bar. Finally, you can translate individual words or phrases with the **Mini Translator**. Just hover over a word or select a phrase with your mouse and the translation is displayed in a small window directly above your selection. You can even hear a pronunciation by selecting the Play button.

Word can translate words from one language to another with the **Translation Tool Tip**. When selected, by hovering the mouse cursor over a word will display its translation in the particular language selected.

- **Sharing Files.** When collaborating with others on a Word 2010 document, you no longer have to waste time with sending the document as an email attachment. You can now simply save the file within Word to an online storage space (e.g., Windows Live SkyDrive) and give other permission to access the file.

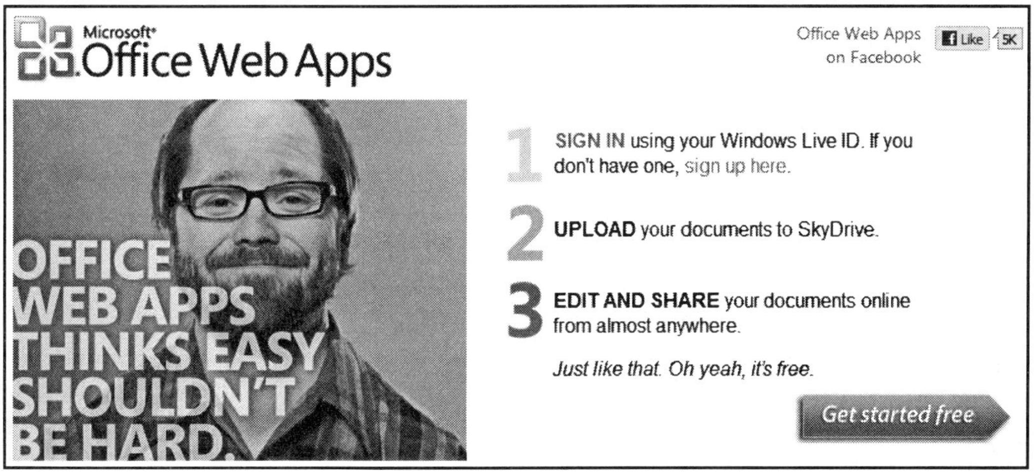

Figure 2.9: Microsoft Skydrive

Microsoft Excel 2010 New Features

Microsoft Excel is a spreadsheet application that enables you to perform numerous calculations with quantitative data. You can also display data graphically in various types of tables, diagrams, and charts. For almost 20 years, Microsoft Excel has been the industry standard for spreadsheets. Lets look at some of the new features that Microsoft has included in Excel 2010.

- **Sparklines.** Sparklines are small charts that fit into a single spreadsheet cell. Sparklines enable you to see a visual representation of your data without having to open another window or search for a graphical representation of your data. You can also see numerous graphical representations of data for easy comparison.

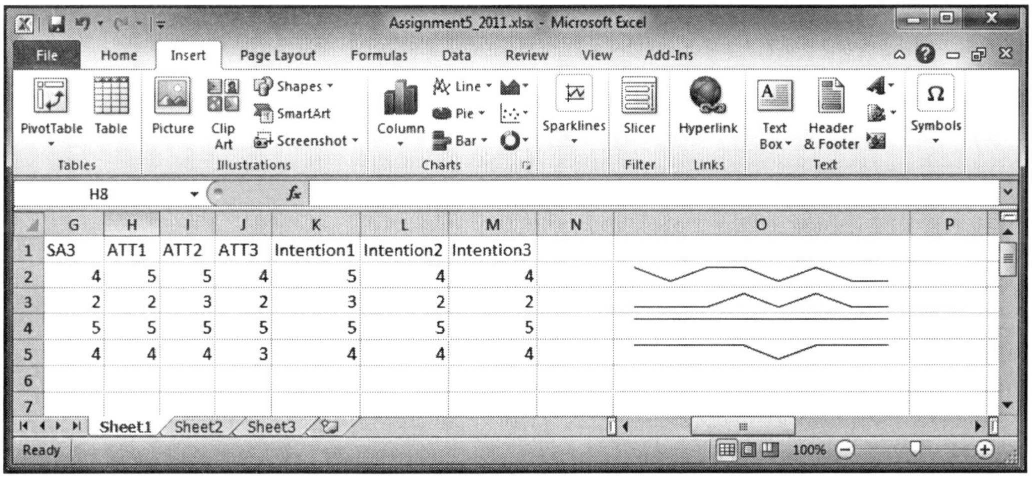

Figure 2.10: Excel Sparkines

- **Better Pivot Tables.** Pivot tables allow you to quickly report and summarize data in lists and tables independent of the original data layout. Pivot table results are displayed in a second "pivot" table showing the desired data. In Excel 2010, pivot table creation is quicker with multi-threading, automatic calculations, and enhanced filtering.

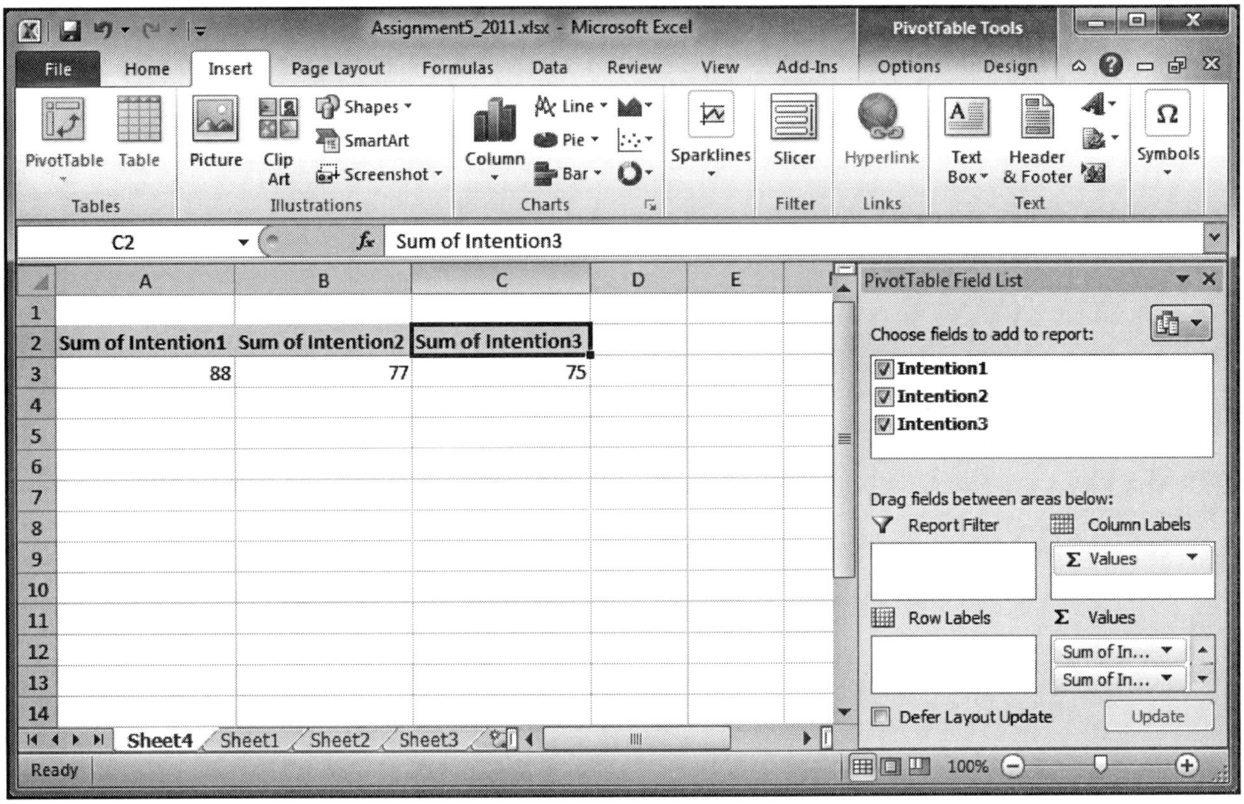

Figure 2.11: Pivot Table

- **Slicers.** Slicers are visual controls that enable you to quickly filter data in a pivot table in a more intuitive way. In Excel 2010, Slicers let you create buttons that enable you to quickly segment and filter data to display just what you want to see.
- **Better Conditional Formatting.** Conditional formatting lets you highlight specific cells or a range of cells that you want to emphasize. You can emphasize data through colors, icons, or bars. Excel 2010 contains new icons sets, more data bar options, and other improvements such as new formatting options.
- **More Themes.** Excel 2010 has more themes than ever before. Themes enable you to apply consistent professional designs across your Excel workbooks. Just select a theme and Excel applies the theme consistently to your data presentations.

> *Excel* can support up to 1,048,576 rows and 16,384 columns in a single worksheet, with 32,767 characters in a single cell.

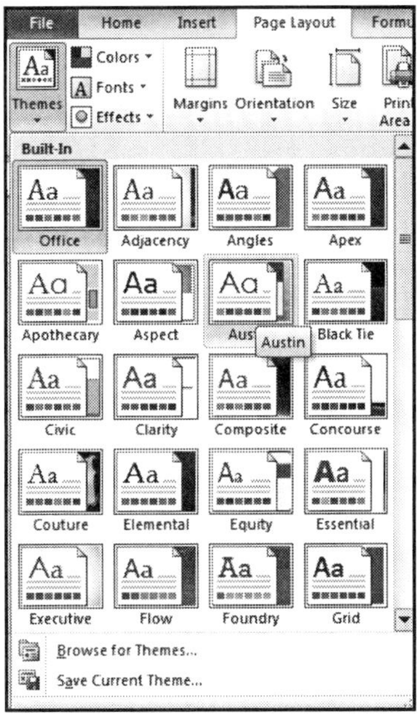

Figure 2.12: Excel Themes

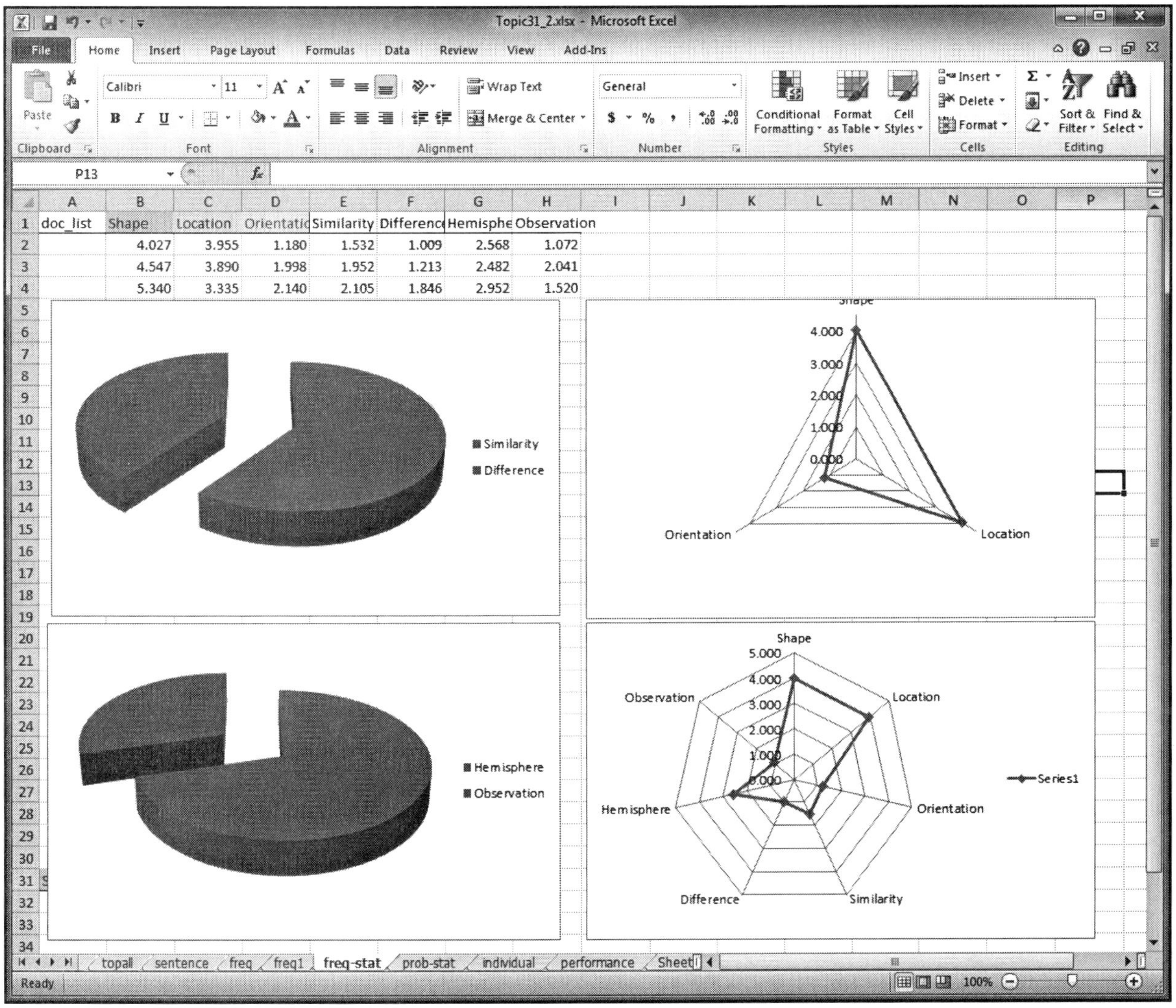

Figure 2.13: Microsoft Excel 2010

Microsoft PowerPoint 2010 New Features

Microsoft PowerPoint is a complete presentation graphics program. With PowerPoint you can create a professional looking presentation with minimal effort. It offers word processing, drawing, graphing, and presentation management tools.

> *Microsoft Office PowerPoint* has become the world's most widely used presentation program.

- **Recover Unsaved Files.** In Word 2010, it's easier to recover an unsaved file, or to return to an earlier version of a file. You can use AutoRecover to automatically save a file at time intervals that you select. This allows you to easily recover files that have accidentally closed. You can also access a list of autosaved files from the Backstage view.
- **Co-author Presentations.** With PowerPoint 2010, two or more co-authors can simultaneously work on a presentation. This prevents authors from being unable to access a presentation file because another author is currently working on it. In short, you no longer have to take turns to work on a co-authored presentation.
- **Slide Sections.** Using Slide Sections in PowerPoint 2010, you can break your presentation down into smaller parts to organize your presentation more effectively. This is somewhat like using folders to organize files in *Windows 7*. You can even assign specific presentation sections to colleagues to make collaboration more efficient.

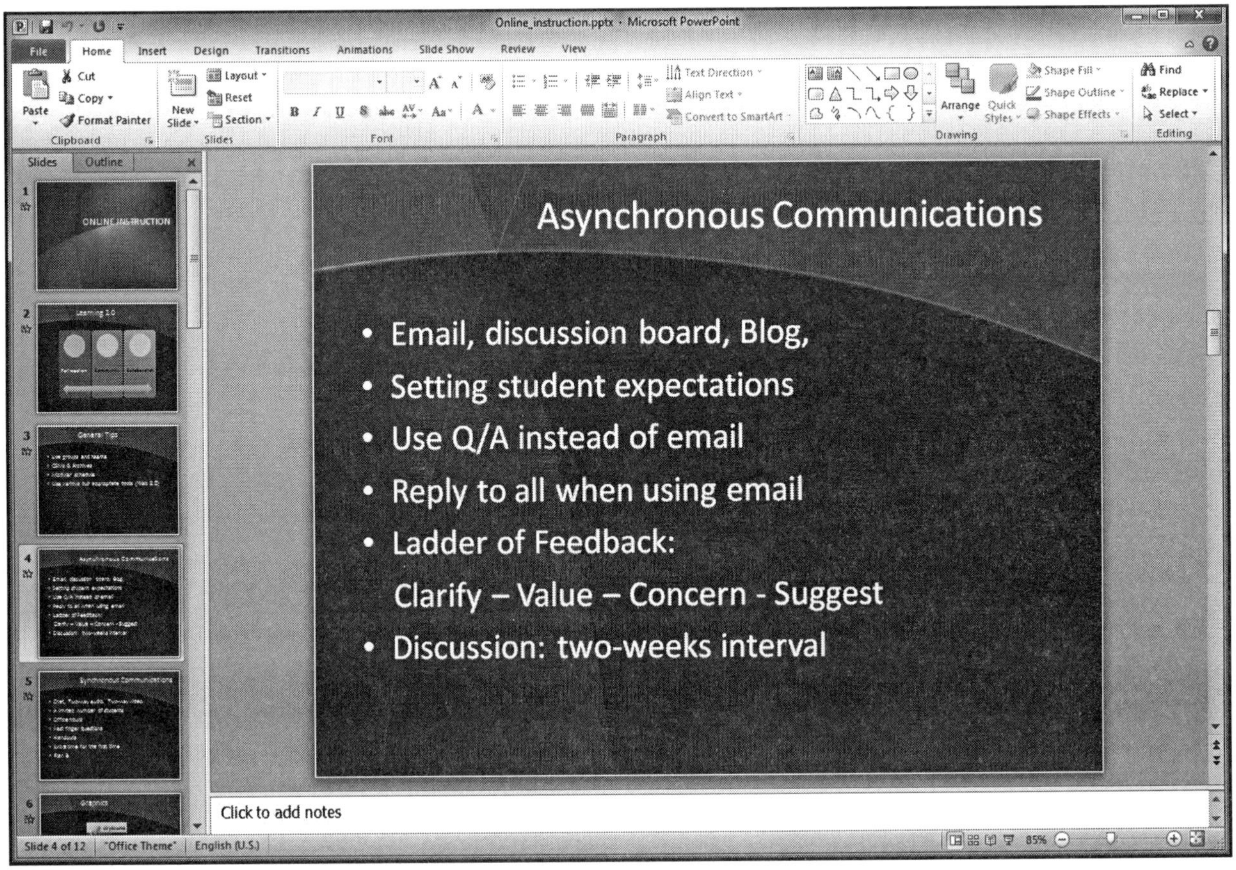

Figure 2.14: Microsoft PowerPoint

- **Improved Video.** In PowerPoint 2010, you can embed a video file directly in a slide. Since video files are embedded directly into the PowerPoint presentation, you no longer have to worry about missing video files when you show your presentation at different locations.
- **Editing Capabilities.** You can now edit audio and video clips in a PowerPoint presentation. For example, you can remove parts of a video or audio clip that is not important to your message. For minor editing, you no longer have to use a separate editing software program--you can do it right in PowerPoint.
- **Media Bookmarks.** You can use bookmarks in PowerPoint 2010 to highlight points of interest in a video or audio clip. You can also use Bookmarks to trigger an animation or to jump to a specific location in your video or audio clip.
- **Video Linking.** With PowerPoint 2010, you can insert videos in your PowerPoint presentation from other websites such as Youtube. As long as the video has an embed code, you can play it in your PowerPoint presentation.

2.9 Conclusion

Office 2010 is a powerful and much improved and expanded suite of programs for a broad range of computer users. The chart which follows summarizes the programs which are included in the various versions of *MS Office.* In this book, we cover use of the core *Offic*e applications. Other advanced applications are described briefly for reader awareness.

All of the exercises and assignments in the following modules in this book are based on *Windows 7* and *Microsoft Office 2010.* In these later modules, you will build on what you have learned in this module to create applications with the enhanced features of *Windows 7* and *Office 2010.*

Key Terms

Aero
Artistic Effects
Background Removal Tool
Backstage View
Core Applications
HomeGroup
Home Premium Edition
Internet Explorer 9
Jump Lists
Live Taskbar Previews
Microsoft Access
Microsoft Excel
Microsoft PowerPoint
Microsoft Word
Mobile Apps
Multitouch
One Box
OneNote
Peek
Pinning
Pivot Tables
Professional Edition
Protected View
Ribbon
Shake
Slicers
SmartArt Graphics
Snap
Starter Edition
Taskbar
Themes
Ultimate Edition
User Account Control
Video Linking
Web Apps
Windows 7 Capable
Windows 7 Premium Ready
Windows Explorer
Windows Media Center
Windows Media Player 12
Windows Search
Windows 7
Office 2010

Assignment 2: Microsoft Office 2010 Questions

Answer the following questions regarding *Microsoft Office 2010* based on the information provided in this module. Either complete and remove this page to submit to your instructor or submit your answers electronically based on your instructor's directions.

1. Office 2010 now includes the _______________ user interface in each suite of Office applications.
2. The ___________ lets you preview the information copied to your clipboard before you actually paste it in your document.
3. The ___________ button on the Insert tab of the Ribbon let you copy and paste screenshots.
4. *SmartArt* can be used to ____
   ____.
5. ___________ enables you to recover an unsaved file, or to return to an earlier version of a file.
6. The world's most widely used presentation tool is _________________________
   ____.
7. What four online applications does Microsoft provide free of charge? _________
   _________________________.
8. Two software programs included in the *Professional Edition* of *Office* which are not included in other editions are ______________________________ and
   ____________________________.
9. The Mini Translator enables users to _________________________.
10. You can use ______________ in PowerPoint 2010 to highlight points of interest in a video or audio clip.

MODULE 3

Word Processing

Word Processing

Word processing is the most common application for which PCs are used, and is probably the most significant advance in the school and the office since the invention of the typewriter. Word processing software, in the hands of an experienced user, produces documents that have been reviewed and revised several times, are correctly spelled, are grammatically sound, and are professionally formatted.

In this module, you will become acquainted with *MS Office* and learn how to use *MS Word 2010* to create your own documents.

Module Objectives

When you have completed this module, you should be able to:

- identify common components of *MS Office* programs;
- use commands common to all *MS Office* programs;
- describe advantages of word processing;
- explain and use the most common *MS Word* menus and tools;
- use *MS Word* to create your own documents; and
- identify the functions of word processing enhancements such as spell check, grammar check, and use of clipart.

Materials Needed to Complete This Module

- This book
- A flash drive (to make 2 copies of your work)
- *Microsoft Word 2010*

***Note:* The instructions and assignments in this module are for *Windows 7* and *Word 2010*. If you are using another version of *Windows* or *Office*, consult your user manual for instructions on completing the exercises and assignments.**

How to Proceed

1. Read this module. From your reading, you will learn about the benefits of word processing. The reading will also describe *Microsoft Word* and provide you with instructions on its use.
2. Review the *Key Terms* at the end of the module.
3. Complete the *Module Review Questions* at the end of the module and check your answers at the end of the book. Use *Microsoft Word* to practice your word processing skills.
4. Complete the *Module Application Assignments*. These assignments include formatting a practice file and writing a 1-page autobiography using *Microsoft Word*. Turn in your assignments to your instructor.
5. Take the Module Test.

3.1 Introduction to Microsoft Office

Microsoft (MS) Office is a collection of application software programs (often called a suite of programs) that work together and have similar interfaces. The versions of *Office* were described in Module 2.

This module, as well as later modules that use the *Microsoft Office* family of programs, assumes the use of *Microsoft Office 2010.* Windows shown in figures are from *MS Office 2010* programs.

Microsoft Word is a powerful **word processing program** that enables users to create many kinds of documents, including letters, memos, and reports. *MS Word* also includes the capability to create mail merges and web pages. Powerful **auto formatting** features allow users to create automatically numbered lists and to print envelopes for letters. Graphics and video clips can be incorporated into *MS Word* documents as well.

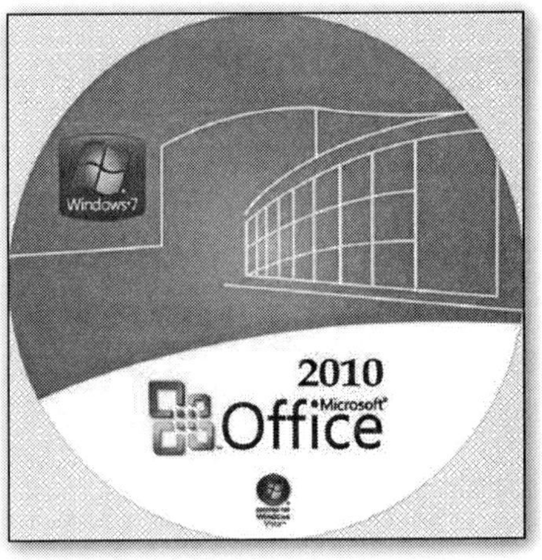

Microsoft Excel is a *spreadsheet program* that allows users to work with numerical information. Common applications for *MS Excel* include budgets, tax calculations, electronic grade books, expense calculations, and statistical analysis.

MS PowerPoint is a **presentation graphics** program that enables users to create slide presentations for meetings, classes, and web publishing.

MS Outlook is an **e-mail management program** that also includes a calendar, contact list, task list, and schedule.

3.2 Common Features of all Microsoft Office Programs

There are several general concepts and elements that are common to all *MS Office* applications. Most of these features are also found in other common productivity software programs. A **document** is any *MS Office* data file. *MS Office* features small colorful pictures called **icons** that represent the software programs on your computer screen. Figure 3.1 shows the window elements: Title bar, Menu bar, Tool bars, Close window button, Maximize window button, and Minimize window button. These **graphical user interface** elements, referred to as **GUI** (gooey), are common to all *MS Office* applications. It is recommended that you familiarize yourself with these window elements as they will be referred to throughout this text.

Microsoft estimates over five hundred million people use the *Office* suite, which includes *Word*. There are also many other commercial word processing applications, such as *WordPerfect*, which dominated the market from the mid-1980s to early-1990s.

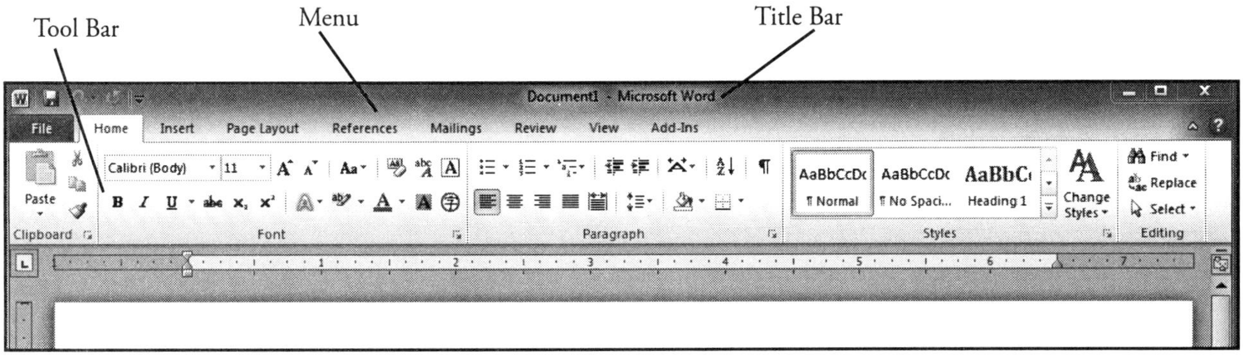

Figure 3.1: GUI Elements Common to *Microsoft Office* Software

GUIs were introduced in reaction to the steep learning curve of command line interfaces (CLI), which require commands to be typed in.

Another feature common to *Microsoft Office* is **dialog boxes.** A dialog box provides users the opportunity to select options. There are many types of dialog boxes. Some of the tasks that are performed with a dialog box are: opening, saving, printing, and selecting preferences. The *Save As* dialog box is found by following the path **File > Save As**. An example of the *Save As* dialog box is shown in Figure 3.2.

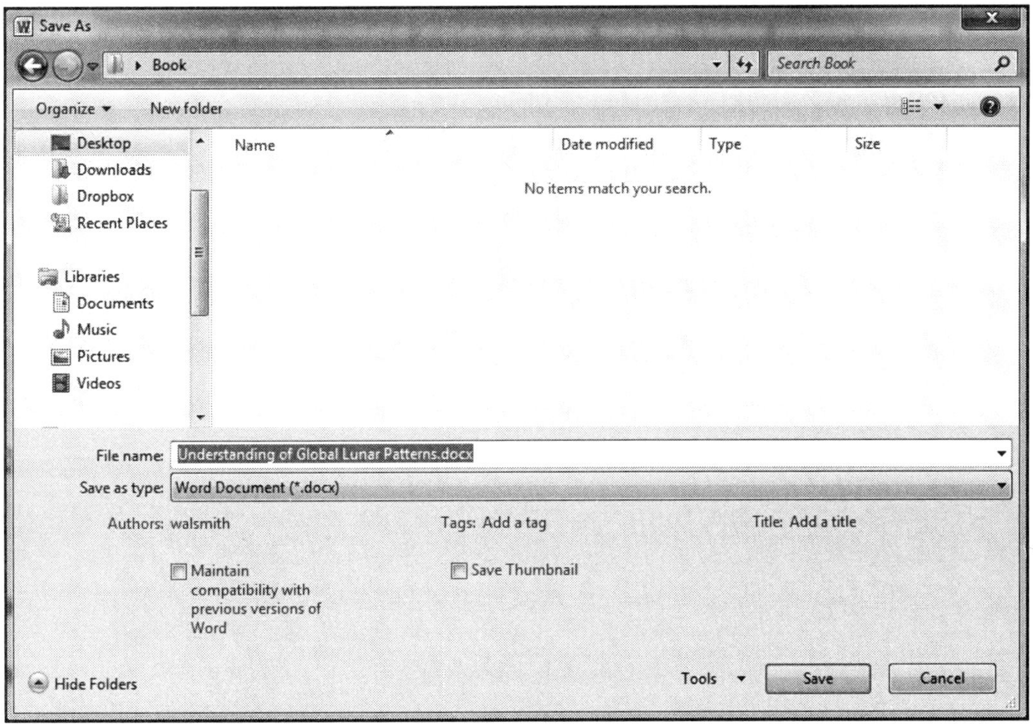

Figure 3.2: *The Save* As Dialog Box

Another GUI dialog box that you may use in *MS Office* is the printer dialog box (Figure 3.3). The printer dialog box enables users to select the printer they wish to use and to specify **parameters** such as the number of copies to be printed and the portion of the document to be printed, either all of the document or only selected pages.

Programs with graphical user interfaces, such as those written for use in *Windows* and *Macintosh* environments, organize their capabilities under **pull-down** or **pop-up menus**.

Users access these menus via the mouse or via keyboard commands. Menus on the far left of a menu bar usually represent basic and important commands, while menus to the right contain program-specific commands.

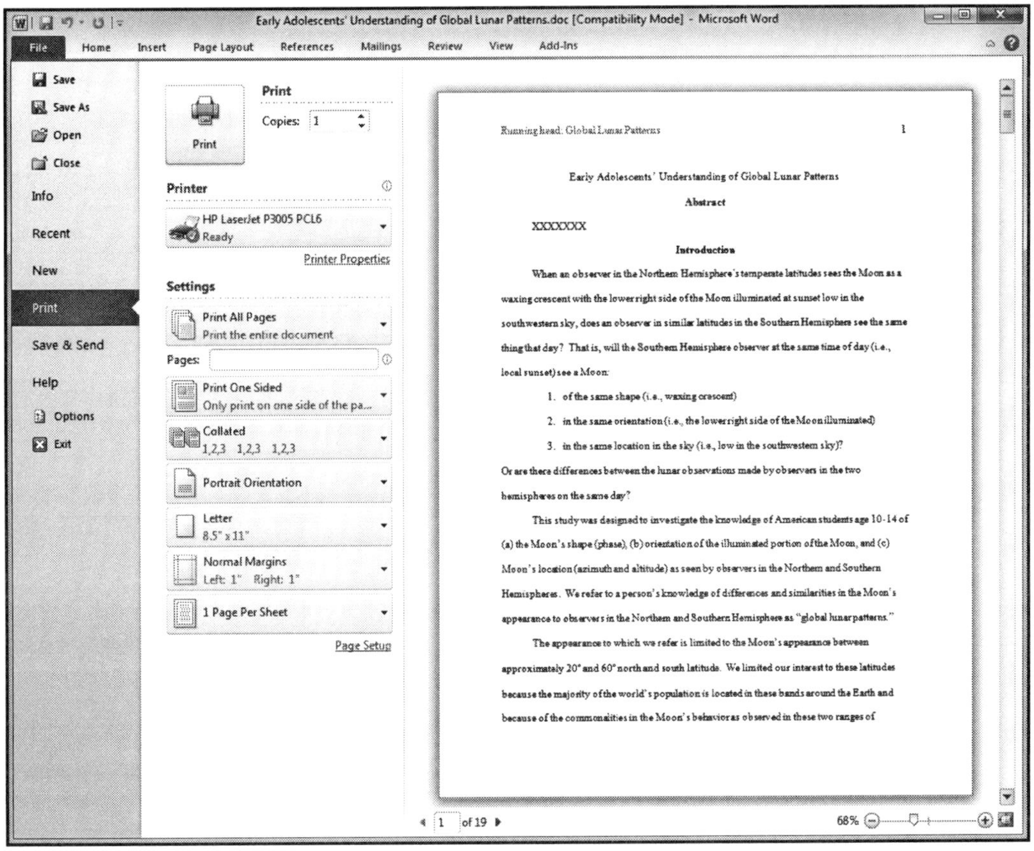

Figure 3.3: *MS Word* Print Dialog Box

Menus will change from program to program, but, in most cases, the **File, Home, Insert, Review**, and **View** menus are common to all programs and are located at the top of the screen. The **File** menu contains commands allowing the user to **Open, Close**, or create a **New** document; **Save** or **Print** an open file; and to quit or **Exit** the program. The **Home** menu contains commands that allow the user to change the contents of a file, such as **Cut, Copy,** and **Paste**. Using these 3 tools, you can incorporate text, pictures, and tables from other documents. After highlighting or selecting text, **Cut** gives the user the ability to cut the selection out of its current position. The **Copy** command works the same way except that it simply duplicates the selected text and leaves the original text in place. Next, you can then **Paste** the selection in another location in the document as desired. **Cut** and **Copy** place the selected text in a portion of the computer's RAM memory called the **clipboard**.

Find and **Replace** are two other powerful editing tools accessible from the Home menu. These commands allow the user to find specific words or text, and to replace it with other words or text. For example, a teacher writing up a student report might search for the word *student* in a document and replace it with a name such as *Nancy*. Using Find and Replace, users can minimize typing and reuse forms by replacing specific information.

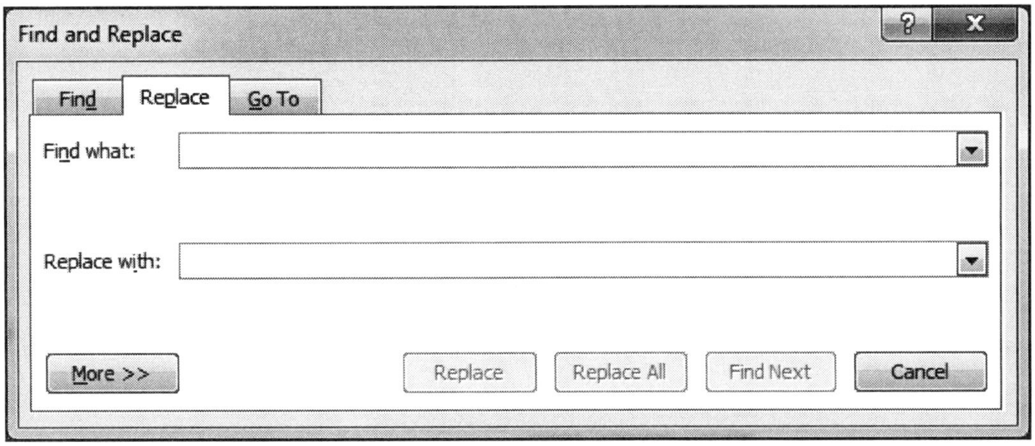

Figure 3.4: Find and Replace

The **Insert** menu enables you to add features to your documents. For example, you can add tables, hyperlinks, and pictures, as well as many other unique features depending on the Office application your are using. Various functions including headers and footers can also be selected from the Insert menu.

The **Review** menu allows you to comment on and edit Office documents. Review in *Word* allows users to check the spelling and grammar in a document, check a thesaurus, or translate a document into another language. The Review menu in other *Office* programs contains different options.

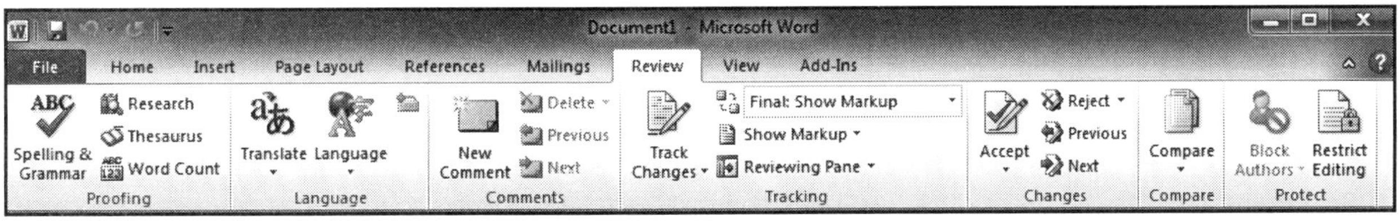

Figure 3.5: Review Options

The **View** menu contains options allowing the user to specify what is to be displayed and how. For example, the View menu in *MS Word* allows users to select a normal (full window) display, a web layout, or a print layout (Figure 3.6). The **View** tools allow the user to easily move from one open file to another by selecting the **Switch Windows** option.

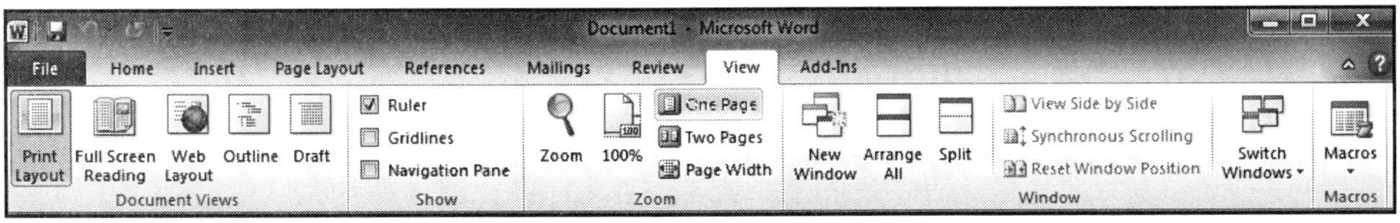

Figure 3.6: View Options

The **Help feature** is the **?** icon located at the right end of the menu bar.

On-screen help files provide answers to common questions about a program and explanations of program operations. The extensive Help feature allows users to enter a specific term or topic or to search a list of topics. Selecting a topic usually reveals several subtopics enabling the user to find an exact match to their question.

Another help feature is **Office.com**. At this site users can get online help while working in *MS Office*. Examples of online help include news articles, software updates, and templates.

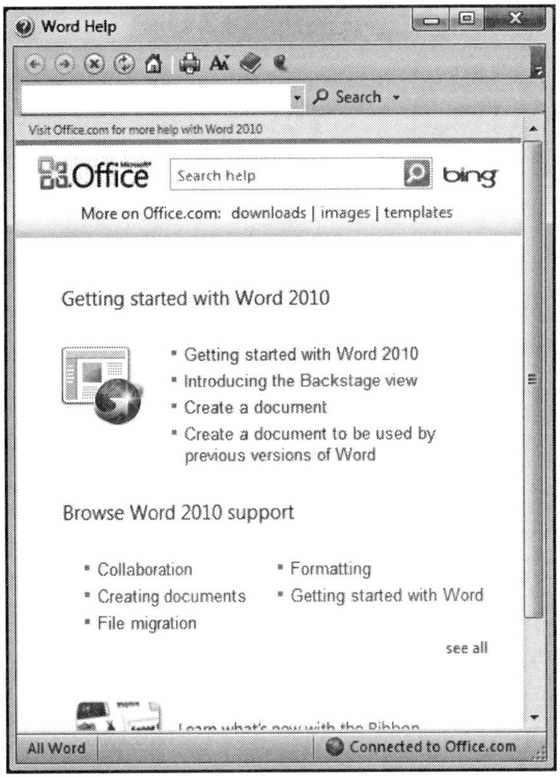

Figure 3.7: *MS Word* Help Features

The **Research** tool enables a user to look up information in a variety of references such as an encyclopedia, atlas, or dictionary.

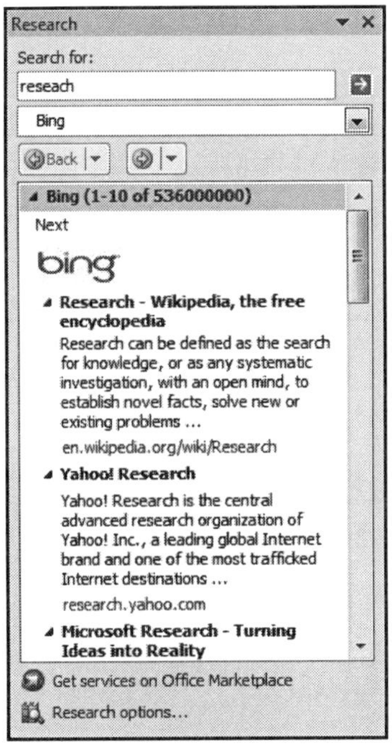

Figure 3.8: The Research Tool

3.3 Introduction to Word Processing

Word processors are valuable personal productivity tools because they improve the quality of writing. They make it easier to correct typing errors, to edit and revise, and to store written documents in a compact manner such as on flash drives. If you need to prepare a term paper or a report, write a letter, or produce other correspondence, then the ability to use word processing is a valuable skill. Businesses use word processing to produce letters, newsletters, business cards, reports, and more. Once computers were used only by scientists and programmers. When computers advanced enough to allow the editing of documents without retyping them, the usefulness of computers for everyone became evident. Had it not been for word processing, computers would not play the central role that they do in our society today. The skills you learn in this module should be of practical use to you now and in the future.

Today, most students are familiar with at least some aspects of using word processor software before they start college. If you are one of these people, this module will serve as a review for you on the basics of using a word processor. Since *MS Word* is part of a software suite, most of the skills that you will learn will also be used in later modules.

3.4 The Evolution of Word Processing

In 1964, *IBM* introduced what it called the magnetic tape ***Selectric* typewriter,** which stored typed text on small cassette tapes (similar in appearance to audio cassette tapes). The *Selectric* did not have a computer monitor to see what was being entered, but it was possible to save text on the cassette tapes and print "hard copies" as desired.

In the early 1970s, "glass-fronted" text editing systems began to appear. Word processing evolved from these text editors. These first text editors were machines with programs designed solely for the task of creating, editing, saving, printing, and maintaining electronic documents. The *Word Pad* and *Note Pad* programs included with *MS Windows* and *Macintosh OS* systems are examples of text editors. Introduced in the 1970s and early 1980s, the first word processing machines were called **dedicated word processors** because they could perform only one task: word processing. The name *word processor* has been maintained even though many current word processors can do much more than just entering and editing text.

Most early word processors were very expensive. For this reason they were used mainly by large businesses. The development of low-cost microcomputers in the mid-1980s made the advantages of word processing with computers readily available to our society. Unlike dedicated word processors, modern personal computers (also called desktop computers) are not limited to word processing.

PC word processing software descended from the early dedicated word processors. Today, many commercial word processing programs are available. Products such as *OpenOffice*, *WordPerfect*, and *Microsoft Word* are just a few of the word processing programs sold in the United States. However, the increasing dominance of *Microsoft Corporation* in the software industry in recent years has made *MS Word* the most popular word processing program by far.

3.5 Advantages of Word Processing

Using a word processor is much easier and more efficient than writing with pens, pencils, and typewriters. A word processing program allows users to type at a computer, alter or change their work electronically on the screen, and then print paper copies of the electronic document.

Word processing programs allow users to manipulate text in many different ways. One important feature of a word processor is **text formatting**, which allows users to define the appearance of text. Using text formatting, users can define its appearance. Text formatting features include the capability to apply styles such as **bold**, *italic*, and underline, and to change the font (text character) style, size, color, and spacing.

Another important formatting feature is **paragraph formatting**. Paragraph formatting changes how a body of text appears on the page. Some of the most common paragraph formatting features are the number of columns, the number and placement of tabs, the alignment or justification (left, right, center, or full justified) of text, and the amount of space before and after paragraphs.

Tables and charts are another useful feature of word processors. Users can create tables and charts by separating text into neat rows and columns and by using such table features as borders, colors, and shading.

Style sheets are great shortcuts to format text in a single step. The style sheet feature of word processors allows users to create text in a particular format and then to apply the sample complex attributes such as font, font size, number of columns, and alignment to other text documents. Common style sheets might be used for greeting cards, business correspondence, reports, and tables.

Some of the advantages of word processors are:

- Typing on a word processor is easier and faster than typing on a typewriter. A feature called **word-wrap** will automatically move to the next line when you come to the right margin. The word processor automatically breaks your line at the last word that fits within the set margins and advances to the next line. There is no need to press the RETURN key!
- Correcting mistakes and revising a document are easier on a word processor. You can change a word, delete a word or series of words, move a sentence or paragraph,

and insert words before printing. Move, copy, search, replace, find, delete, merge, and many other options permit the user to easily organize and alter information within a document. The word processor will correctly adjust the spacing of lines in your document whenever changes are made. These features can help make writing more precise and creative.

- You can save your work in progress to enable revision and updates at a later time. Your electronically created documents can all be saved on a flash drive, hard drive, CD, or online. Large amounts of text can be saved on any of these media. A single page of printed text in *Microsoft Word* requires about 2 K (kilobytes) of computer memory. A 3-1/2" inch data disk can hold 1.44 MB or 1440 K, the equivalent of about 720 pages of text. Much more text can be stored on CDs and hard drives.
- **WYSIWYG** (pronounced "wiz-e-wig") is an acronym for "What-You-See-Is-What-You-Get." WYSIWYG word processing programs display text on the screen exactly as it will appear when printed on paper.
- **Spell checkers and grammar checkers,** which are built into all modern word processors, help users correct spelling errors and grammatical mistakes. These tools are not intended to replace a computer user's natural skills, but to correct "typos" and other mechanical errors. Spell checkers may improve a student's ability to spell words correctly by identifying spelling errors and providing a set of options from the spell checker's internal dictionary. Spell checkers cannot detect grammar errors. If you typed "too" instead of "two," a spell checker could not detect an error since both are spelled correctly. You still need to check your work for errors even when using a spell checker.
- A **thesaurus,** which is included with most word processors, allows the user to select from a list of synonyms and antonyms of common words, and then exchange one word for another. If a word appears many times in a document, and the user desires another word with the same or related meaning, using a thesaurus will enable the user to quickly locate additional word choices.

3.6 Using Microsoft Word

The MS Word Icon

To start *MS Word* in *Windows 7*, click on the *MS Word* icon on the desktop. If the *MS Word* icon does not appear on the desktop, open the *Start Menu*, select *All Programs*, select *Microsoft Office*, and then select *Microsoft Word 2010.*

To create a new document, select **File>New** from the menu bar at the top of the screen.

3.7 Orientation to the Document Window

Microsoft Word and similar computer applications operate according to **WIMP** (Windows, Icons, Menus, and Pointing devices) principles. WIMP describes the interface and operating characteristics of a computer system. Operations in *MS Word* are performed in a **document window**. See Figure 3.9.

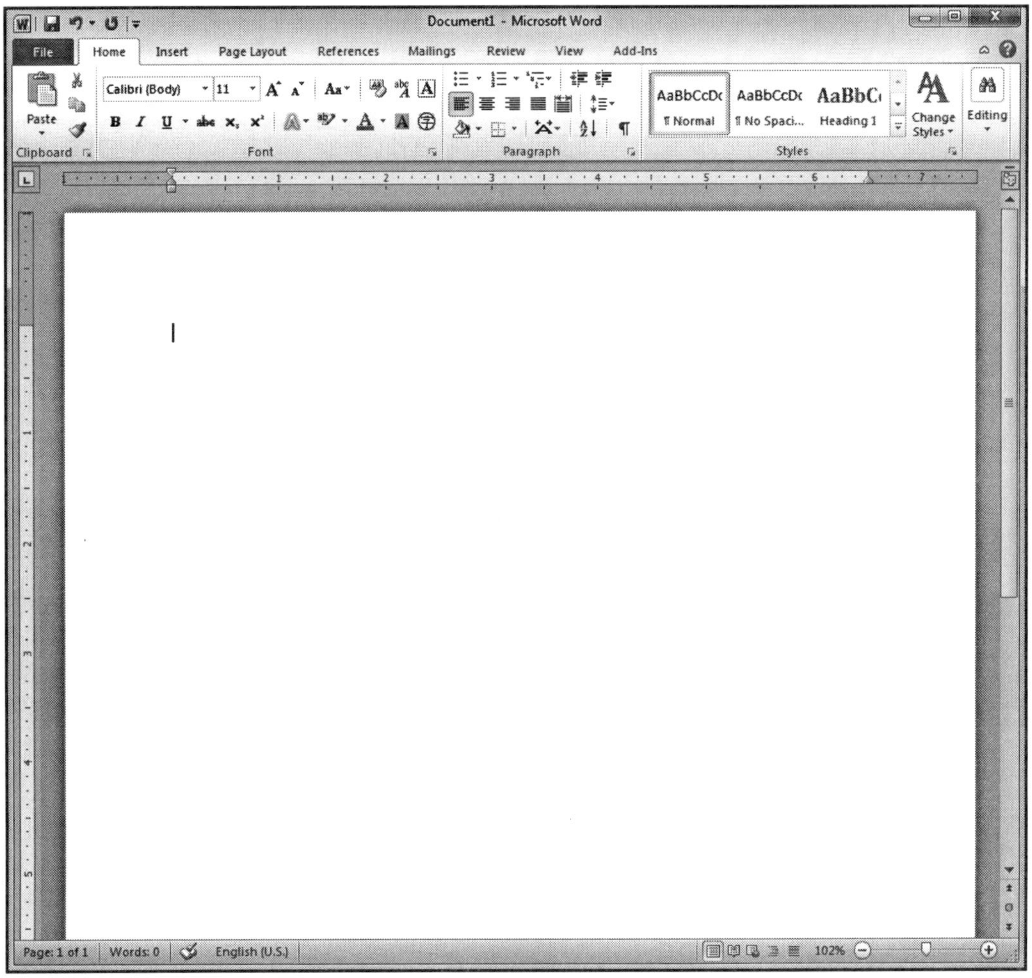

Figure 3.9: The Document Window

3.8 Menu Commands

Commonly used *Microsoft Word* menu commands are described in this section. A series of menu tabs provide the primary tool bars. Please note that the items displayed on the next few pages reflect the *Windows* version of *Microsoft Word*. The options differ slightly between *Macintosh* and *Windows* versions of *MS Word*. Many of the advanced commands are beyond the scope of this book. You can learn more about using advanced commands by opening the *MS Word* **Help** menu.

> Microsoft has made available a free add-on known as the "Microsoft Office Compatibility Pack" that lets *Office 2000-2003* editions open, edit, and save documents created under the new *Office 2010* formats.

3.9 File Tab

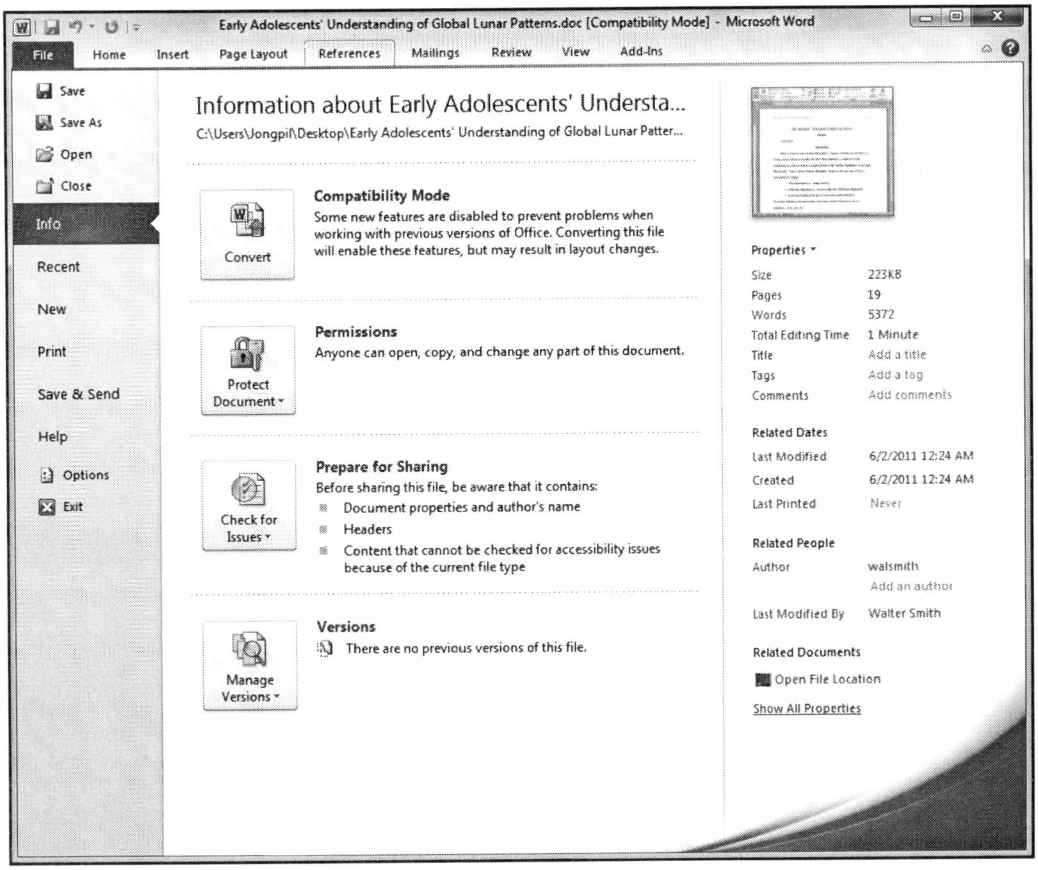

Figure 3.10: *Word 2010* File Tab

The newer ".docx" extension signifies Office Open XML and is used by Word 2010 for Windows and Word 2011 for the Macintosh.

- **New:** Creates a new word processing file in a new document window.
- **Open:** Allows you to retrieve and display an existing file in a new document window.
- **Close:** Enables you to close the current document.
- **Save:** Saves a copy of the current document with the same name. If the document has not been previously saved, you will be prompted to give the document a name.
- **Save As:** Saves a copy of the current document with a different name. Save As also gives you the opportunity to save the document to a different location such as a flash drive or public folder.
- **Print:** Provides options for printing parameters such as which pages to print and the number of copies to print.
- **Info:** This tool provides the means to edit the document properties, such as title, author, and keywords and to encrypt or restrict access to the document.
- **Save and Send:** This tool provides the options of sending the document as an email or fax. You can also use this tool to create a blog post or sharing the document on a server.
- **Recent:** Users can use this tool to view and access recently used documents.

3.10 Home Tab

The *Home Tab* tools provide the main *Word* editing options including font selection, size and style, paragraph layout, print color and style, and basic editing features including selection, find, and replace.

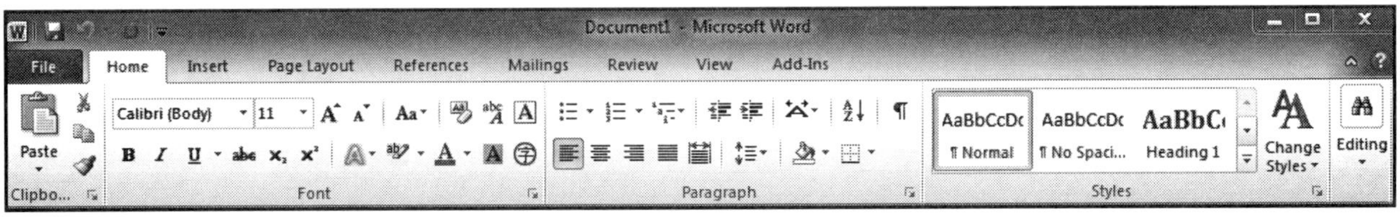

Figure 3.11: *Word* 2010 Home Tab

The primary tools on the *Home* tab are described below:

- **Fonts:** Text attributes such as boldface, italic, color, etc may be selected.
- **Text alignment:** Sets text alignment to left, center, full, or right justification.
- **Bullets and Numbering:** Formats selected text as a numbered or bulleted list.
- **Indentation:** Provides for automatic indentation of text.
- **Line spacing:** Sets line spacing as desired such as single space or double space text.
- **Style Sheets:** Style sheets are a set of preset attributes such as page and text color, text styles, indentations and other layout features. Selecting a style sheet formats a document in the predetermined style.
- **Editing:** Provides tools for selecting, finding, and replacing text in a document.

3.11 Insert Tab

The Insert tab provide the means to add tables, pictures, clip art, smart art, charts, hyperlinks, headers, footers, page numbers and various other options.

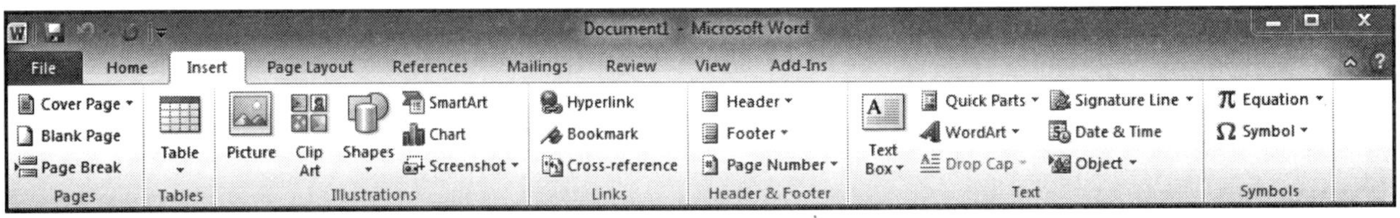

Figure 3.12: Word 2010 *Insert* Tab

Some of the main objects on the Insert menu are described below:

- **Blank Page:** Inserts a blank page in the document.
- **Page Break:** Ends the current page at the location of the cursor.
- **Table:** Inserts a table of rows and columns into a document. The grid may be shown or invisible.

- **Picture:** Allows users to insert a picture or graphic into a document.
- **Clip Art:** Allows users to insert a graphic from the built in clip art collection into a word document.
- **Chart:** This tool uses Microsoft Excel to create a chart such as a pie chart or a line chart into a document.
- **Hyperlinks:** Links to sites on the world wide web may be inserted into a document so that users can jump to a web resource from within a Word document.
- **Headers and footers:** These are lines on the top or bottom of each page which may contain a running head title or page numbers.
- **Page numbers:** These may be inserted into headers or footers to provide for automatic numbering of pages throughout a document.
- **Date and Time:** Like page numbers, the current date and time may be inserted into a header or footer or the body of the text.

3.12. Page Layout Tab

The Page Layout tab provides tools for setting themes, margins, number of columns, indentations, spacing, page color, and other page layout options.

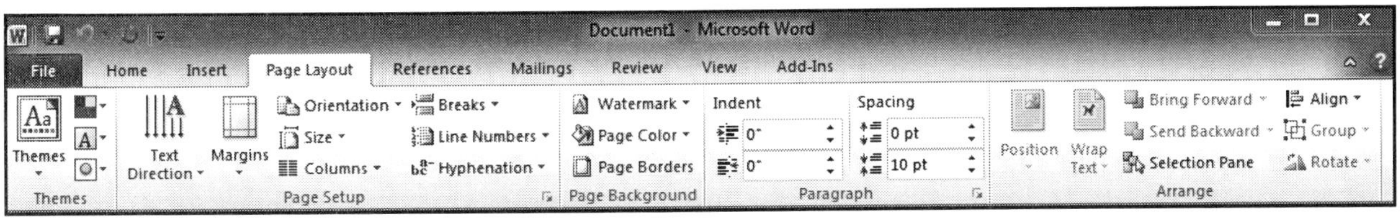

Figure 3.13: Word 2010 Page Layout Tab

Some of the primary layout options are described below:

- **Themes:** Themes are similar to style sheets and provide a means of changing the overall design of a document with preset colors, fonts, and effects.
- **Margins:** The top, bottom, left, and right margins for an entire document or a part of a document may be changed from the default settings.
- **Columns:** Full page layout is the default setting. This may be changed to provide for two or more columns which are of equal or unequal size.
- **Page Color:** The user may change the background color of the page from the default white background.
- **Page Borders:** A frame or border may be added to the page. Various colors and styles are available.
- **Paragraph indentation:** If indentation is desired, it may be set in inches to be applied to the document. Block style is the default setting.

3.13 References Tab

The References tab provides a means of creating and modifying a table of contents, entering footnotes, inserting citations, and entering cross references to other items within the document.

Figure 3.14: Word 2010 References Tab

The primary References options are described below:

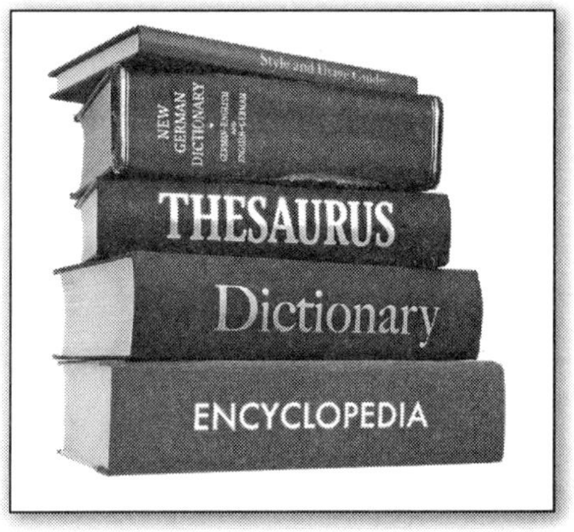

- **Table of Contents:** A table of contents may be added to a document. Once you have added a table of contents, entries may be added with the Add Text button.
- **Insert Endnote:** An endnote is a footnote that appears at the bottom of a page.
- **Insert Citation:** Books and journal citations may be inserted in the body of a document. The user may choose a style from a list of options.
- **Mark Entry:** Provides a means of entering selected text into an index which can be added to the end of a document.

3.14 Mailings Tab

The Mailings tab provides tools for formatting envelopes and mailing labels and creating a mailmerge with and address database.

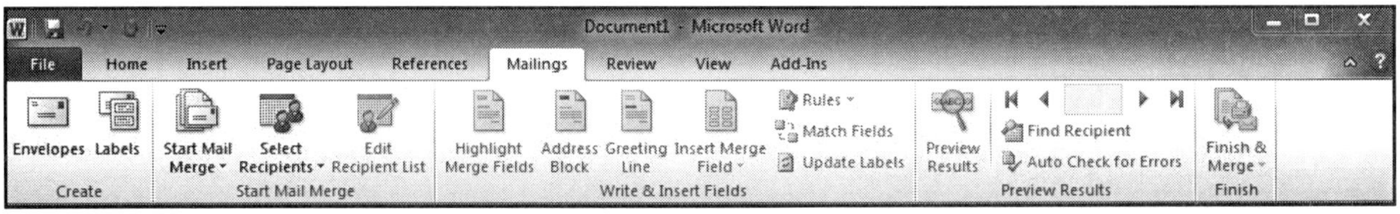

Figure 3.15: Word 2010 Mailings Tab

The primary Mailings options are described below:

> Mail merge is a software function describing the production of multiple (and potentially large numbers of) documents from a single template form and a structured data source.

- **Envelopes:** This tool provides a means of printing standard size envelopes with mailing and return addresses.
- **Labels:** The Labels tool enables users to create and print labels from a number of popular sizes and styles.
- **Start Mail Merge:** Mail Merge is used to create a form letter (either an email or printed letter) which you intend to send to

multiple recipients. You can insert fields such as name and address or other information from a database. Once a mail merge has been started, the Write and Insert Fields tools are used to create the mail merged letter.

3.15 Review Tab

Selecting the Review tab displays tools to check spelling and grammar, translate the document into a different language, find similar words in a thesaurus, insert non-printing comments into a document, and inserting editing marks into a document.

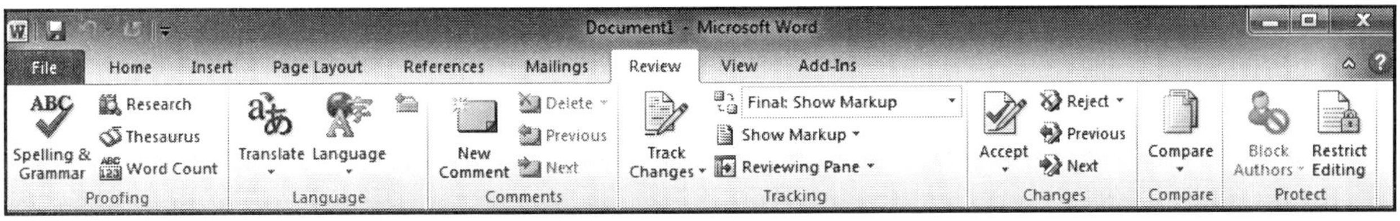

Figure 3.16: Word 2010 Review Tab

The primary Review options are described below.

- **Spelling and Grammar:** This familiar tool enables the user to check the spelling and grammar of a document. Word also checks spelling "on the fly" as a document is created and attempts to correct spelling and typing errors.
- **Thesaurus:** By selecting a word, users can use the thesaurus to suggest other words with a similar meaning.
- **Translate:** The tool provides the ability to translate a word or sentence into a different language. Translation is accomplished by sending the selected text over the internet to a translation web site.
- **New Comment:** This tool allows users to insert comments into a document. Various colors and styles may be used for comments. Instructors might use this tool to critique student work.

3.16 View Tab

The View tab includes various means of displaying the document on the screen including WYSIWYG print layout, web layout, and full screen display. A zoom tool allows the user to zoom in or out and the Window tool allows users to switch between documents or show 2 or more documents or pages on the screen at one time.

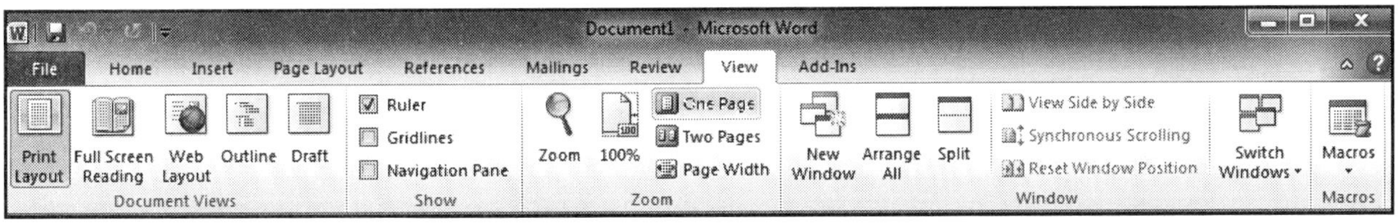

Figure 3.17: Word 2010 View Tab

The primary view options are described below:

- **Print Layout:** The pre-set view of the page. This is a general purpose view for typing, editing, and formatting text. Print Layout view shows text editing but simplifies the layout of the page so that you can type and edit easily.
- **Web Layout:** A view that simulates how the document will appear as a web page. Text appears larger and wraps to fit the window.
- **Full Screen Reading:** Displays 2 pages, side by side using the full monitor screen.
- **Outline:** Shows an outline view of the document.
- **Ruler:** Sets increments of the ruler above the current document window.

3.17 Help Button

Microsoft has recognized that people typically don't like to read user manuals and has built some very good help features into Word 2010 so that they can learn about *Word* as they use it. When the cursor is placed over any tool on the menu, a pop up balloon provides a description of the tool.

3.18 Formatting Text with MS Word

When you open *MS Word*, it is ready to go with present default parameters. These include page margins, line spacing, justification, tab settings, etc. However, users may change these settings. The most common text formatting methods are described in this section.

Changing Line Spacing

To change line spacing in a document:

1. Select the text to be reformatted.
2. Click on the spacing tool button in the *Home* tab.
3. From the dialog box, click on the desired spacing.

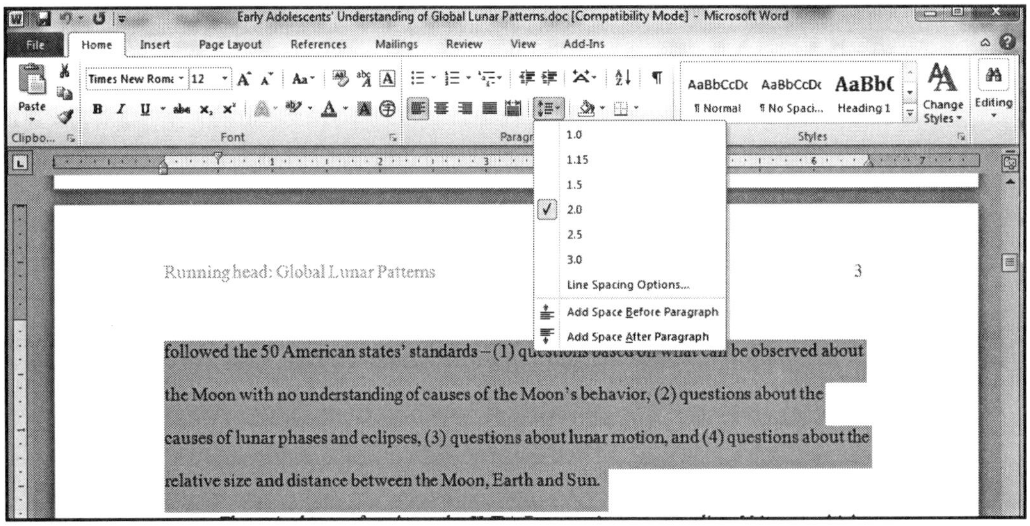

Figure 3.18: Changing Line Spacing

Setting Text Justification

To change the justification of text:

1. Select the text to be reformatted.
2. Click on the desired text alignment tool from the paragraph frame of the *Home* tab.)

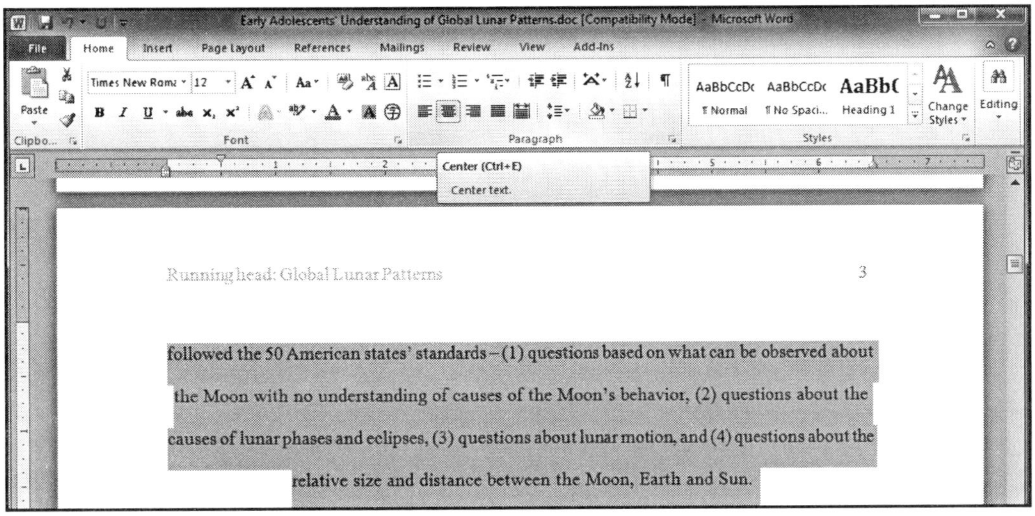

Figure 3.19: Text Justification

Setting Margins

To change the margins from the default settings:

1. Select the text to be reformatted.
2. Click on the *Margins* tool located in the *Page Setup* frame on the *Page Layout* tab. Choose from the present options or enter the settings desired.

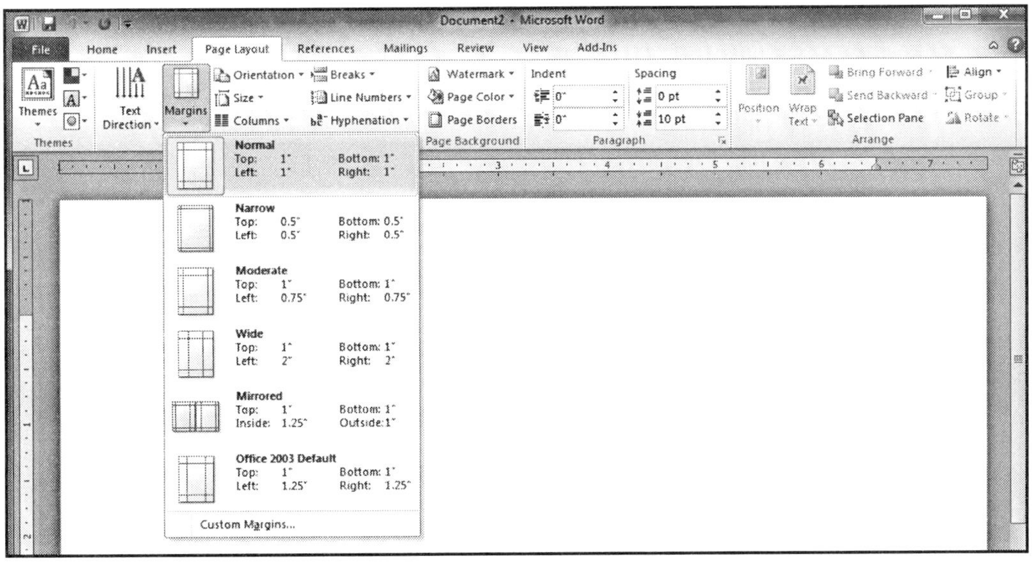

Figure 3.20: Setting Margins

Setting Tabs

To set a tab in *Microsoft Word*:

1. *Select All* or select the part of the document to be reset.
2. Click on the location of the desired tab setting in the ruler, located at the top of the document window.

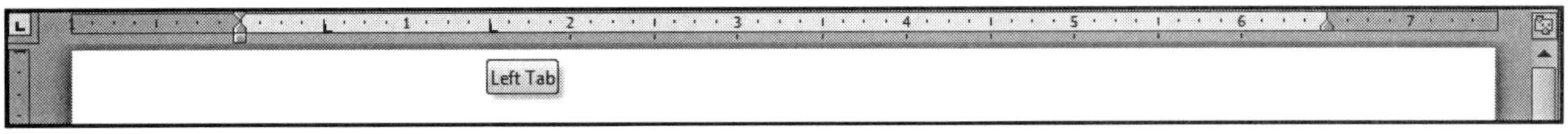

Figure 3.21: *MS Word* 2010 Tab Settings

3.19 Inserting Pictures and Clip Art

Microsoft Word provides for the inclusion of pictures and clip art within text.

Clip art, in the graphic arts, refers to pre-made images used to illustrate any medium. The term "clip art" originated through the practice of physically cutting images from pre-existing printed works for use in other publishing projects. Before the advent of computers in publishing, clip art was used through a process called paste up. To insert a graphic, follow these steps:

1. Place the cursor at the location in the document where you want the graphic to appear and left click to anchor the cursor.
2. Choose the *Picture* tool from the *Illustrations Pane* of the *Insert* menu.
3. Select the desired picture by browsing the files on your computer.

Alternatively, you may select the clip art or another illustrations tool. MS Office comes with a set of clip art preinstalled. To locate an image from the database, enter a search term as shown in the following figure. Double click on the image to insert it into the document. Additional clip art images may be downloaded from Office Online. Once the image has been inserted in the document, you can size the image by clicking on it to select it and dragging one corner to achieve the desired size. You can align the image using the left, center, or right align icons in the tool bar.

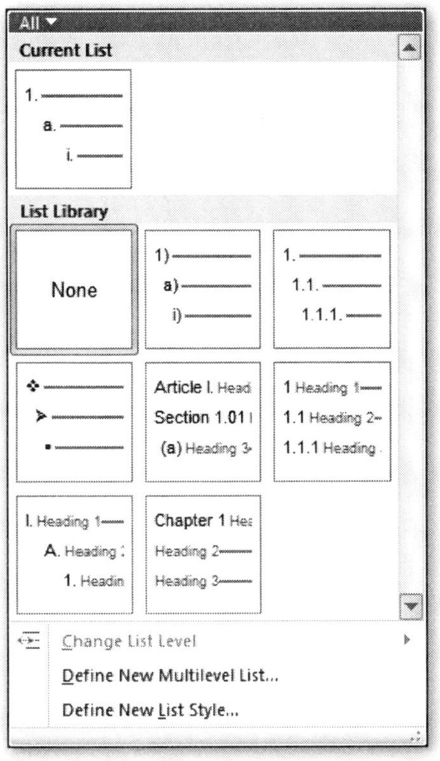

3.20 Formatting Lists

Microsoft Word allows the automatic formatting of many kinds of lists, such as numbered and bulleted lists. Automatic formatting includes proper indentation and symbols for a professional appearance. You can see the list options by selecting either the number or bullet tool from the Paragraph frame on the *Home* menu. Several styles of numbered and bulleted lists are available. See Figure 3.20

The list tools can be used in one of two ways: (1) select the type of list you want before you type the list; or (2) select and reformat existing text.

3.21 Saving and Backing Up Your Work

You should save and **back up** (save a second copy of your work) frequently as you work to avoid data loss should a program, disk, or the computer crash or if a power failure should occur. *MS Word* normally saves to a default location on the computer's internal hard disk (the C drive) and the *My Documents* folder for saving documents.

To save a backup copy of your work or to select an alternate to the default location for saving, follow these steps:

1. Open the document to be backed up or create a new document with *MS Word.*
2. Choose *File>Save As. . .*
3. Select the file format desired, usually *MS Word* format.
4. Choose the drive and folder where you wish to save your work. You can specify a flash drive, CD, or another drive. You will be prompted for a file name. You may use the same file name or a different one such as *Backup of My Document.* If you are unable to save your work to a flash drive or your own disk, on many networked computers you can save your work to the computer's *public folder.*

3.22 Conclusion

This module has introduced you to the most popular productivity software suite, *Microsoft Office,* and to word processing. Every aspect of *MS Word* was not presented, but the information covered should allow you to use this popular program to create your own documents effectively. More information on using *MS Word* and other *MS Office* programs are presented in later modules.

Key Terms

Back up
Clip art
Clipboard
Dedicated word processor
Dialog box
Document
Document window
Formatting
GUI
Help
Icons
Menu bar
MS Excel
MS Office
MS Outlook
MS Word
MS PowerPoint
MS Office Online
Parameters
Pop-up menu
Presentation graphics
Pull-down menu
Save
Save As
Selectric typewriter
Shortcut keys
Spell checker
Style Sheets
Thesaurus
Mail Merge
Tool bar
WIMP
WYSIWYG
Word-wrap

Computer Application Assignments

There are 2 parts to the computer application assignment for this module:

1. Practice Document: *How Computers Work and*
2. *Autobiography.*

Assignment 1: How Computers Work

The purpose of this assignment is to provide you with the opportunity to use the word processing skills that you have learned in this module. When you have completed this assignment, you will have a printout of a document titled *How Computers Work* that you have formatted and changed as explained below. You will use practice files included with this book to complete this assignment. Refer to the information given in this module to complete this assignment.

1. Start *Microsoft Word,* and then open the Module 3 practice file titled *How Computers Work.*
2. Save the file to your own disk or flash drive.
3. Make the following format changes to this document:
   a. Select the entire document and change the font to Verdana.
   b. Change the text size of the entire document to 11 point.
   c. Change the line spacing for the entire document to 1 ½ space.
   d. Add your name and the current date to the upper left hand corner of the document. Place a blank line after this.
   e. Add the following title on the first line above the document text: *How Computers Work.* Center, boldface, and set the text size to 14 point for the title. Place a blank line after the title.
   f. Locate the list in the third paragraph, which begins with "Let's take a look at the main components . . ." and reformat it as a numbered list. You may select any of the bulleted list options.
   g. Insert a computer diagram just before the last paragraph.
   h. Spell and grammar check the entire document. Correct any misspelled words.
4. Save your revised document and print it out to turn in to your instructor. It is also a good idea to save a back up copy of your work.

Assignment 2: Autobiography

Write a 1-page autobiography. The information that you include is up to you. This assignment may help your instructor get to know you better. Review the information given in this module as needed to complete the assignment as you work. Follow these steps to complete this assignment:

1. Start *Microsoft Word* and open a new blank document. Title your document: "Your Name" Autobiography.
2. Type a 1-page autobiography.
3. Format your autobiography to include the following elements:
   - The entire document should use Verdana font.
   - The title should be bold and centered.
   - The title should be sized at 16-point text and the rest of the document should be 12-point text.
   - Both margins should be justified. This means that both the left and the right margins should be straight.
   - The document should be double spaced and 1-2 pages long.
   - When your autobiography is complete, check the spelling and grammar.
   - Save your autobiography. It is also a good idea to save a back-up copy of your autobiography.
   - Print a copy of your autobiography to turn in to your instructor.

MODULE 4

Advanced Word Processing

Advanced Word Processing

Advanced word processing features discussed in this module provide an introduction to computing tools commonly used in business and educational settings, including use of form letters, mail merges, and the integration of word processing with electronic spreadsheet files, graphs, and graphics. *MS Word* supports some database functions, mainly form letter applications.

In this module, you will learn to use *Microsoft Word's* advanced word processing features to create a mail merge and a letter, which includes a table produced by an electronic spreadsheet.

Module Objectives

When you have completed this module, you should be able to:

- identify advanced word processing features and functions;
- differentiate between a field, a record, and a file in a database;
- recognize advantages and applications of using an electronic database;
- perform a mail merge from an address database using *MS Word*; and
- create a letter that includes a table and graphics using *MS Word.*

Note: Instructions and assignments given in this module are for *Office 2010.*

Materials Needed to Complete This Module

- This book
- *Microsoft Word 2010* or later edition
- Disks or other storage media on which store your work.

How to Proceed

1. Read this module.
2. Review the *Key Terms* at the end of the module.
3. Complete the *Module 4 Review Questions* at the end of the module.
4. Complete the *Module 4 Computer Application Assignments*. In the computer application assignments for this module, you will create a newsletter and a mail merge letter, which includes a table imported from an electronic spreadsheet. Specific instructions for these assignments are provided later in this module. Print the instructions to turn in to your instructor.
5. Take the Module 4 test.

4.1 All About Fonts and Type

Fonts are resources used by a computer to produce type on a screen or via a printer on a page. *Microsoft Word* comes with a variety of **fonts** or **typefaces** installed. Libraries of fonts can also be purchased on CD or downloaded over the Internet. Some popular fonts sizes are:

This is 9 point type.

This is 10 point type.

This is 12 point type.

This is 18 point type.

This is 24 point type.

The main body type used in this book is 12 point type. Fonts of 10 or 12 points are considered to be acceptable sizes for body text. They are easy to read for most people. Larger point sizes are used for headings and subheadings in manuscripts.

Fonts can be enhanced with a variety of font styles. Some of these are shown below.

This is boldface text.

This is italic text.

This is underlined text.

~~This is strikethrough style.~~

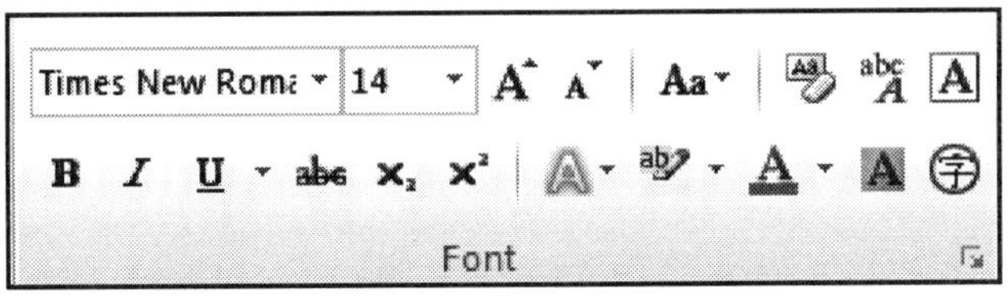

Figure 4.1: Font Tab

Also, *Word 2010* comes with a set of font style templates. Font styles may be accessed with the ***Change Styles*** tool located in the *Styles* pane of the *Home* menu. Style sheets are listed in the following figure.

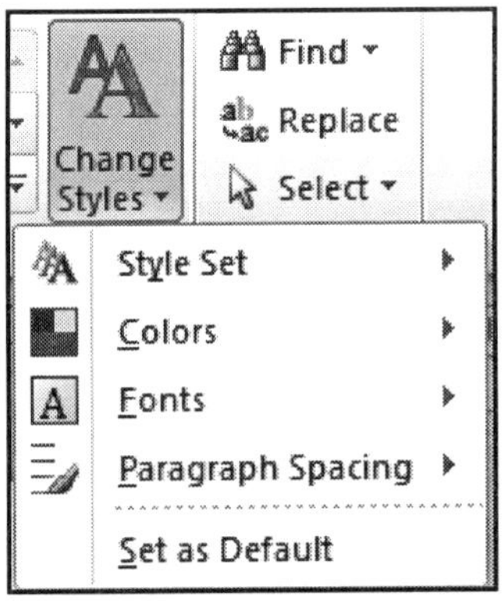

Figure 4.2: Font Styles

Times New Romans
Calibri
Garamond
Arial
Impact
Helvetica

There are three main kinds of fonts: bitmap fonts, PostScript fonts, and Truetype fonts. **Bitmap fonts** are composed of tiny dots. These fonts tend to print poorly and are now rarely used. **PostScript fonts** avoid the jagged appearance of bitmap fonts because they are described mathematically using a printer language called PostScript. However, PostScript fonts must be used with PostScript printers, which are generally more expensive. Most laser printers are PostScript printers. Less expensive printers usually use a different printer command language called Printer Command Language (PCL). **TrueType fonts** are also described mathematically but can be used with either PostScript or PCL printers.

The choice of fonts is largely an individual choice. However, you should not get too carried away with ornate and unusual fonts.

MS Word contains many useful, advanced word processing features. We can not cover all of them but some of the more popular advanced features are described in the next part of this module.

4.2 Templates

One of the most useful ways to extend the power of *MS Word* is though the use of **templates.** *MS Word* templates are available from a variety of sources. Templates are available from the *Microsoft* web site at **<office.microsoft.com/en-us/templates>**. The Microsoft site contains a template gallery for *MS Word* that includes a wide variety of templates such as those for greeting cards, form letters, letterhead, legal forms, mailing labels, calendars, resumes, and more. These templates can be downloaded for free. They can be easily customized for various projects that enhance the usefulness of *MS Word.*

Figure 4.3: *Microsoft Clipart Gallery*

4.3 Clip Art

In addition to the limited amount of clip art that comes with *Word* (see *Clip Art* from the *Insert* menu), a large assortment of searchable clip art is available on the *Microsoft* web site at **<office.microsoft.com/en-us/images>**. Images can be downloaded at no cost and may be used in a wide variety of ways with *MS Word* as well as with other *Microsoft* applications. Clip art includes drawings, animations, sounds, and stock photography.

4.4 The Quick Access Toolbar

The **Quick Access Toolbar** is a customizable toolbar that contains a set of commands that are independent of the tab that is currently displayed. The default location of the *Quick Access Toolbar* is in the upper left corner of the screen, but you can move it below the ribbon if you desire. You can also easily add buttons that represent commands to the *Quick Access Toolbar*. The *Quick Access Toolbar* is shown in the following figure. The sample toolbar shown in Figure 4.4 includes a Quick Save feature (the disk icon), an undo typing feature, a repeat typing tool, and the autotext tool.

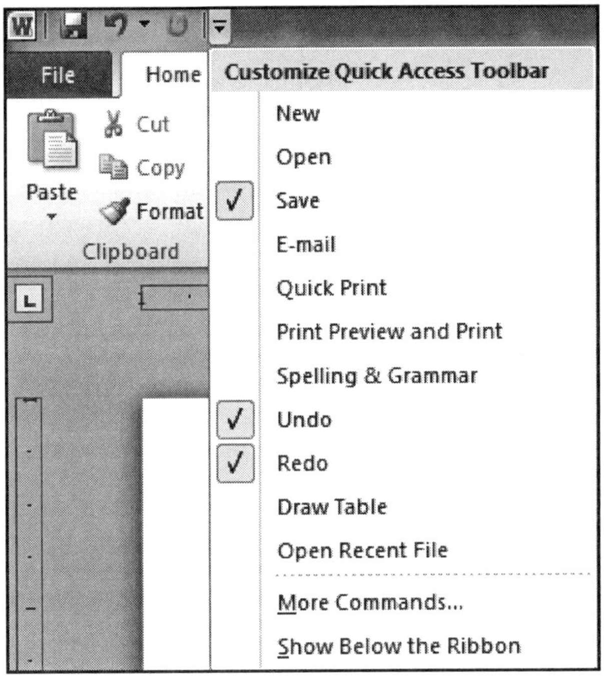

Figure 4.4: The Quick Access Toolbar

4.5 AutoText

The **AutoText tool** allows you to insert completely preformatted text into a document, a real timesaver. You can put anything into AutoText that you wish. Examples include a document letterhead, a form for data entry, or a standard paragraph of information that you may want to insert into a letter or document. In Word 2010, each AutoText entry is called a building block.

Follow these steps to add a building block to your AutoText gallery in Word 2010:

1. Select the text you want to save as a building block. Graphics or pictures may be included.
2. Click *Insert* > *Quick Parts* (located in the *Text* task pane)
3. Click *AutoText* > *Save Selection to AutoText Gallery* (bottom of dialog box)

Once an entry has been added to the *AutoText* gallery, you can add an AutoText building block to a document by selecting the desired building block from the *Auto-Text* dialog box.

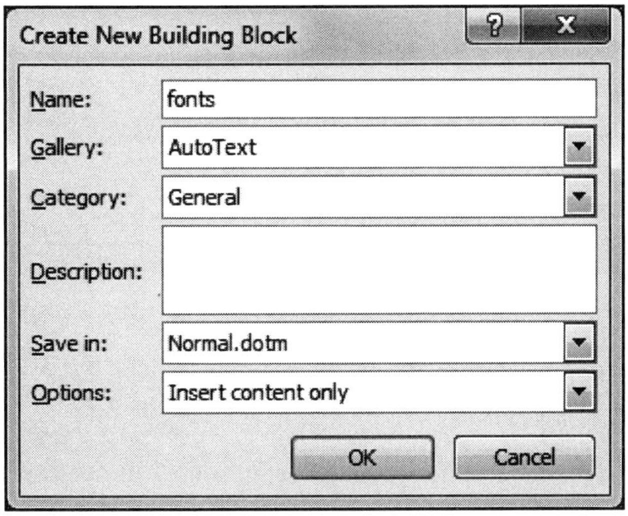

Figure 4.5: New Building Block for Auto Text

4.6 Footnotes and Endnotes

Footnotes and Endnotes explain, comment on, or provide references for a designated part of the text in a document. You can include both footnotes and endnotes in a document. Footnotes appear at the end of a page in a document, while Endnotes appear at the end of a document.

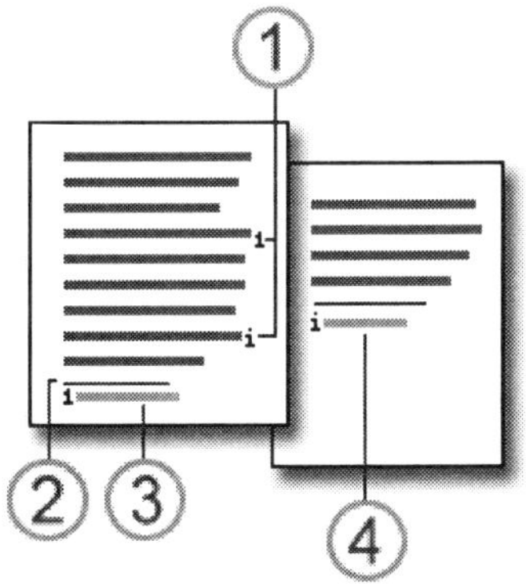

1. Footnotes and endnotes reference marks
2. Separator Line
3. Footnote text
4. Endnote text

From office.microsoft.com

Figure 4.6: Footnotes and Endnotes

Footnotes and endnotes consist of two linked parts: the note reference mark and the corresponding note text. In Word 2010, you can use automatically numbered marks or create your own custom marks. When you add, delete, or move notes the note reference marks are automatically renumbered. To insert a footnote or endnote, follow these steps:

1. Click *View* > *Print Layout*
2. Click where you want to insert the note reference mark.
3. Click *References* > *Insert Footnotes*, group, click *Insert Footnote* or *Insert Endnote.* The following figure shows the *Insert Footnote* dialog box.

Figure 4.7: The *Insert Footnote* Dialog Box

You can customize formatting options for footnotes and endnotes by opening the *Footnote and Endnote* dialog box. Just click the dialog box launcher in the lower right corner of the *Footnotes* pane.

4.7 Comments

Comments can be used to add non printing comments to a document. Comments are a popular way for teachers to provide feedback on student work. You can add comments of any length to a document and format the text just as you would any other text. To add comments to a document in Word 2010, follow these steps:

1. Select the text or item that you want to comment on, or click at the end of the text passage.
2. Click *Review* > *New Comment* > (from the *Comments* group).
3. Type the comment text in the comment balloon.

Opening a *Word* Document file in a version of *Word* other than the one with which it was created can cause incorrect display of the document.

Figure 4.8: The Comment Dialog Box

To view a comment, rest the pointer on the comment reference mark in the document. The comment appears above the mark.

4.8 Bookmarks

A bookmark is a location or selection of text that you name for reference purposes. *MS Word* marks the location with the name you specify. Bookmarks can be used to create and number cross-references in a long document. You might also use a bookmark to identify a location that you wish to revise at a later time to eliminate the need to scroll through a document to locate it. Bookmarks can create cross reference hyperlinks that jump to a predetermined place in a document. To create a bookmark, follow these steps:

1. Place the cursor at the desired location where a book mark is to be located.
2. Click *Insert* > *Bookmark* (from the *Links* group).
3. Give the bookmark a name, such as *Bookmark 1*, when the dialog box appears.

Below are shortcut keys for working with cross-references, footnotes, and endnotes that make document editing more efficient.

Action	**Key combination**
Mark a table of contents entry	ALT+SHIFT+O
Mark a table of authorities entry	ALT+SHIFT+I
Mark an index entry	ALT+SHIFT+X
Insert a footnote	ALT+CTRL+F
Insert an endnote	ALT+CTRL+E

Figure 4.9: *MS Word* Shortcut Keys for Notes

4.9 Indexes

When working with long documents, it is often helpful to include an index. An index is basically a more detailed table of contents located at the end, rather than the beginning, of a document.

To create an index, you must first mark your index entry (words or phrases) in your document. Once you have marked all the entries to be included in your index, you can build the index by following these steps:

1. Select the text in your document that you wish to use as an index entry.
2. Click on *References* > *Mark Entry (from the Index* group)

After you mark all the index entries, you choose an index design and build the finished index. *Word* collects the index entries, sorts them alphabetically, references their page numbers, finds and removes duplicate entries from the same page, and displays the index at the end of document.

Figure 4.10: The *MS Word* Index Tool

4.10 Tables of Contents

A table of contents is useful in books or any long document. You create a table of contents by choosing the heading styles — for example, Heading 1, Heading 2, and Heading 3 — that you want to include in the table of contents. *Word* searches for headings that match the style that you choose, formats and indents the entry text according to the heading style, and then inserts the table of contents into the document.

An ergonomic keyboard

Word provides a gallery with multiple table of contents styles to choose from. Mark the table of contents entries, and then click the table of contents style that you want from the gallery of options. *Word* automatically creates the table of contents from the headings that you marked.

To create a table of contents, follow these steps:

1. Click where you want to insert the table of contents.
2. Click *References* > *Table of Contents* > *Insert Table of Contents* (from the *Table of Contents* group)
3. Click *Options.*
4. Under *Available styles*, find the style that you applied to the headings in your document.
5. Under *TOC level*, next to the style name, type a number from 1 to 9 to indicate the level that you want the heading style to represent.
6. Repeat step 4 and step 5 for each heading style that you want to include in the table of contents.

Figure 4.11: The *MS Word* Table of Contents Tool.

4.11 Tables

A table is a collection of information organized in rows and columns. Tables can contain numbers, text, or combinations of numbers and text. Each row and column intersection is called a cell. Word allows users to either create a table by choosing from a selection of preformatted tables, called Quick Tables, complete with sample data or you may create a table from scratch using your own specifications.

To create a QuickTable in MS Word using a template, follow these steps:

1. Click where you want to insert a table.
2. Click *Insert* > *Table* > *Quick Tables* (from the *Tables* group) and then click the template that you want.
3. Replace the data in the template with the data that you want.

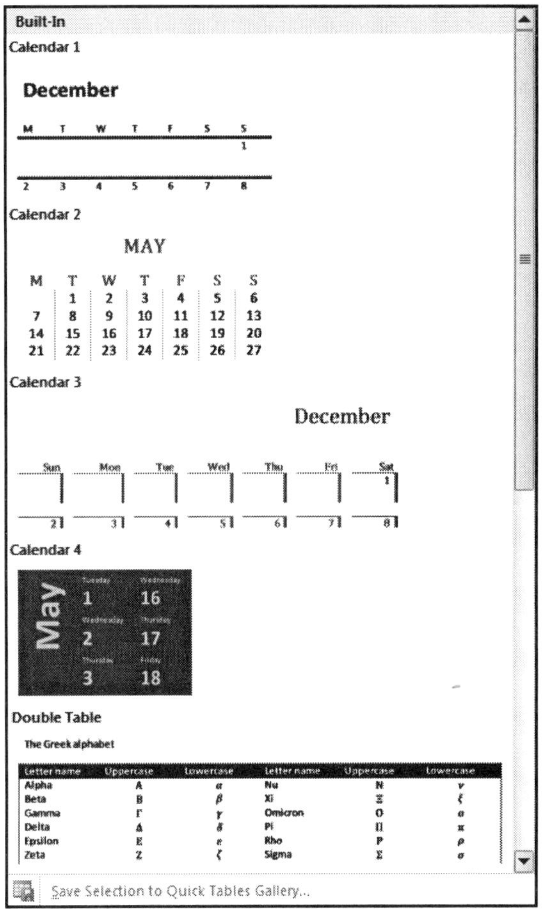

Figure 4.12: Some Examples of *Word Quick Tables*

4.12 Envelopes and Labels

The *Word Mailings* feature, allows users to print envelopes and labels either individually or as a mail merge using a database of names and addresses. *Word* allows you to print envelopes and labels using pre-defined label formats based on commonly-used commercial label formats. To create a single envelope or label, click on either *Envelopes* or *Labels* from the *Create* pane of the *Mailings* menu. Enter the mailing address and a return address in the dialog box.

You will need to insert an envelope or a sheet of mailing labels into your printer and you will need to place the envelope face down and adjust the paper guides to fit the envelope before you click on *Print.*.

Clicking on the **Labels** property sheet tab will display options pertaining to printing labels. When you click **Options**, the next dialog box gives you the option of changing the label product name and of choosing from a list of commonly used commercial label formats. For example, suppose you would like to print out your greeting card mailing list on a set of standard gummed labels. You could purchase a package of labels from an office supply store. Using the **Mailings>Letters and Mailings>Envelopes and Labels** feature in *MS Word*, you select the product number that corresponds to the product number on the package of labels you purchased and create a new document for your labels. Figure 4.10 shows what a pre-defined commercial label format might look like in *MS Word*. In this example, *Avery* standard 160 Mini Address Labels have been selected. The label maker allows you to print a full page of the same address or print single labels from a list of addresses.

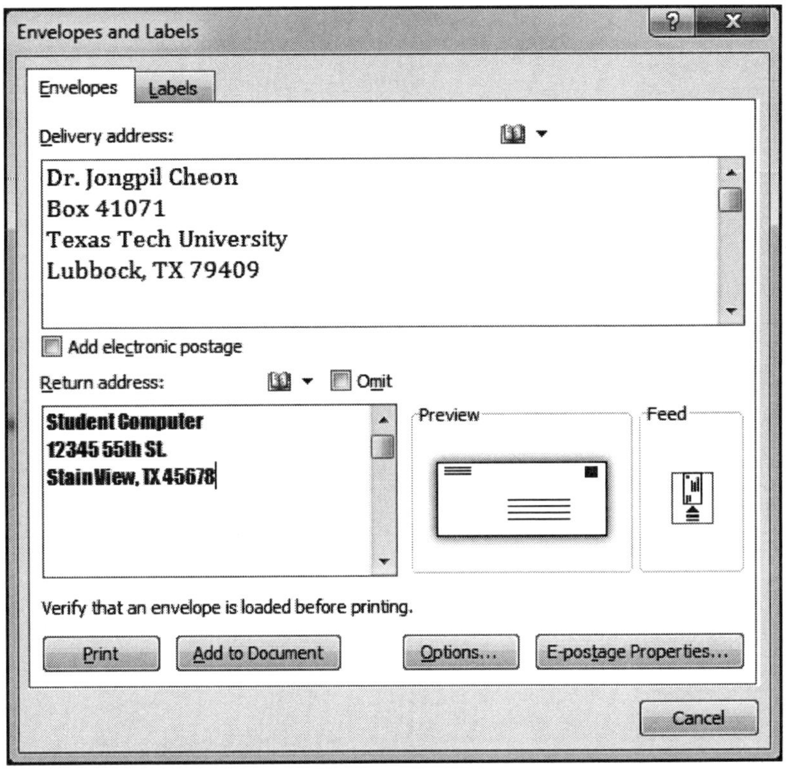

Figure 4.13: The Envelopes and Labels Dialog Box

4.13 Creating a Mail Merge with Microsoft Word

Mail merge is a useful feature for creating mass mailings. *Microsoft Word's* mail merge feature consists of two parts: the **main document** (a single document that functions like a template and contains the text and graphics that stay the same for each version of the merged document), and the **data source** (the file that contains the names, addresses and other information used in the mail merge process). The data source can be created from within *MS Word* or it can originate in *Microsoft Outlook, Microsoft Access,* or *Microsoft Excel.* You will complete a mail merged letter in the assignments for this module. To create a mail merge for a letter using *MS Word*, follow the steps below.

1. Click on *Start Mail Merge* from the *Mailings* Menu.
2. Click on *Letters* from the *Mail Merge* Submenu.

Figure 4. 14: Starting a Mail Merge

3. Create a letter. A business letter could be a letter written to a particular business requesting information or it could be one business writing to another business. Figure 4.12 is a sample business letter from a college student requesting information regarding an internship.

Mail merge is a software function describing the production of multiple (and potentially large numbers of) documents from a single template form and a structured data source.

The **heading** for the business letter includes the writer's complete address and the date. The heading is spaced about an inch from the top of the page.

The **current date** should be placed on the letter below the heading. To insert the current date, skip a space below the heading and select Date and Time from the Text pane of the Insert Menu.

The **inside address** is placed on the left margin, 4 to 7 line spaces below the heading. It should include the name and address of the person and/or company to whom the letter is being sent.

The **salutation** is placed two line spaces below and directly under the inside address. The most common salutations when addressing a company or firm are *Gentlemen:, Dear Sir:, or Dear (Company Name).* If you are writing to an individual within the company, you should address him or her as *Dear Mr. Smith, Dear Miss Jones*, or *Dear Ms. Watson.*

The **body** of the business letter is the same in form as the body of any letter. It should be single-spaced (unless it is very short: 7 lines or less) with a double space between paragraphs.

The **closing** comes between the body and the signature. The most commonly used closings for business letters include *Very truly, Very truly yours, Sincerely yours*, or simply *Sincerely*. The **signature** of a business letter should always include a handwritten signature of the writer, followed by the typed name and title of the writer. Use your own name in the signature.

A sample form letter is shown on the following page.

John Doe
1234 Memphis Avenue **: Heading**
Lubbock, Tx 79423

6/16/2011 **: Current Date**

Howard World Communications Co.
2090 West Buena Vista Dr. **: Inside Address**
San Diego, CA 12345

Dear: **: Salutation**

I am writing you to inquire about the summer internship program for which your company is so highly acclaimed. I am a Junior Communications Studies major at Central State University with a speciality in Corporate Organization Communications. My dream is to one day be the head of my own business. This summer internship program would provide me with the hands-on experience that would show me what to expect in the business world.

I have spoken with some employees at your company, and I am convinced that this would be the perfect job for me. I am hard-working, competitive, and dependable. I am also extremely motivated to put forth 110% in any endeavor into which I enter. I would be grateful if you could send me further information on the internship program. You can reach me at home at 806-555-1234 or on my cell at 806-444-1478 or by email at joedoe@ttu.edu. Thank you for your time and consideration.

Sincerely, **: Closing**

Your Name **: Handwritten Signature**

Your Name **: Typed Signature**

Figure 4. 15: A Form Letter For A Mail Merge

4. After creating a letter, Click on *Select Recipients* from the *Start Mail Merge* panel of the *Mailings* menu.
5. Select *Type New List.*
6. Type in a list of 5 names, entering information in the *Title, First Name, Last Name, Company Name, and Address 1, Address 2, City, State*, and *Zip* fields. You may make up the names and addresses or use real ones. You may leave the other fields blank. Use the tab key to scroll from field to field. See the following figure for an example of a name entry. Repeat the data entries until you have entered 5 names.

You use mail merge when you want to create a set of documents that are essentially the same but where each document contains unique elements. For example, in a letter that announces a new product, your company logo and the text about the product will appear in each letter, and the address and greeting line will be different in each letter.

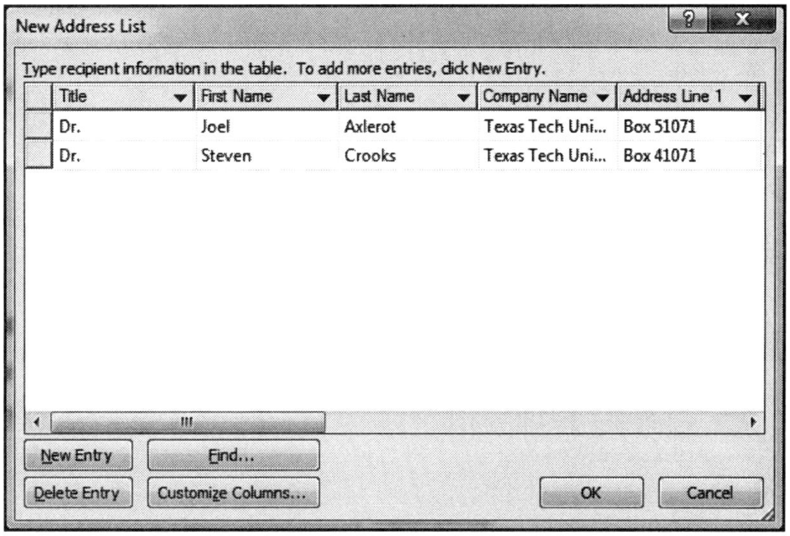

Figure 4.16: Creating A Mailing List

7. Click *OK* when you are finished entering the 5 names and addresses and give your address file a name and save it when prompted. By default, your name and address file will be saved in a folder named ***My Data Sources***.
8. After saving your address file, to continue the mail merge, click on *Select Recipients* from the *Start Mail Merge* panel of the *Mailings* menu.
9. Click on *Existing List* and locate your address file in the *My Data Sources* folder.

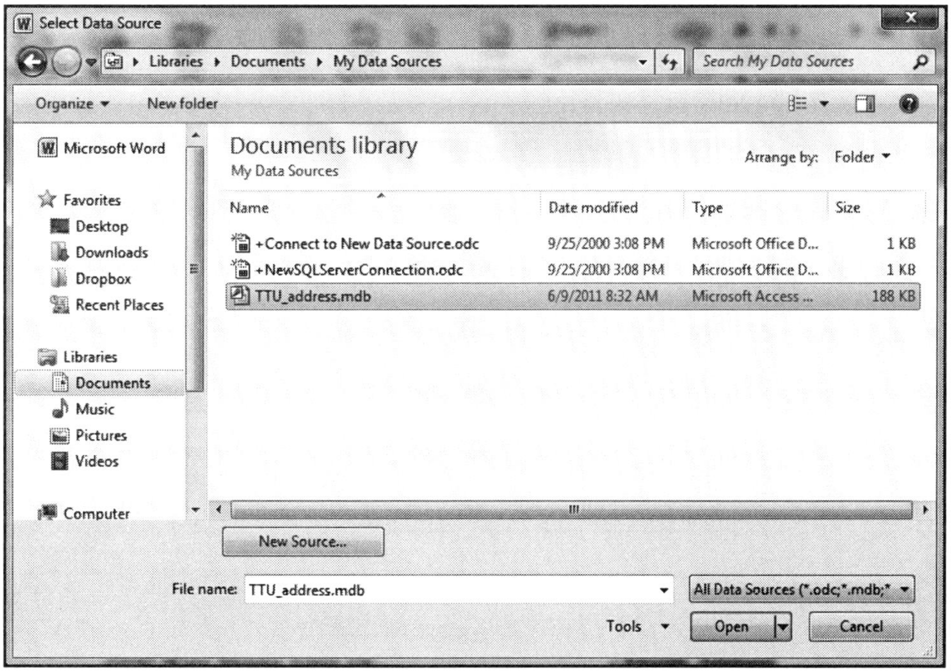

Figure 4.17: Selecting The Mailing List

10. Click on *Address Block* from the *Write and Insert Fields* pane of the *Mailings* Menu. Select the recipient's name, company name, address to insert into the form letter and click OK.

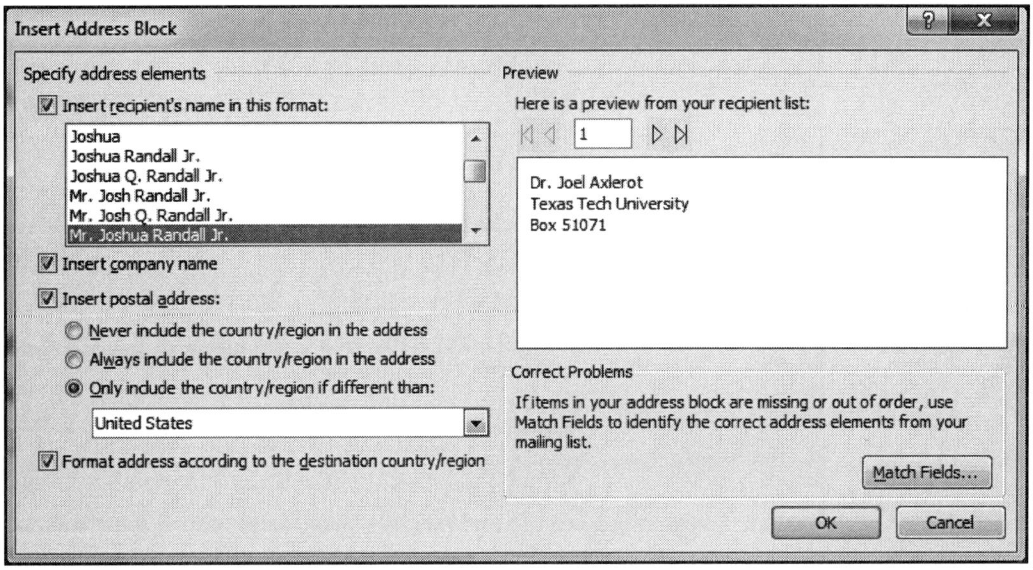

Figure 4.18: Inserting an Address Block

11. Place the cursor in the salutation line.
12. Click on *Greeting Line* from the *Write and Insert Fields* pane of the *Mailings* menu.
13. Choose the Format: Dear Mr. Randall by inserting the title and last name field into the salutation. These are the default settings.

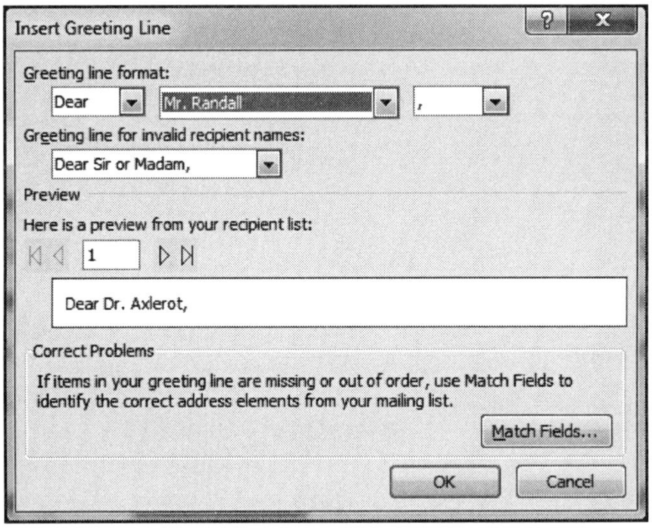

Figure 4. 19: Inserting a Salutation

14. Place the cursor on the first line of the 2nd paragraph of the letter just before the words your company. Delete the words your company.
15. Click *Insert Merge Field* from the *Write and Insert Fields* pane of the *Mailings Menu* and select the *Company Name* field. This will place the company name into the body of your form letter.

The following figure shows part of a completed form letter with the mail merge fields.

John Doe
1234 Memphis Avenue
Lubbock, Tx 79423

6/16/2011

«AddressBlock»

«GreetingLine»,

I am writing you to inquire about the summer internship program for which your company is so highly acclaimed. I am a Junior Communications Studies major at Central State university with a speciality in Corporate Organization Communications. My dream is to one day be the head of my own business. This summer internship program would provide me with the hands-on experience that would show me what to expect in the business world.

I have spoken with some employees at **«Company_Name»**, and I am convinced that this would be the perfect job for me. I am hard-working, competitive, and

Figure 4.20: A Form Letter Showing the Mail Merge Fields

Once you select Preview Results pane, you will see the completed mail merged from the letter as follows;

John Doe
1234 Memphis Avenue
Lubbock, Tx 79423

6/16/2008

Mr. John Howard
Howard World Communications
2080 117th St.
Dallas, Tx 78503

Dear Mr. Howard,

I am writing you to inquire about the summer internship program for which your company is so highly acclaimed. I am a Junior Communications Studies major at Central State university with a speciality in Corporate Organization Communications. My dream is to one day be the head of my own business. This summer internship program would provide me with the hands-on experience that would show me what to expect in the business world.

I have spoken with some employees at Howard World Communications, and I am convinced that this would be the perfect job for me. I am hard-working, competitive, and dependable. I am also extremely motivated to put forth 110% in any endeavor into which I enter. I would be grateful if you could send me further information on the internship program. You can reach me at home at 806-555-1234 or on my cell at 806-444-1478 or by email at johndoe@ttu.edu. Thank you for your time and consideration.

Sincerely,

John Doe

John Doe

To print the form letter showing the mailing list fields, just use the *Print* command from the *Home* menu.

To print the mail merged letters with the fields inserted, just click on *Finish and Merge* from the *Finish* panel of the *Mailings* menu.

Mail merges and form letters are a convenient means of creating personalized form letters for a large number of individuals. They eliminate the need to retype each letter. In this example, we included only 5 records. A real mailing list might include hundreds or even thousands of records. Personalized form letters could be sent to all of them accurately and efficiently using a mail merge.

Some Mail Merge Applications:

- A set of labels or envelopes.
- A set of form letters, e-mail messages, or faxes.
- A set of numbered coupons.

Computer Application Assignments

There are 3 computer application assignments for this module: a technology report, a form letter with mail merge, and a questionnaire on database management.

Assignment 1: Technology Report

Create a brief report (about 2 pages) on any aspect of technology and computers using the Internet and/or a library as a resource. Give your report a title and place your name and date below the title. Some possible topics are: The History of Computing; Trends and Future Directions in Technology; Computer Applications in... (Art, Architecture, Business, Education, Health and Medicine, Law, etc.); Computer Security; Computers and Society. These are suggestions only. Any topic related to technology or computers is acceptable. Do not copy and paste your report directly from the Internet or other sources. Write your own paper. Your report should include the following elements covered in Module 5:

- Use appropriate fonts and text styles to enhance your paper,
- An appropriate picture or clip art obtained from the *Microsoft* Web site or another source of your choice,
- A table,
- Two or more footnotes documenting sources of the material that you included in your report. Use current references that are not more than one year old. Any footnote format is acceptable, and
- A brief index or table of contents (choose either one) for your report.

The purpose of this assignment is to give you experience and skill using some of *MS Word's* advanced features. The content of your report is not the major concern here.

Print your report to turn in to your instructor with the other 2 parts of the Module 5 Assignment.

Assignment 2: Mail Merge

In this assignment, you will create a mail merge using a source document and a mailing list that you will create. Follow these steps:

1. Open the Form Letter practice file. This letter is similar to the sample letter in the *Mail Merge* section of this module. This will be your main document for the mail merge.
2. Follow the instructions given in Section 5.12. of this module on creating a mail merge with *MS Word* to create your letter using an *MS Word Mail Merge*.
3. Include the following fields in your mailing list:

- Title
- First Name
- Last Name
- Company Name
- Address Line 1
- City
- State
- ZIP Code

4. Enter 5 fictitious records. Make up the names and data for your mailing list.
5. Enter your name and address at the top of the letter and insert the fields into the main document letter as shown in the sample below. Do not simply type in the name and address information. This information must be inserted using a *Mail Merge*. (Note the insertion of the company name in the second line of the first paragraph). Also, type your name at the bottom as the author of the letter. See the sample letter on the facing page.
6. Save and print the form letter showing the fields inserted. This should look similar to the sample letter shown on the next page.
7. Save and print the 5 mail merged letters to turn in to your instructor.

Your Name
Your address
Your Name
Your Address
Your City, State, Zip Code

Current Date

«AddressBlock»

«GreetingLine»,

I am writing to inquire about the summer internship program for which **«Company_Name»**, is so highly acclaimed.

I am a Junior Communications Studies major at Texas Tech University with a speciality in Corporate Organizational Communication. My idea is to one day be the head of my own business. This summer internship program would be a great stepping stone on my path.

The program would provide me with the hands-on experience that would show me what to expect in the business world. It would also be great to work under people who have experiences in the field that I plan to spend the rest of life in.

Sincerely,

Your Name Handwritten

Your Name Typed

Figure 4:21: A Sample Mail Merge Letter Showing Fields

MODULE 5

Spreadsheets

Introduction to Electronic Spreadsheets

From civilization's need to keep track of objects and money arose written language and number systems. Once people started manipulating numbers – adding, subtracting, multiplying, and dividing – they soon developed the desire to automate this laborious process. The abacus was an early device for mechanizing the manipulation of numbers.

Management of financial affairs in today's complex world cannot be done easily by just using a calculator, a pencil, and a sheet of paper. Before the advent of electronic spreadsheets, such mathematical computation tasks such as budgets, income taxes, and expense ledgers usually involved many hours of tedious and time-consuming calculations. Even worse, these projects often included errors because of the many calculations involved.

Just as a word processor automates portions of the writing task, an electronic spreadsheet can automate many of the repetitive chores involved in mathematical calculations. Electronic spreadsheets can be used for a number of tasks and are not limited to just business uses. They can be used for budgeting, for household expenses, balancing checkbooks, calculating interest on savings or on loans, maintaining class grade books, or any other task requiring multiple calculations. The electronic spreadsheet is the second most popular computer productivity tool (after word processing).

Module Objectives

When you have completed this module, you should be able to:

- identify the basic functions of and the terminology associated with, an electronic spreadsheet;
- recognize the advantages of using electronic spreadsheets;
- identify the types of electronic spreadsheet data such as labels, values, formulas, and functions;
- discuss features common to most electronic spreadsheets; and
- produce a *Microsoft Excel* spreadsheet, and make printouts of the requested information.

Note:* The instructions and assignments given in this module are for *Office 2010.

Materials Needed to Complete This Module

- This book
- *Microsoft Excel 2010*
- Flash drive to store your work

How to Proceed

1. Read this module. Many parts of this module are detailed and somewhat technical. Carefully read this module to familiarize yourself with the electronic spreadsheet prior to beginning your work on the Module 5 *Computer Applications Assignments.* This will save you time and frustration.
2. Review the *Key Terms* at the end of this module.
3. Complete the *Module 5 Review Questions* at the end of the module. Remember to check your answers at the end of the book.
4. Complete the *Module 5 Applications Assignments.* Complete the practice Grade Book and print it with formulas showing. Create a personal budget, including a graph, using *Microsoft Excel.* Specific instructions are provided later in this module. Print your budget on 1 page.
5. Staple your printouts together to turn in to your instructor.
6. Take the Module 5 Test.

5.1 Introduction to Electronic Spreadsheets

Electronic spreadsheet applications are useful tools for any numeric application.

In simple terms, a **spreadsheet** is a table of information that is primarily numeric. Traditionally, spreadsheets have been used for preparing budgets and for financial forecasting. The original spreadsheet was the accounting ledger book, which was primarily used for organizing numerical information.

Early manual spreadsheets were large sheets of paper with letters across the top representing columns and numbers along the left side that represented rows. These large sheets of paper were sometimes spread out across a table or desk and thus became known as spreadsheets. The **columns** (vertical) and **rows** (horizontal) on spreadsheets form a grid. Specific **cells** within the grid can be designated with the column and row coordinates such as A1 or D5. These spreadsheets helped accountants and budget planners organize information for ease of understanding. They also made it easier to find specific data.

An electronic spreadsheet (Figure 5.1) can be thought of as a computerized version of the traditional manual spreadsheet consisting of a grid of rows and columns that can be used to store and manipulate any kind of numerical data.

When electronic spreadsheets were introduced in the in the late 1970s, both small and large businesses immediately recognized their importance as tools for improving productivity. Instead of large sheets of paper, which had to be recalculated manually whenever a single figure changed, electronic spreadsheets on computers could perform these calculations automatically. Many computer users already had word processing technology in the form of dedicated word processors. Most word processors could not perform the functions of a spreadsheet program, so purchasing a spreadsheet meant that the business had to buy a microcomputer also.

The first popular electronic spreadsheet program was ***VisiCalc***, "visi" for "visible" and "calc" for "calculator." In the early 1980s, when executives and other business managers became more acquainted with the power of electronic spreadsheets, the sale of microcomputers skyrocketed! The introduction of *VisiCalc* has been credited for the sale of thousands of *Apple* computers. Today there are many electronic spreadsheets on the market. In addition to *Microsoft Excel,* some of the popular commercial spreadsheet titles include *Quattro Pro, Lotus 1-2-3,* and *AppleWorks.*

5.2 Microsoft Excel Basics

Microsoft Excel is a powerful spreadsheet application that allows you to create budgets, business plans, accounting worksheets, or other documents that contain calculated numbers.

> **A** spreadsheet is a computer application that simulates a paper worksheet. It displays multiple cells that together make up a grid consisting of rows and columns, each cell containing either alphanumeric text or numeric values. A spreadsheet cell may alternatively contain a formula that defines how the contents of that cell is to be calculated.

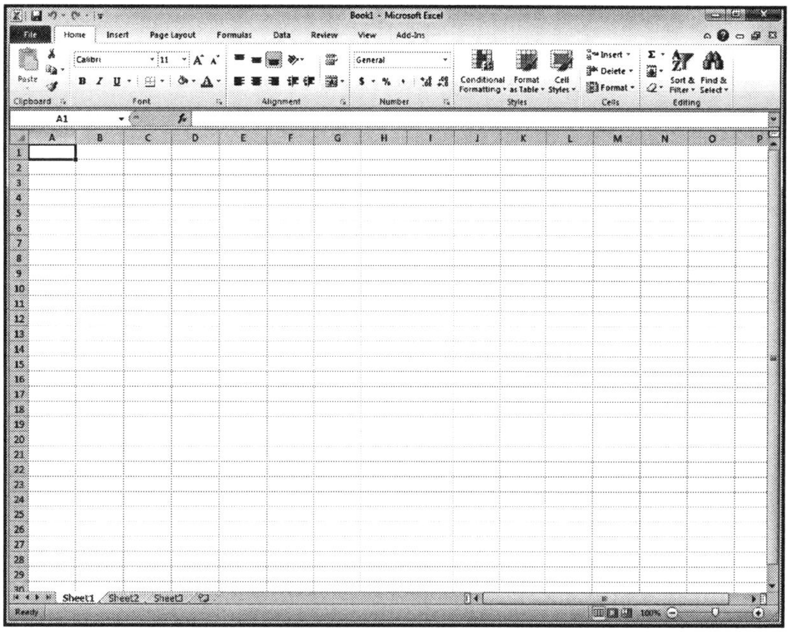

Figure 5.1: An Empty Electronic Spreadsheet

The document that you create in *MS Excel* is called a **workbook**. A workbook contains one or more worksheets. A **worksheet** is a collection of rows and columns that hold text and numbers. In *MS Excel*, there is no limit to the number of worksheets a workbook may contain. On start up, blank workbooks contain three worksheets named Sheet 1, Sheet 2, and Sheet 3 (See Figure 5.2). When you click a sheet's tab, that worksheet is displayed.

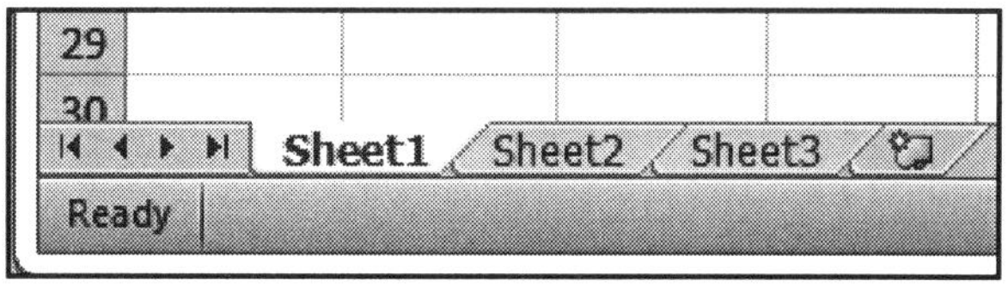

Figure 5.2: The *MS Excel* Worksheet Tabs

Rows: Spreadsheet rows run horizontally from left to right on your computer screen. Each row is numbered (See Figure 5.1).

Columns: Spreadsheet columns run vertically from the top to the bottom of your computer screen. Individual columns are identified by letters, e.g., A, B, C, etc. (See Figure 5.1).

Cell: The intersection of a row and column is known as a **cell**. When you move your mouse over a worksheet, you will notice that your mouse pointer turns into a cross as you point to a cell.

Cell Coordinates: Cells are identified by their coordinates. Rows and columns form a set of cells that are identified by alphanumeric coordinates (column letter and row number). For example, A1 is a coordinate that refers to the information in the cell located where column A and row 1 meet (Figure 3.1). Cell A1 is located at the top left most position in the worksheet. Likewise, cell D76 would refer to the cell located at the intersection of row 76 and column D.

5.3 Entering Data

Microsoft Excel works with the following kinds of data:

- Labels
- Numbers
- Formulas

Labels are alphanumeric entries. Alphanumeric data consists of any combination of text and numbers. It is not possible to perform computations using alphanumeric data so electronic spreadsheets consider them to be labels. Labels are used for titles of worksheets, of individual columns and rows, and for other comments or subtitles within a worksheet.

Numbers can be expressed in different forms, with or without decimals, or even as scientific notations.

A **formula** is any type of mathematical expression, such as average for computing averages, and sum for creating totals. Formulas can be much more complex, calculating the interest on savings or the amortization of a loan, for example.

A **cell** can be thought of as a box for holding data. A single cell usually referenced by its column and row. For example, Cell A2 would represent the cell located at the intersection of Column A, Row 2.

B8 | *fx* =AVERAGE(B3:B6)

	A	B	C	D	E
1	Name	Grade			
2					
3	T. Ahem	85			
4	S. Crooks	90			
5	J. Cheon	75			
6	B. Price	100			
7					
8	Average	87.5			
9					

Figure 5.3: Spreadsheet Data Entries

The contents of the selected cell also appear in the edit line near the top of the worksheet noted with the *fx* symbol. In the sample grade book spreadsheet shown in Figure 5.3, several names (labels) are listed in column A. Grades (numbers) are listed in column B. Cell B8 contains a formula for computing grade averages. Since cell B8 is selected, the formula is shown in the *fx* line, while the calculated average appears in the cell.

To begin developing an understanding of how electronic spreadsheets work, first look at the main *Excel* **menu commands.**

5.4 Excel Operations

All *MS Office* programs operate with the same GUI interface and similar commands. In this section, we will review the main operational features of *Excel.*

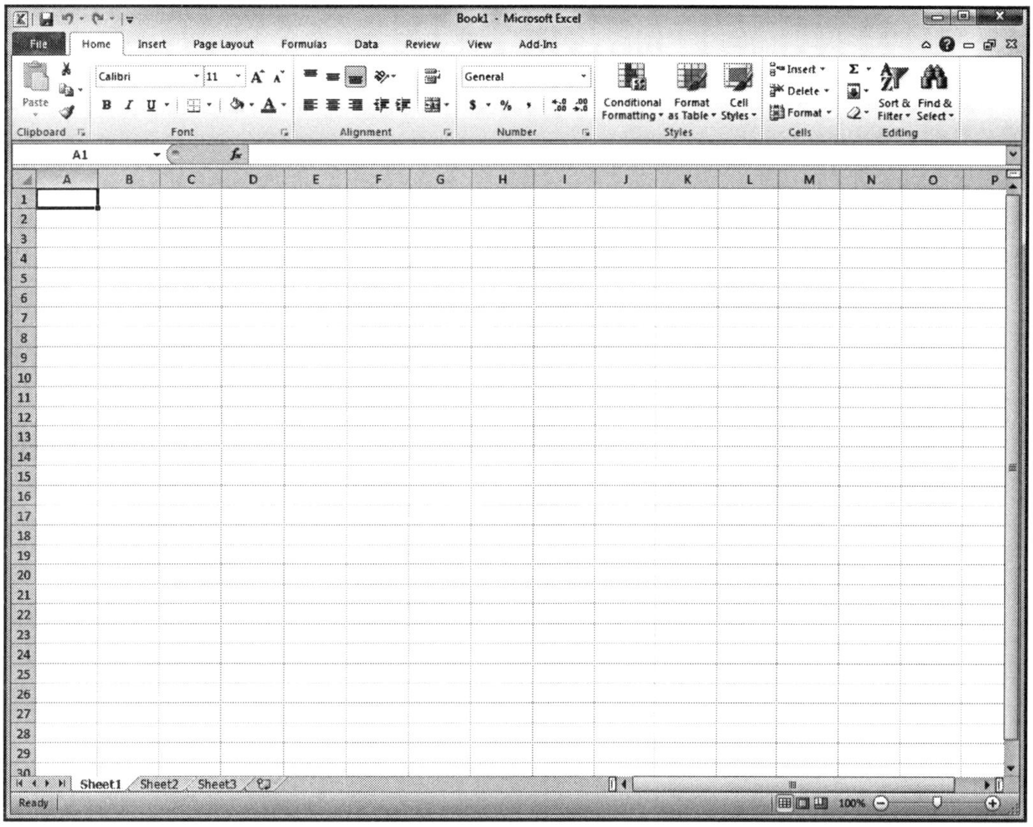

Figure 5.4: An *Excel* Worksheet

5.5 Similarities Between MS Word and Excel

You should recall from *Module 3* that there are several common features in all *MS Office* programs. These were reviewed in section 3.2 of *Module 3*. You may wish to look over this section of *Module 3* again if you need a review. The *File Menu* with the *Print* and *Save* features work the same in *Excel* as they do in *Word*. The *View Tab Menu, Page Layout,* and the *Help* features also work the same in *Excel* as they do in *Word*. Text formatting features are also very similar in *Excel* and *Word*.

5.6 The Home Menu

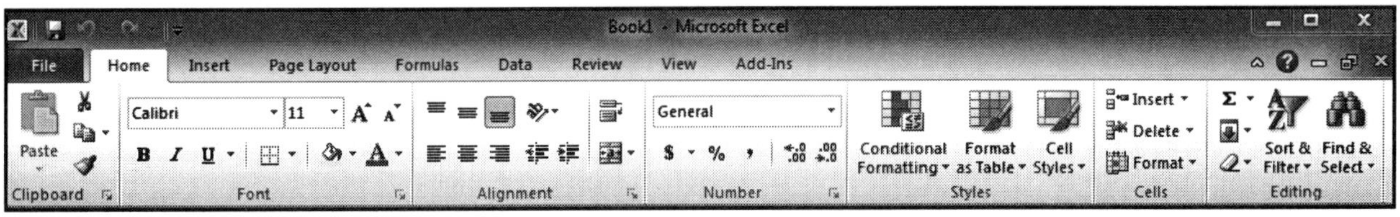

Figure 5.5: The *Home* Menu

Figure 5.5 shows the *Excel* **Home** menu. The **Font** and **Alignment** panels look similar to those found in *MS Word.* Since these were covered in *Module 3,* we will not review them again here. The **Number Panel** is unique to *Excel.* The **Format Window** lets the user choose how numbers will be displayed-as currency, time, percentages, dates, etc. The **General format** is the default setting and is just numeric with no specific setting. Other number format buttons allow users to select the number of decimal places desired, to select various currency notations, and to display data as a percentage.

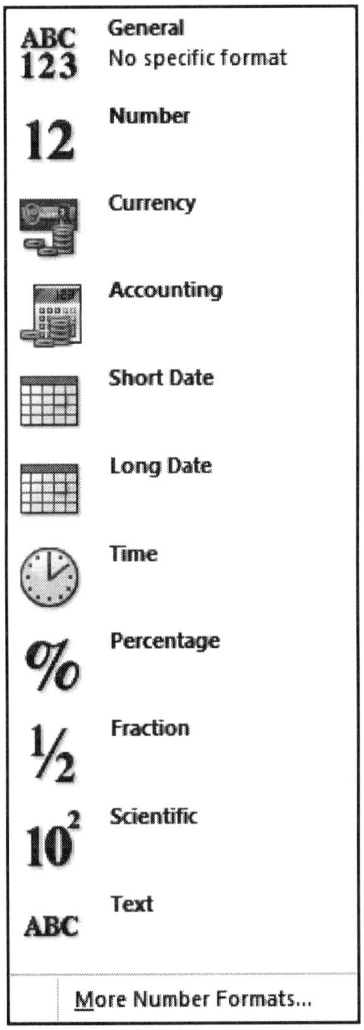

Figure 5.6: Number Formatting

Visicalc is usually considered the first electronic spreadsheet (although this has been challenged), and it helped turn the Apple II computer into a success and greatly assisted in their widespread application.

Electronic spreadsheets are used on job sites for calculations.

Excel offers a wide variety of options of displaying information. The ***Styles Panel*** offers users the option of selecting various colors and styles for data. The ***Conditional Formatting*** tool allows user to highlight unusual cells, visualize data using color scales, and to incorporate icon sets into the spreadsheet for data representation. Figure 5.7 shows the *Conditional Formatting* tool options. Each submenu will display various choices when selected.

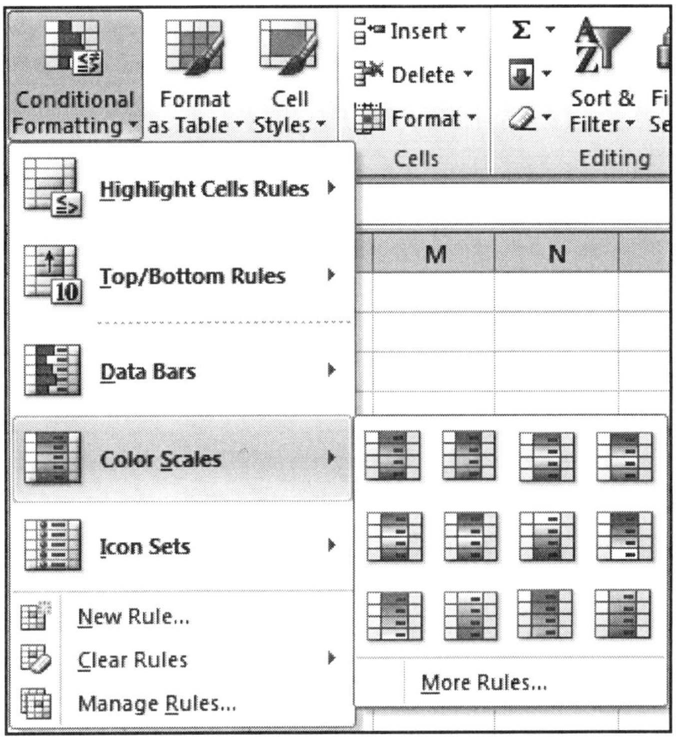

Figure 5.7: *Conditional Formatting*

The ***Format as Table*** tool provides users with a means of quickly formatting a range of cells and converting them to a table. A number of predefined table types and styles are available. The ***Cell Styles*** tool (adjacent to *Format as Table* tool) allows users to choose from a variety of predefined styles to customize the worksheet.

The **Cells Panel** provides for easy editing of the data. The **Insert** tool allows users to insert cells, rows, or columns. The **Delete** tool allows users to delete rows, cells, or columns. The **Format** tool allows users to change row or column size or to protect or hide cells. **Protection** keeps data secure so that others may view but change data in a spreadsheet. **Visibility**, hides a cell or range of cells from view. This is useful in case a user wishes to hide sensitive data such as financial figures, grades, or salaries from general view.

The ***Editing Panel*** provides a means to arrange and filter the data into meaningful ways. The ***AutoSum*** tool displays the sum of a range of numbers directly about the selected cell. The ***Fill*** tool is used to fill a range of cells, which can be below or to the left or right of a selected cell with the same value or formula. The ***Clear*** tool (eraser icon) provides a means of clearing data from a cell or range of cells. The ***Sort and Filter*** tool

(A-Z and Funnel icon) is a very useful tool which allows data to be rearranged as desired. For example a user may wish to sort student grades from highest to lowest or a business might wish to sort a list of customers into alphabetical order. Data can be rearranged in this manner even after it is entered in a random manner.

Figure 5.8: The *Editing* Panel

5.7 The Insert Menu

The Insert Menu provides for various objects such as charts, tables, pictures, clip art, hyperlinks, and text boxes to be added to the worksheet.

Figure 5.9: The *Insert* Menu

5.8 The Formulas Menu

The ***Formulas*** tab provides a means of inserting functions, which are built in formulas, into the worksheet. Electronic spreadsheets are useful and powerful tools because of their ability to manipulate data. Formulas are therefore one of the main spreadsheet tools. The most often used function is the **SUM** function which simply adds up a defined range of cells. The *Formula* tool is used by highlighting a range of cells by clicking and dragging and then choosing the SUM function (e.g., within *AutoSum*). Other functions include **AVERAGE**, **MAX**, which finds the largest value in a range of numbers, **MIN**, which finds the smallest number in a range of numbers, and many others. *Excel* provides many other functions, some of which are very complex. The function tool even allows user to enter a description for what they want to do and then choose from a list of options. Figure 5.10 shows a function search dialog box in which the term "loan amortization" has been entered. The **PMT function** is located in the example. This function will determine the required payment for a loan of a given length and specified interest rate. Users may also enter and save their own formulas to supplement those provided by *Excel*.

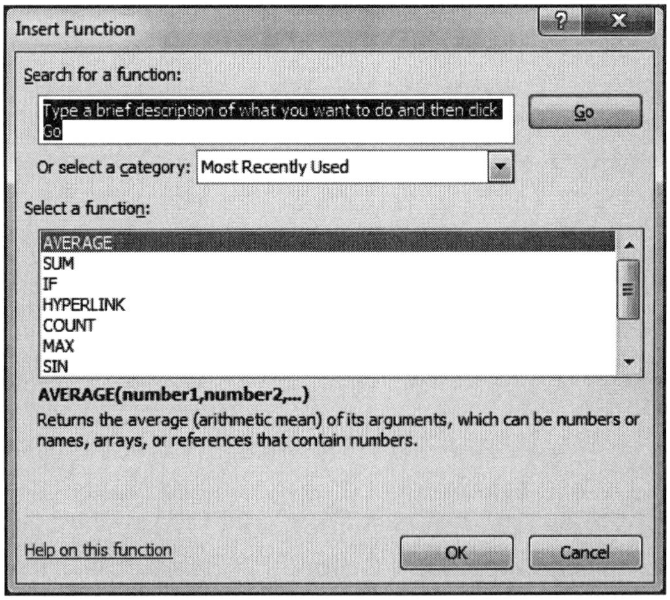

Figure 5.10: The *Functions* Dialog Box

The ***Formula Auditing*** panel provides tools to check errors and trace incidences of values in large tables of data and to change the default. A detailed description of the *Formula Auditing* panel is beyond the scope of this book. The ***Calculation*** options, which are used to change the default method formula operation, are also beyond the scope of this book.

5.9 The Data Menu

The ***Data*** menu is shown below. The *Get External Data* panel provides a means to import data from *Microsoft Access*, the world wide web, text documents, or other software programs such as *Microsoft Money*. The *Connections* panel is used to establish and display external network connections which may be used to obtain data for use in an *Excel* worksheet. The *Sort and Filter* panel is the same as the one included on the *Home* menu. The *Data* tools panel provides several useful tools for manipulating information. For example the ***Text to Columns*** tools may be used to divide a list of names into first name and last name columns. The other tools in this panel are more advanced and beyond the scope of this book.

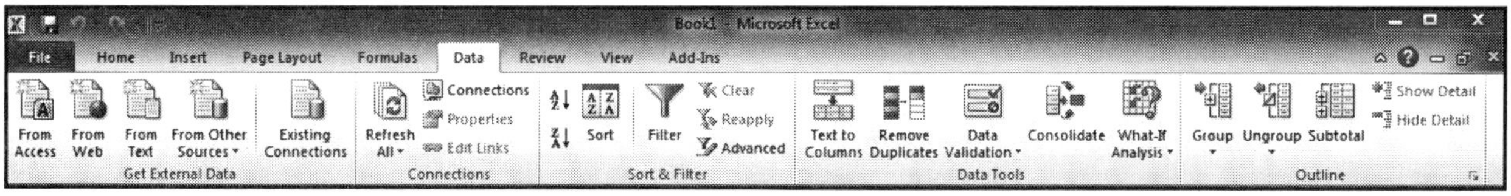

Figure 5.11: The Data Menu

5.10 The Review Menu

The ***Review*** tab provides some familiar tools and some new ones. As in *Word*, a spell checker, and a thesaurus are provided. A ***Translate*** tool for the purpose of translating text into other languages is also provided. The ***Changes*** panel provides tools to lock a worksheet or a workbook to prevent unauthorized or accidental changes and deletions. The ***Share Workbook*** tool provides a means for sharing with other users so that multiple people can work on the same workbook. The ***Track Changes*** tool tracks the changes such as deletions, data changes, and format changes made in a worksheet.

Figure 5.12: The *Review* Menu

5.11 The View Menu

The ***View*** menu provides a variety of ways to view a spreadsheet. The ability zoom in and out is particularly useful for large spreadsheets. Users may choose to display or hide such features as the Formula Bar and grid lines may be hidden or shown with the *View* tools.

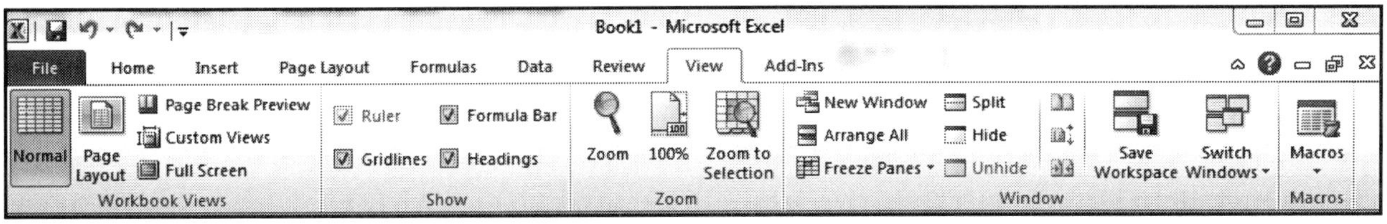

Figure 5.13: The *View* Menu

5.12 Using Excel

Once you are familiar with the *MS Excel* menus and tools, you are ready to begin using the program. The following sections provide an explanation of using *Excel*.

5.13 Entering Labels in Microsoft Excel

As you type the first character into a spreadsheet cell, *MS Excel* will automatically determine whether the entry is a label (text), a value (number), or a formula. A key concept in understanding *MS Excel* is being aware of the type of information being entered into a cell. This awareness will save you much time and frustration when working in *MS Excel*. After a cell entry (label, value, or formula) has been typed, it is entered into the cell when the *Enter* key, the *Tab* key, or an arrow key is pressed, or when the mouse pointer is moved to another cell. *MS Excel* uses the following criteria to differentiate between labels, values, and formulas.

> A value can be entered from the computer keyboard by directly typing into the cell itself. Alternatively, a value can be based on a formula which might perform a calculation, display the current date or time, or retrieve external data such as a stock quote.

- Any entry starting with a letter is considered to be a **label**.
- Any entry starting with a number is considered to be **value**.
- Any entry starting with an equal (=) sign is considered to be a **formula**.

Care should be taken when entering information into a worksheet to ensure that *MS Excel* interprets it correctly. For example, typing the social security number 792-98-6594 will result in a "value." A spreadsheet will not try to perform any calculations on a "value." However, inserting an "equal" sign such as: =792-98-6594 indicates a formula and the spreadsheet will calculate the result.

For a number, such as a ZIP Code, to be treated as a label entry, a single apostrophe (') is placed before the number. Therefore, **79413** would be typed **'79413** in the cell. If a text entry is longer than a cell, *MS Excel* will do one of the following, depending on the contents of the adjacent cell:

- When long labels are entered, if the cell to the right of the entry is empty, *MS Excel* will display the entire entry by spreading it across adjacent cells to the right.

- If the adjacent cell contains data, *MS Excel* will **truncate** (shorten) the entry and only display as much of the label as the cell's width will accommodate.

5.14 Entering Numbers in Microsoft Excel

To enter a number in *MS Excel*, just select the desired cell and type the number, then press the *Enter* key. Sometimes users will wish to repeat the same number in a number of cells. For example, a rent payment in a monthly budget will probably remain consistent for each month. *MS Excel* uses data fills to copy entries from one cell to adjacent cells. In Figure 5.14, the figure $450 has been copied from the first entry in cell A6 to cells B6 through D6 by using the ***Fill*** tool, located in the *Editing* pane.

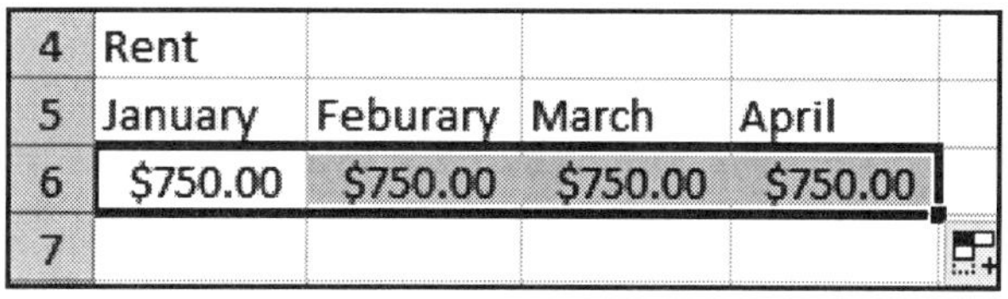

Figure 5.14: Using The *MS Excel* Fill Tool

MS Excel is able to anticipate your intentions and complete some entries automatically. A feature called **AutoFill** automatically fills common text labels such as:

- names of the days of the week
- abbreviations of the names of the week (Mon, Tue, etc.)
- month names month abbreviations (Jan, Feb, etc.)

To use AutoFill, type the first item in the series (such as the name of a month) in the desired cell, then click and drag on the **fill handle** (the small black square in the lower right hand corner of the selected area of cells) across the cells that you wish to fill. When you point to the fill handle, the pointer will change to a black cross. Releasing the mouse button causes the selected cell to be filled automatically, as illustrated in Figure 5.15.

A formula identifies the calculation needed to place the result in the cell it is contained within.

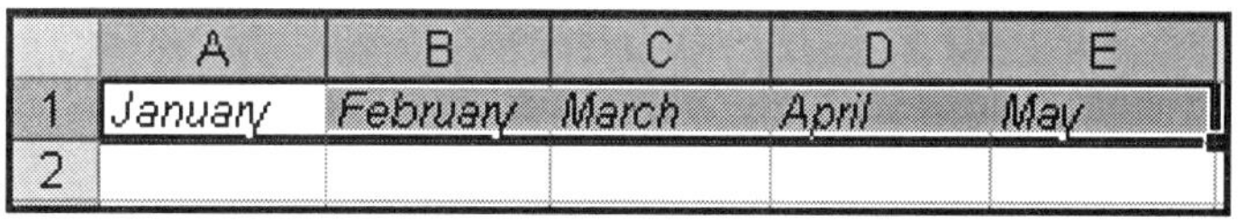

Figure 5.15: The *MS Excel* AutoFill Feature

5.15 Editing Cells

Selecting cells in the *Microsoft Excel* spreadsheet is accomplished by using either the arrow keys or the mouse cursor (the mouse cursor appears as a fat plus sign in the spreadsheet).

To **edit a cell**, follow these steps:

1. Move the cell pointer to the cell you want to change.
2. Double-click the cell.
3. Press the "insert" key to toggle between overtype mode and insert mode.
4. Press *Enter.*

Cutting and pasting with *Excel* works much like it does in *Word.* To copy and paste the contents of one cell to another follow these steps:

1. Select the cell.
2. Right click the mouse to display the *Quick* **menu.**
3. Choose **Copy** from the *Quick* menu.
4. Move the cursor to the cell where you wish to paste the entry,
5. Right click the mouse to display the *Quick* menu again.
6. Choose a **Paste** option from the *Quick* menu.

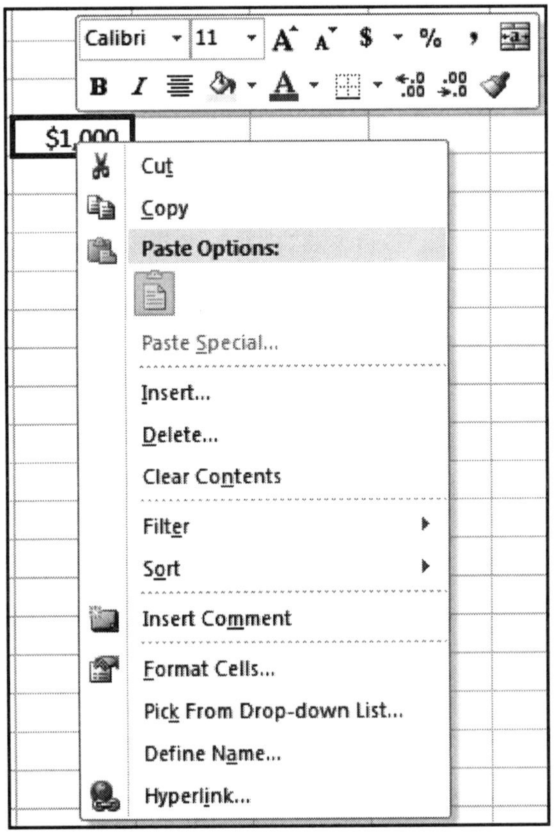

Figure 5.16: The Excel *Quick* Menu

When entering a formula into a Microsoft Excel cell, you must precede the formula with an equal (=) sign.

You can also clear data from a cell using the Quick menu. **Clearing data** deletes information within the cells of your spreadsheet without altering the row or column formatting. *Clear Contents* is not the same as *Copy* or *Cut*. Data that is **cleared** is permanently deleted. To quickly and completely erase everything in the cell, just select the desired cell and press the **Delete** key

No worksheet program prior to *Microsoft Excel* included a **spell checker**. The spell checker will check the worksheet that is currently on your screen. You can check your worksheet's spelling by clicking on the *Review* tab and selecting the spell checker.

Microsoft Excel lets you either insert or delete rows or columns without changing existing information in other parts of the spreadsheet. However, when a row or column is deleted, any data within it is also lost.

When you select **Delete** from the Quick menu, you are presented with a Delete dialog box (see Figure 5.17), which gives you the option of deleting cells or entire rows and columns. The dialog box also gives you the option of how your worksheet will be adjusted after deleting a cell: shift left or shift up.

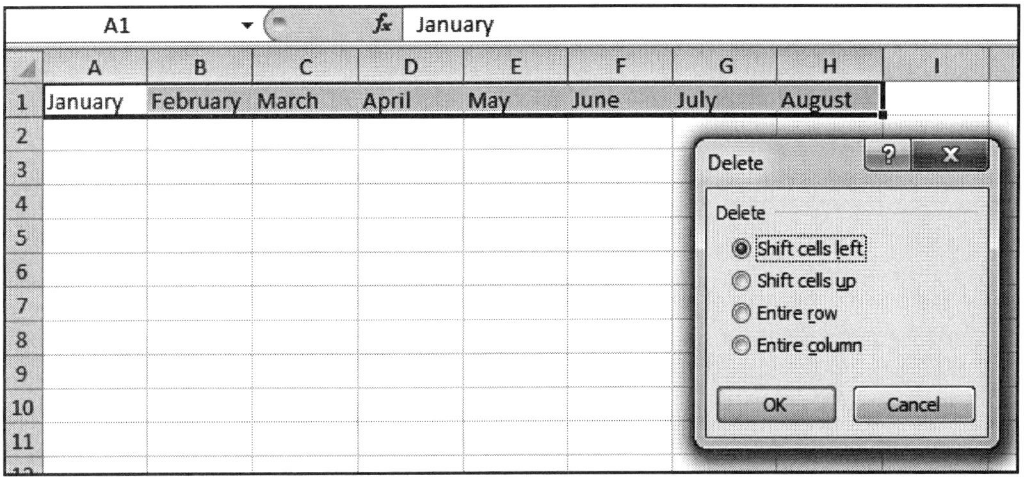

Figure 5.17: The Delete Dialog Box

When you **insert a cell**, the worksheet cells move to the right and down to make room for the new cell. To correctly insert a cell, follow these steps:

1. Select the cell that will appear *after* (to the right or below) the inserted cell.
2. Select ***Insert*** from the *Cells* pane of the *Home* menu.
3. Click either the **shift cells right** or **shift cells down** option to determine which way you want the worksheet adjusted.
4. Click **OK**.

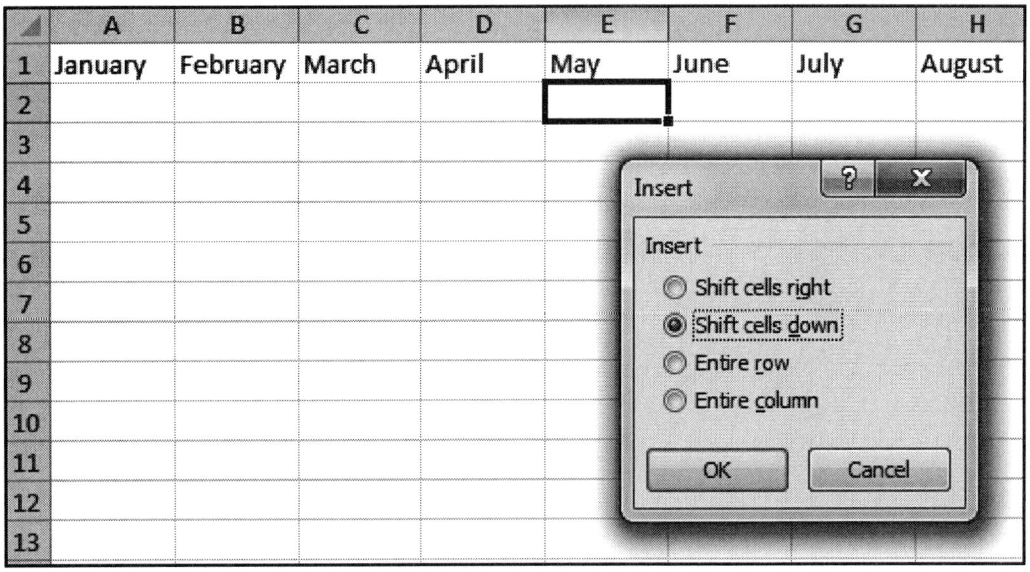

Figure 5.18: Inserting a Cell

When you **insert a row,** you will move the other rows down, and when you **insert a column,** you will move the other columns to the right. To insert a row or column:

1. Select the row or column that will appear <u>after</u> the inserted row or column.
2. Click the row or column header to select the entire row or column.
3. Select **Insert** from the *Cells* pane of the *Home* menu. The existing rows or columns will be shifted to make room for the new insertion.

To delete a row or column (i.e., take out the row/column and all its contents):

1. Select the row or column to be deleted.
2. Select Delete from the Cells pane of the Home menu. The existing rows or columns will be shifted accommodate the deletion.

A worksheet range is a rectangular group of cells that is described by its upper-left-hand cell address, called an anchor point (Figure 5.19). Ranges allow large worksheets to become more manageable. For example, in a budget, you might assign a range name of Expenses to expenses and of Income to income contained in the budget.

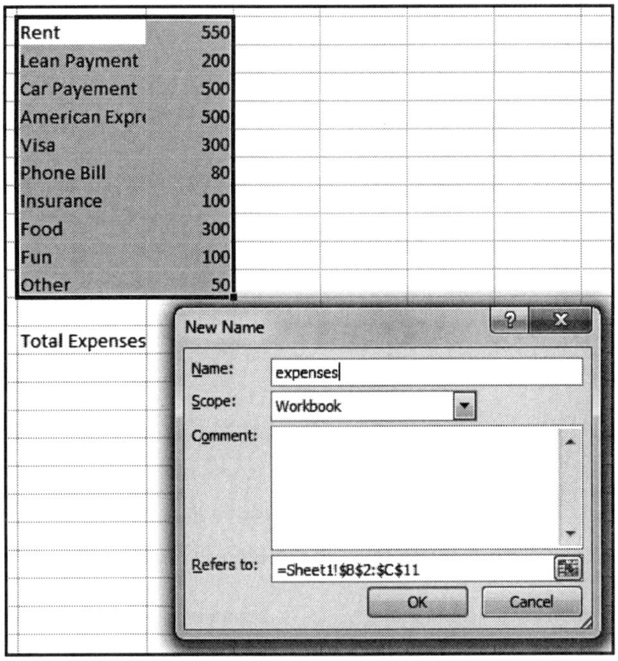

Figure 5.19: A Range of Cells

To name a range of cells, follow these steps:

1. Select the desired range of cells by clicking and dragging the mouse.
2. Right click to bring up the Quick menu.
3. Select *Define Name* from the Quick Menu and enter a name in the dialog box.

Once you have created the range, you can use a range name in a formula by typing the name anytime you would type the range. For example, instead of typing =Sum (F4:F15), type the formula =Sum (Expenses).

5.16 Formulas and Functions

Arithmetic operators perform mathematical operations on data in spreadsheet cells. The symbols that represent commonly used mathematical operators are:

Add	+ (upper case "=")
Subtract	- (lower case dash)
Multiply	* (upper case "8")
Divide	/ (be sure not to use \)

MS *Excel* uses the carat (^) character to indicate exponentiation. 2^2 (two squared) would be entered as 2 ^ 2 while 2^3 (two cubed) would be entered as 2 ^ 3.

Formulas are very important time-saving and general purpose tools. On a calculator you type a formula and press the equal sign to obtain the result. In *MS Excel*, formulas begin with an equal (=) sign. Formulas may look like a simple arithmetic problem, such as: **=5+2+7+8** or a formula may look more like an algebra equation such as: **=42 * (9 / 3) – 77.**

Operational hierarchy is the order in which computations are made in formulas. *Microsoft Excel* first computes exponentiation, then multiplication and division in left-to-right order, (i.e., the first one to appear is computed first), then addition and subtraction (also in left-to-right order), and then logical operators (see #5 below). For example, the following formulas return a value of 14 because *MS Excel* computes exponentiation (^), followed by division, followed by multiplication, and ending with subtraction.

=18 - 2 ^ 3 / 4 * 2

In this example, if you want to override the automatic operational hierarchy, you would put parentheses around the parts to be executed first. See the example below.

=(18-2) ^ 3 / 4 * 2

This formula computes to 2,048. Quite a difference!

To recap, the order of priority for calculation (operational hierarchy) is performed according to normal algebraic standards and follows this order:

1. Anything enclosed in parenthesis.
2. Exponentiation.
3. * and / (Multiplication and Division).
4. + and – (Addition and Subtraction).
5. = , > , >= , < , <= , or <> (Logical operations such as: equal; greater than; greater than or equal to; less than; less than or equal to; and not equal to).

Study the examples given below to review how these calculations were obtained.

2+8*3 = 26	20/5+2 = 6
2+6+(9/3) = 11	10/(5+5) = 1
4-2/2 = 3	5+6+22*4 = 99

Both numbers and formulas may be used in spreadsheet calculations. For example, see Figure 5.16. This is a simple spreadsheet in which cell B33 contains a number ($2,678), cell B34 contains a formula that calculates 22% of the number in cell B33, and cell B36 contains a number derived by subtracting the value of B34 from the value of B33. The formulas for B34 and B36 are shown beside these cells.

19	income		
20			
21	Salary	$4,678.00	
22	Deductions	$243.26	fx =B21*0.052
23			
24	Net Income	$4,434.74	fx =B21-B22

Figure 5.20: *MS Excel* Calculations Using Numbers and Formulas

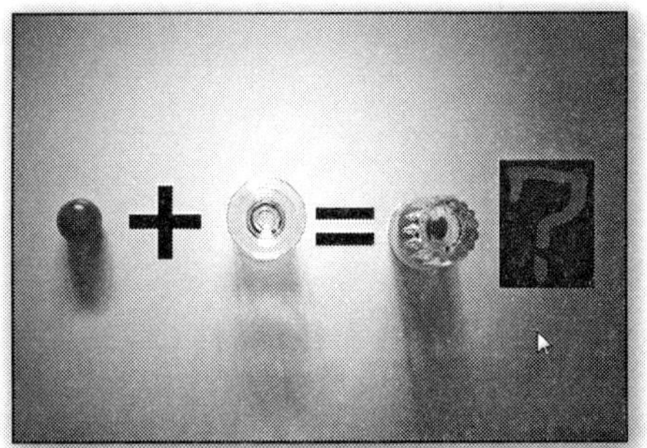

If you changed the value in cell B33, the spreadsheet would automatically recalculate the new answers and display them in cells B34 and B36. This is an example of the power of an electronic spreadsheet. You can change data or enter new values, let the computer do the work and display the result instantly. In this example, if you got a raise or the percentage of your deductions changed, you could enter the new numbers and *MS Excel* would automatically include these changes into the calculations.

A **calculation** is a deliberate process for transforming one or more inputs into one or more results, with variable change.

Once the formulas are written, the spreadsheet user can ask "what if" type questions by entering new or differing values into cells. For example, if you wanted to know what your net income in this example would be if the deductions changed from 22% to 27%, it would be easy to find out. This simple calculation is used to illustrate a point. In real spreadsheets, calculations are usually much more complex.

Moving or copying formulas in *MS Excel* is easy. To copy a formula to an adjacent cell, follow these steps:

1. Select the cell that contains the formula you want to move or copy.
2. Select **Copy** from the **Quick** Menu
3. Select the cell that you want to copy to.
4. Select **Paste** from the **Quick** Menu.

A **function** is a built-in mathematical process. Functions are used instead of having to write a complicated formula manually. For example, most spreadsheets know how to perform the functions of sum, average, square, and square root. For example, in the formula =Sum(B3:B6), Sum is a function that means "add up the values in the following cells or cell range." The colon between B3 and B6 tell *MS Excel* to use all of the cells between B3 and B6. Therefore, (B3:B6) stands for cells B3, B4, B5, and B6. After the sum of cells B3 through B6 is calculated, the answer would be displayed in the selected cell in which the function is entered. The =Sum function is used to simplify the writing of the formula.

AutoSum: AutoSum is an easy-to-use function that helps quickly total or sum a selected row or column of numbers.

To perform AutoSum, follow these steps:

1. Select the range of data that you want to sum.
2. Click the **AutoSum** toolbar button and click on *Sum*.
3. Press the *Enter* key.

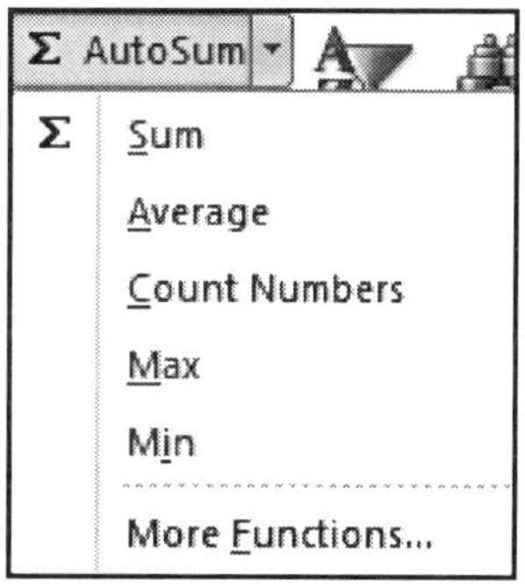

Figure 5.21: The *AutoSum* Toolbar

5.17 Worksheet Formatting

Row height and **column width** can be changed by dragging the boundary between the column or row headings. To size a column to fit the widest cell entry, double-click the right boundary of the column in the shaded column letter heading and drag it to the desired size. To resize a row, double-click the bottom boundary of the row in the shaded row number and drag it to the desired size.

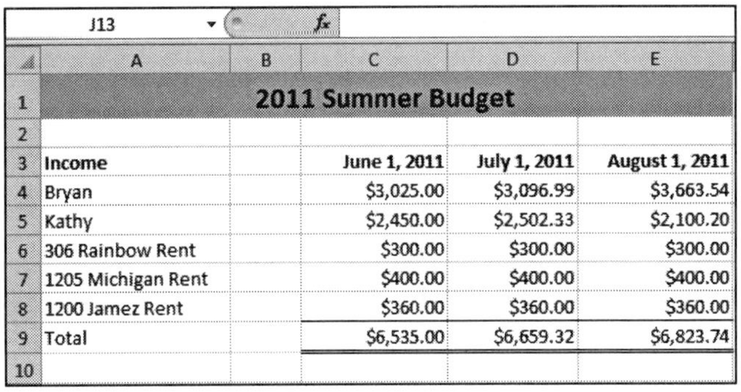

	A	B	C	D	E
1	2011 Summer Budget				
2					
3	Income		June 1, 2011	July 1, 2011	August 1, 2011
4	Bryan		$3,025.00	$3,096.99	$3,663.54
5	Kathy		$2,450.00	$2,502.33	$2,100.20
6	306 Rainbow Rent		$300.00	$300.00	$300.00
7	1205 Michigan Rent		$400.00	$400.00	$400.00
8	1200 Jamez Rent		$360.00	$360.00	$360.00
9	Total		$6,535.00	$6,659.32	$6,823.74
10					

Figure 5.18: Various Size Columns

Number formatting can be changed in the *Number* pane of the *Home* menu. Data can be formatted in a wide variety of colors and styles. The primary *Cell Style* options are described below.

Format Name	Description
General	Numbers appear just as you enter them.
Number	Allows setting of decimal places.
Currency	Displays dollar sign and two decimal places.
Accounting	Aligns currency and decimals.
Date	Displays numbers as date and time.
Percentage	Multiplies the cell by 100 and displays percent sign.
Fraction	Displays numbers as fractions.
Scientific	Scientific notation.
Text	All data is formatted as text (e.g., ZIP codes)

Figure 5.19: Cell Styles

Numbers can be formatted with the options shown in the *Numbers* pane. Numbers can be either left justified, right justified, or centered within their cells. Examples of *Excel* number formats are shown in the following figure.

A **number** is a mathematical concept used to describe and assess quantity.

	A	B	C
1	Number formats		
2	100	Number	
3	$100	Currency	
4	14-Jun-11	Date	
5	20%	Percentage	
6	1.00E+00	Science Notation	
7	12:00:00 AM	Time	
8			

Figure 5.20: Some *MS Excel* Number Formats

To align data in selected cells, use the alignment buttons on the **Home** tool bar. Centering labels over several columns can also be accomplished by using the alignment buttons on the formatting tool bar.

Sometimes a worksheet will become so large that it is impossible to view the entire file on the screen at once. In this case the computer screen becomes a window that allows the user to look at a portion of the spreadsheet. Using the **scroll bars** at the right and on the bottom of the spreadsheet window allows users to move to other parts of the spreadsheet. To view two workbooks at the same time, you can align them side by side using **View Side by Side** tool located in the *Windows* pane of the *View* Menu. You need to open two Excel files first and select View Side by Side tool.

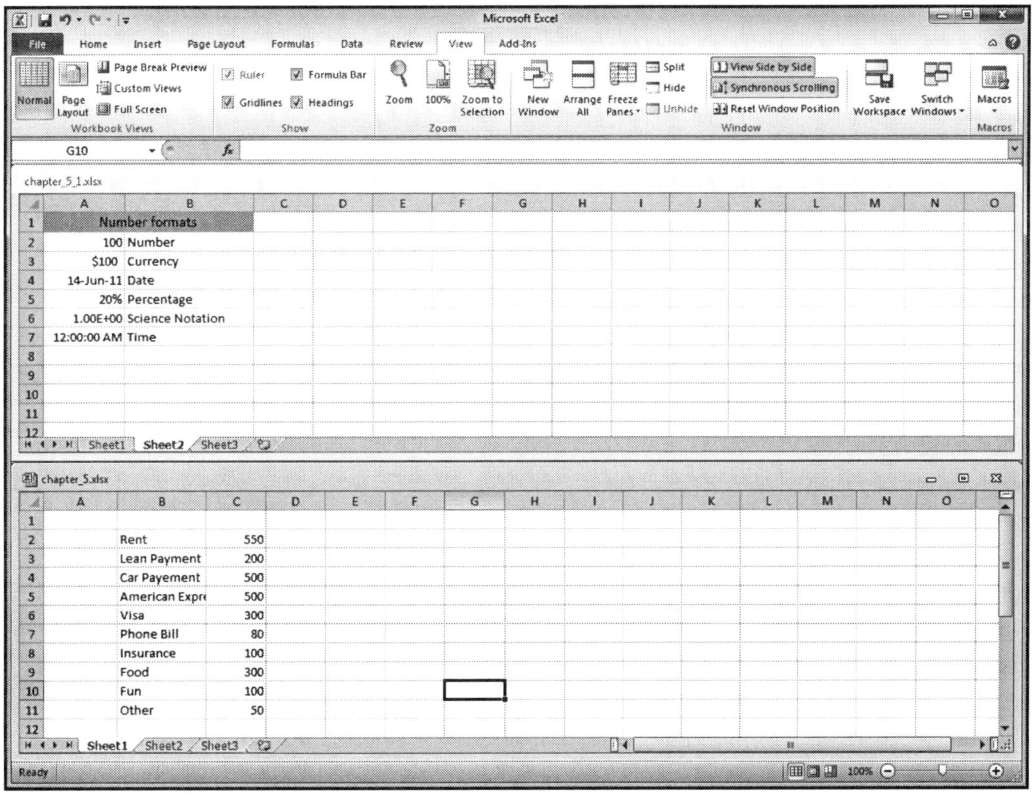

Figure 5.21: The View Side by Side Tool

Users can also zoom in on a part of the worksheet by using the **Zoom tools** which are also located in the *View* menu.

5.18 MS Excel Special Effects

Format as Table saves time in creating attractive worksheet formatting. *MS Excel* provides the AutoFormat feature to apply predefined formatting to your worksheet. To automatically format a worksheet as you type, follow these steps:

1. Select cells in your worksheet.
2. Select ***Format as Table*** from the Styles panel.
3. Click the style you want.

Frenchman Blaise Pascal is credited with inventing the first calculating machine in 1642. It was a numerical wheel calculator called the Pascaline to help his father, a French tax collector, count taxes.

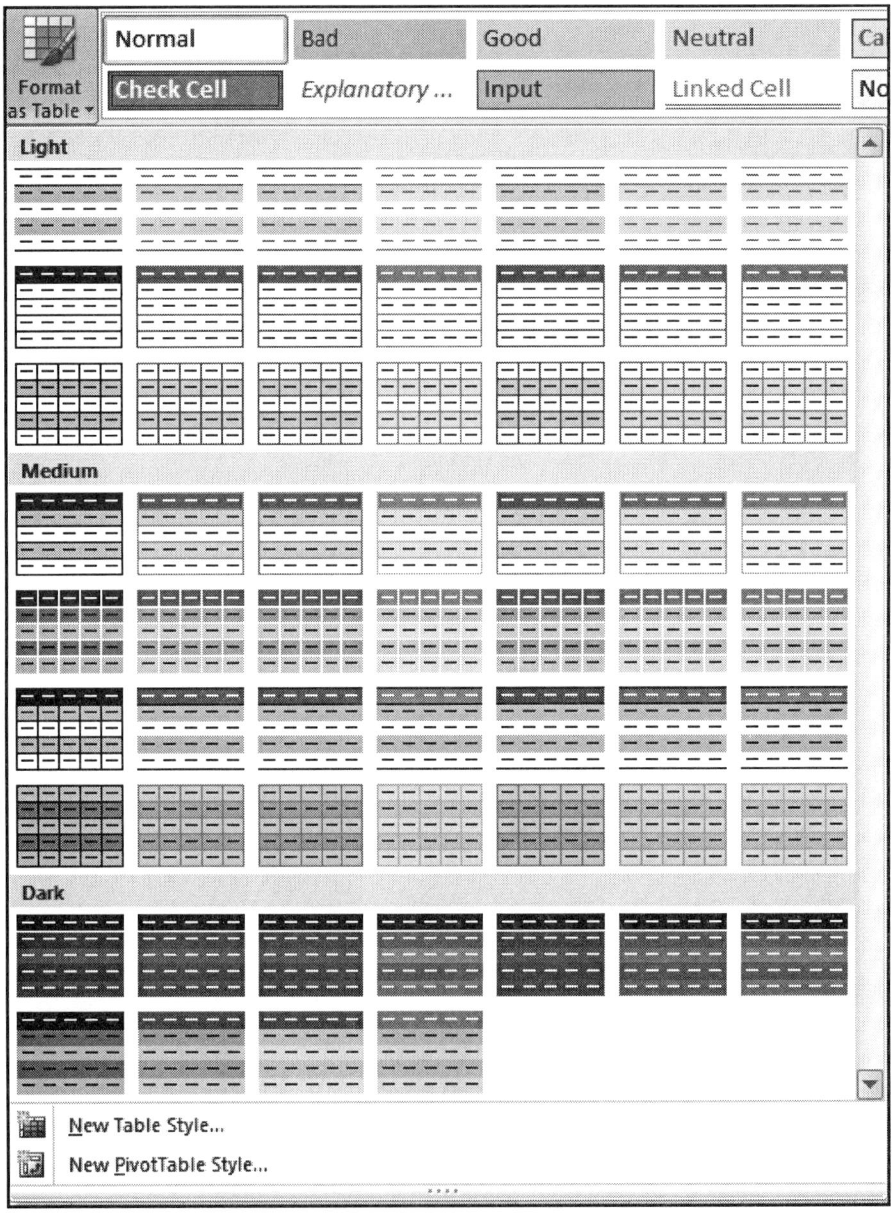

Figure 5.22: Auto formatting a Document

5.19 Creating Charts with Microsoft Excel

MS Excel can produce great-looking graphs from worksheet data. The **Chart tool** is an *MS Excel* wizard that uses worksheet data to produce **graphs** and **charts**. A **data series** is a data set that is selected from a column or row. **Pie charts** show single data series while other types of graphs show comparisons between two or more data series. To create a graph from a set of numbers, follow these steps:

1. Select the cells of data to be used to make the graph.
2. Click one of the ***chart tools*** from the *Chart* pane of the *Insert Menu.*
3. Choose one of the options from the dialog box.

A data chart will be created to represent the selected data. To experiment with different graphs, just delete a graph and repeat the procedure selecting a different type and style of graph. Tip: Avoid using a large amount of data to make a chart. Charting a large set of data tend to look confusing and is hard to read.

The information on the spreadsheet in Figure 5.24a is shown as a bar graph in Figure 5.24b and as a pie chart in Figure 5.24c.

A chart or graph is a type of information graphic or graphic organizer that represents tabular numeric data and/or functions.

	A	B	C	D	E	F
1	LeAnn's Personal budget					
2	Expenses	January	February	March	April	
3	Rent	$600	$600	$600	$600	
4	Utilities	$150	$175	$145	$157	
5	Phone	$50	$75	$55	$60	
6	Car	$250	$250	$250	$250	
7	Insurance	$100	$100	$100	$100	
8	Entertainment	$50	$75	$85	$70	
9	Visa	$200	$200	$200	$200	
10	Expenses Totals	$1,400	$1,475	$1,435	$1,437	
11						
12	Income	January	February	March	April	
13	Loan	$1,000	$1,000	$1,000	$1,000	
14	Job	$500	$500	$450	$483	
15	Income Totals	$1,500	$1,500	$1,450	$1,483	
16						

Figure 5.24a: Sample Spreadsheet Data for Graphs

Charts are often used to make it easier to understand large quantities of data and the relationship between different parts of the data. Charts can usually be read more quickly than the raw data that they come from.

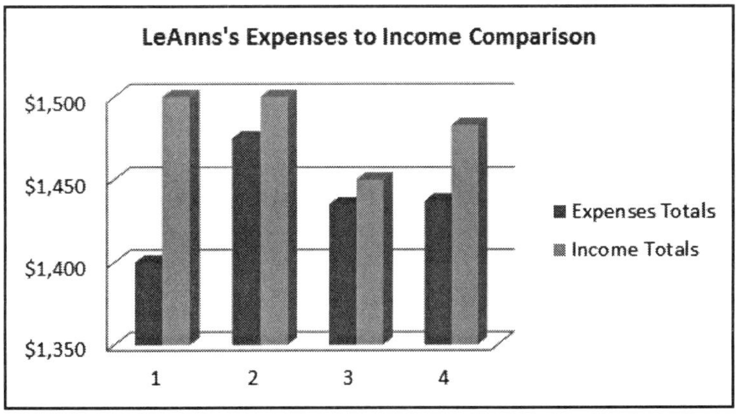

Figure 5.24b: Bar Graph of Sample Spreadsheet Data

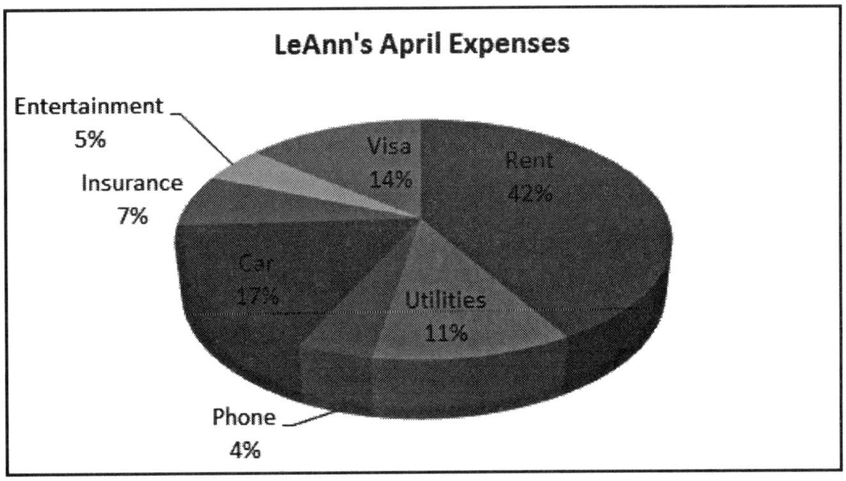

Figure 5.24c: Pie Chart of Sample Spreadsheet Data

5.20 Printing Options

Excel provides various printing options. Two of the most useful options enable the user to print only a part of spreadsheet or printing formulas instead of the numeric values created by the formula.

Printing a Portion of a Spreadsheet. To print part of a spreadsheet, follow these steps:

1. Select the cells of the worksheet which you wish to print clicking and dragging the mouse.
2. Choose *Print* from the *File* menu.
3. Choose *Print Selection* under the *Settings* section.
4. Choose *Print* under the *Print* section.

This will print only the selected portion of the worksheet.

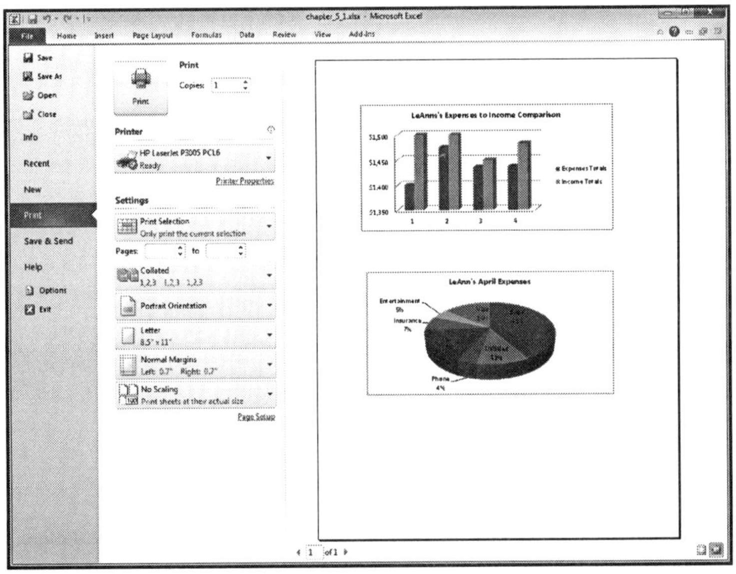

Figure 5.25: Printing Part of a Worksheet

Printing Formulas: By default, *MS Excel* prints the values in cells that contain formulas. To view and/or print the formulas instead of their values, follow these steps:

1. On the formula tab, in the formula auditing group, click the show Formulas button.
2. With the formulas displayed, print the worksheet as you normally would any other report.
3. Return the worksheet to normal by clicking the Show Formulas button again or press the Control key plus the accent (') key (next to the 1 key) on the keyboard together.

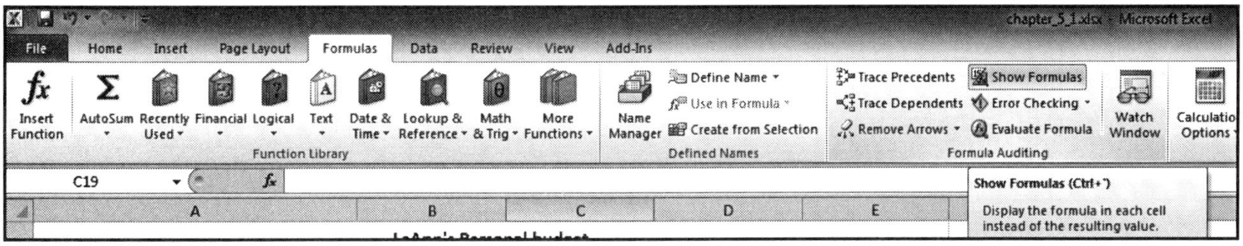

Figure 5.26a: Show Formulas Menu

	A	B	C	D	E
1	LeAnn's Personal budget				
2	Expenses	January	February	March	April
3	Rent	600	600	600	600
4	Utilities	150	175	145	157
5	Phone	50	75	55	60
6	Car	250	250	250	250
7	Insurance	100	100	100	100
8	Entertainment	50	75	85	70
9	Visa	200	200	200	200
10	Expenses Totals	=SUM(B3:B9)	=SUM(C3:C9)	=SUM(D3:D9)	=SUM(E3:E9)
11					
12	Income	January	February	March	April
13	Loan	1000	1000	1000	1000
14	Job	500	500	450	483
15	Income Totals	=SUM(B13:B14)	=SUM(C13:C14)	=SUM(D13:D14)	=SUM(E13:E14)

Figure 5.26b: The Spreadsheet Showing Formulas

5.21 A Spreadsheet Grade Book

A useful tool for teachers is the computerized grade book. By using an electronic spreadsheet, grades can be easily recorded, edited, weighted, and averaged. Class rankings can also be included. Once the formulas are entered, teachers may enter student scores and have the grades calculated automatically. It takes a little time and organizing to set up a spreadsheet (especially the formulas), but once the spreadsheet is set up, it will save a great deal of time in mathematical calculations. See Figure 4.27 for an example of a spreadsheet grade book.

EDIT 2318 Module3: Spreadsheets				
Name	Test 1	Test 2	Test 3	Average
Kent, C.	99	93	97	96.33
Lane, L.	98	92	94	94.67
Olson, J.	90	91	89	90.00
White. P.	95	96	92	94.33
Cheon, J.	98	94	94	95.33
Crooks, S.	90	90	98	92.67

Figure 5.27: An Electronic Grade Book

> The concept of grading students' work quantitatively was developed by a tutor named William Farish, and first implemented by the University of Cambridge in 1792.

Look at the sample grade book. Note that it is made up of 5 columns and 8 rows. Columns are identified by letters of the alphabet and rows by numbers. The label *EDIT 2318 Module 3: Electronic Spreadsheets* is contained in the top row. The label *Name* is an entry in cell A3. The labels in row 3 show *Test 1, Test 2, Test 3,* and *Average.* The value *98* is a value assigned to L. Lane for Test 1. It appears in cell B5. The lowest score for J. Olsen (91 for Test 2) is a value. It appears in cell C6.

The formulas to make the calculations in this sample spreadsheet are not shown, but are stored in cells E4, E5, E6, E7, and E8. The formula for cell E4 would be: (+B4+C4+D4)/3. Exactly, the same result could be achieved with the function =AVERAGE(B4:D4). If the **average function** were used, the formula for cell E5 would be: =AVERAGE(B5:D5).

Any new value entered in columns B, C, or D will automatically be calculated correctly in column E. The formulas in column E operate upon any value entered in columns B, C, or D. All calculations are performed electronically by the computer. Computations are accurate and immediate.

Sorting data is another useful function of electronic spreadsheets. The following figure shows a portion of a grade book for which names have been sorted alphabetically based on the last name column. To alphabetize the list, follow these steps:

1. Select all of the rows to be sorted by clicking and dragging the mouse.
2. Choose *Sort* tool from the *Data* menu.
3. Choose *A-Z* icon to sort the names into alphabetical order.

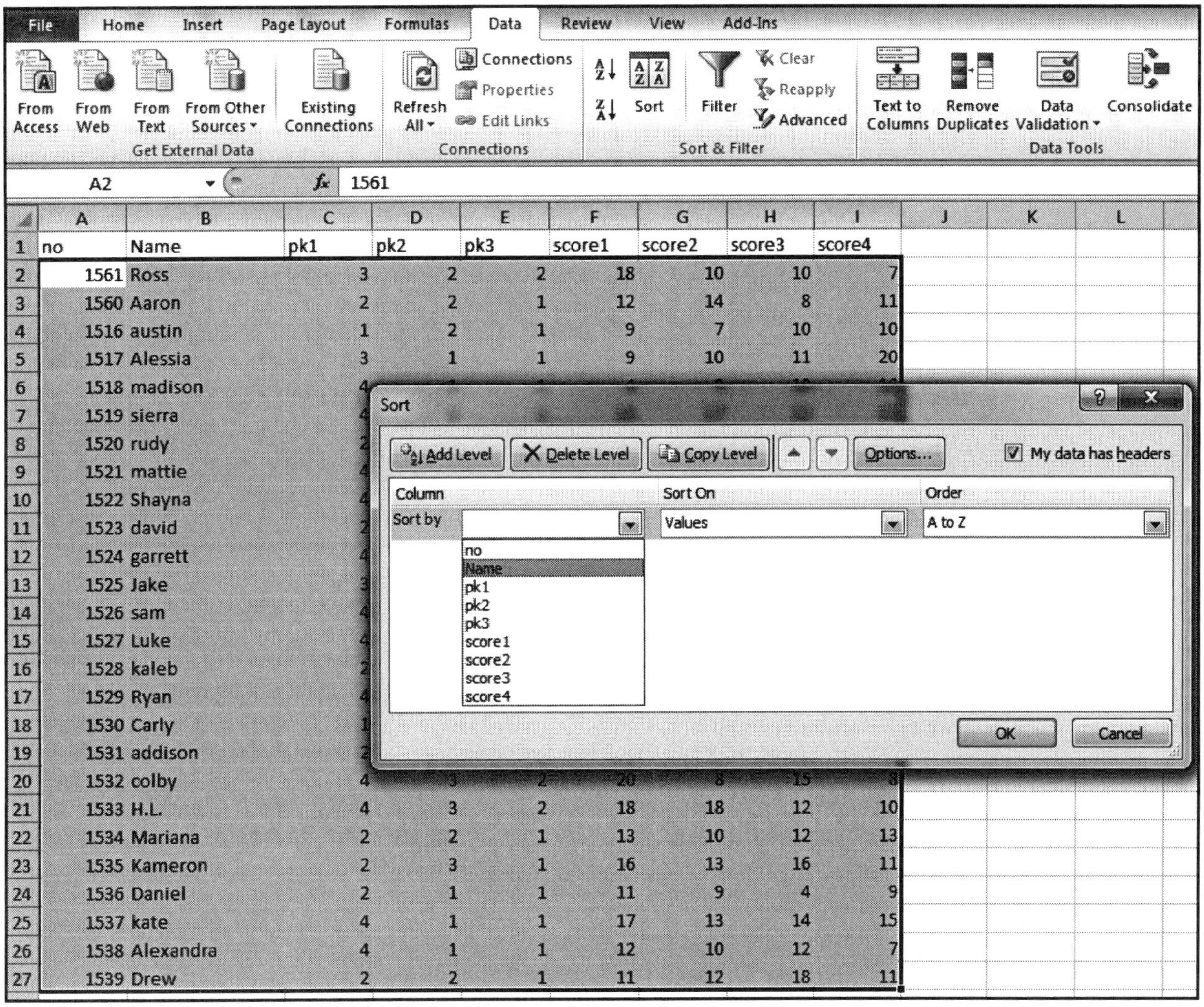

Figure 5.28: Alphabetizing a list of names with the Sort dialog box superimposed over the grade book spreadsheet

Another useful way to sort data is **numeric sorting**. For example, to sort the grades in our sample spreadsheet from highest to lowest based on their final grades, a teacher would select the *Final Grade* column and sort the grades in descending order by selecting the *Z – A* icon using the *Sort* tool as in the previous example.

5.22 Conclusion

In this module you have seen how electronic spreadsheets can automate many of the repetitive chores involved in mathematical calculations. You have seen how electronic spreadsheets can be used for a variety of tasks and how they can make working with numeric data easier than working with manual calculations. We have covered the basics of using *MS Excel*. While it is beyond the scope of this book to cover all aspects of *Excel*, you should now be able to use *Excel* to create various types of electronic spreadsheets. In the application assignments for this module, you will use *MS Excel* to produce a grade book and also to create a personal budget.

Key Terms

Alignment
AutoFill
AutoFormat
AutoSum
Cell coordinate
Cells
Chart Wizard
Charts
Clearing data
Columns
Data range
Data series
Delete
Fill handle
Formulas
Function
Graphs
Hidden cells
Insert
Labels
Locking cells
Menu commands
MS Excel
Numbers
Number formatting
Numeric sorting
Operational hierarchy
Operators
Rows
Sorting
Values
VisiCalc
Workbook
Worksheet
Worksheet range

Important Symbols and Operators

/ Divide

* Multiply

- Subtract

+ Add

‘ Denotes numerical entries that are to be read as text.

Computer Application Assignments

There are 3 application assignments for this module. In the first assignment, you will use a practice spreadsheet file to practice formatting, entering calculations, and creating charts. In the second assignment, you will create a personal budget from scratch. Use *MS Excel* to complete these assignments. Save your work. Refer to the information provided in this module for information on using electronic spreadsheets and *MS Excel*. The third assignment is a spreadsheet questionnaire.

Assignment 1: Format and Manipulate a Grade Book Spreadsheet

First, create a new *MS Excel* file and enter the text and numbers as shown in Figure 5.29. Once you complete it, save it to your computer, disk, or other storage device. This file contains a simple but incomplete grade book spreadsheet, which you will complete and enhance. Follow these steps to complete this assignment. Save your spreadsheet after you complete each step.

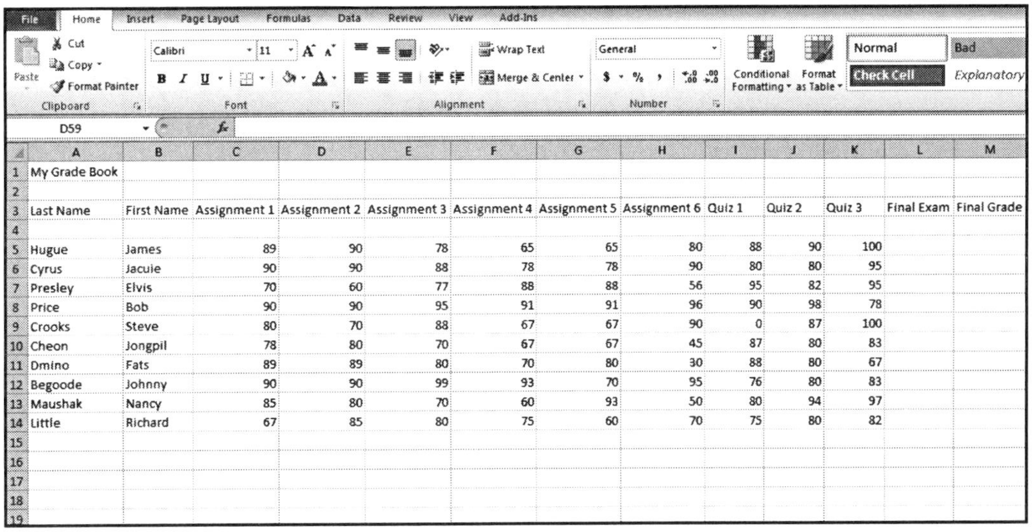

	A	B	C	D	E	F	G	H	I	J	K	L	M
1	My Grade Book												
2													
3	Last Name	First Name	Assignment 1	Assignment 2	Assignment 3	Assignment 4	Assignment 5	Assignment 6	Quiz 1	Quiz 2	Quiz 3	Final Exam	Final Grade
4													
5	Hugue	James	89	90	78	65	65	80	88	90	100		
6	Cyrus	Jacuie	90	90	88	78	78	90	80	80	95		
7	Presley	Elvis	70	60	77	88	88	56	95	82	95		
8	Price	Bob	90	90	95	91	91	96	90	98	78		
9	Crooks	Steve	80	70	88	67	67	90	0	87	100		
10	Cheon	Jongpil	78	80	70	67	67	45	87	80	83		
11	Dmino	Fats	89	89	80	70	80	30	88	80	67		
12	Begoode	Johnny	90	90	99	93	70	95	76	80	83		
13	Maushak	Nancy	85	80	70	60	93	50	80	94	97		
14	Little	Richard	67	85	80	75	60	70	75	80	82		
15													
16													
17													
18													
19													

Figure 5.29: The Practice Grade Book File

1. Replace *My Grade book* with your name in Row 1.
2. Center and bold all of the column titles in Row 3.
3. Enter names and grades for 5 more students following those that are already listed. You may make up the names and grades.
4. Enter a final exam grade for all students. You may make up the grades.
5. Average the final grade for the students. To do this, enter the *AVG function* into cell L5 and select the range of cells with the grades that are to be averaged. For this example, we will assume that all grades count equally. After you have entered the formula, use the *Fill* command to fill in the formula in column L for the rest of the students.

6. Sort the students from highest grade to lowest based on their final grade.
7. Now assume that the teacher would like to know the average grade as well as the highest grade and lowest grade for the class on each assignment. In column A beginning in cell A21, enter the labels: *Class Average, Highest Grade,* and *Lowest Grade.* In cell C21, enter the *AVG formula* and select the range of cells from C5 through C19 to include all of the grades for *Assignment 1.* In cell C22, use the *MAX function* to find the highest grade in range of grades. To do this, select the *MAX function* from the function tool in the tool bar and then select the range of cells containing the grades for Assignment 1 as you did for the assignment average. In cell C23, enter the *MIN function* to find the lowest grade in the range of grades using the same procedure as you used to find the highest grade. After entering these functions in cells C21, C22, and C23, select all 3 of these cells and use the *Fill* command to copy the formulas into rows 21, 22, and 23 into columns D through M.
8. Steve Crooks took make-up tests, so replace the zeros in cells I19 with grades. Enter any grades you wish. Note that their grade average is automatically updated as is the class average for Quiz 1.
9. Make a block from C21 to M21, and change the numbers with one decimal places using Format Cells menu.
10. Now create a chart of the final grades. To do this, follow these steps:
    - Select all of the final grades by clicking and dragging the mouse.
    - Click on the *Column* graph tool in the *Charts* pane of the *Insert* menu.
    - Choose one of the 3D column formats.
    - Enter *Grade Distribution* for the chart name using *Chart Layouts* pane
11. Your chart will appear in your spreadsheet. Click on your chart and drag it to an appropriate location for printing.

Your completed grade book spreadsheet should look similar to the one shown in the following figure except that your grade book will be sorted based on grades and will include your chart. First, print or save your grade book with the formulas displayed. Second, print or save your grade book with the values displayed. Submit both versions of your spreadsheet to your instructor.

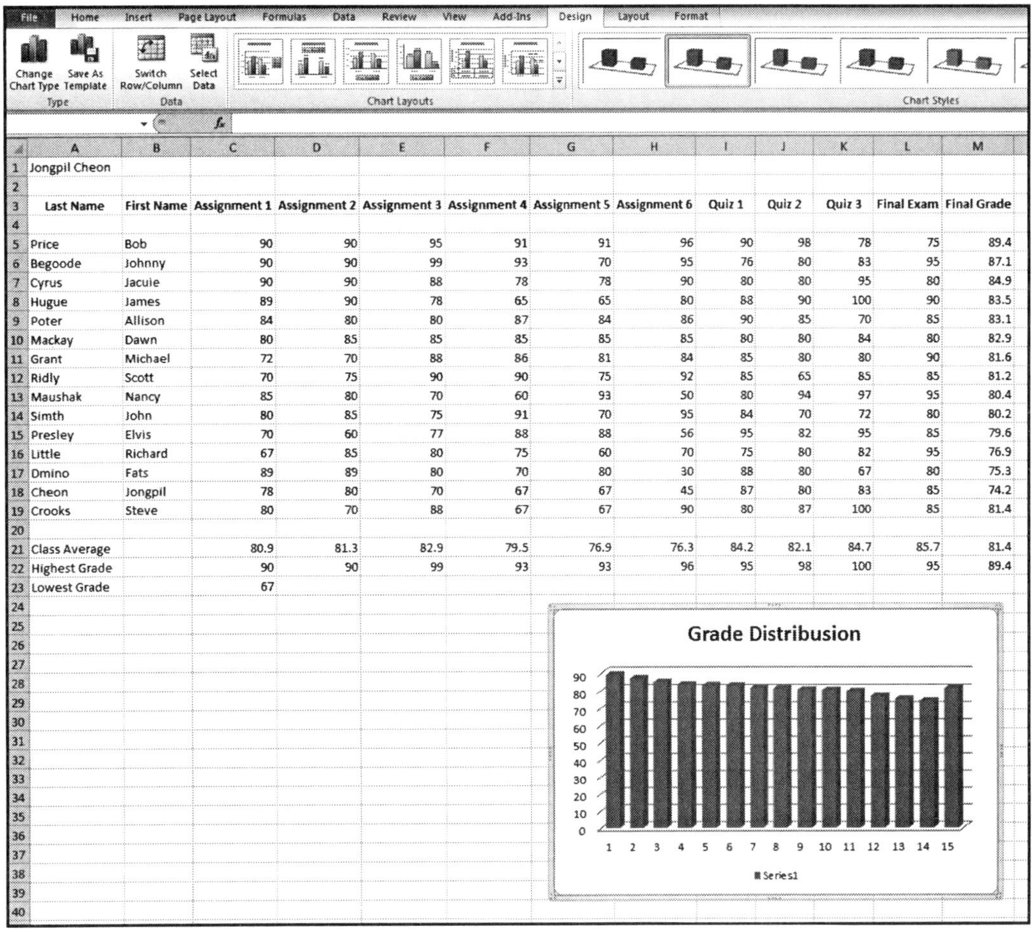

	A	B	C	D	E	F	G	H	I	J	K	L	M
1	Jongpil Cheon												
2													
3	**Last Name**	**First Name**	**Assignment 1**	**Assignment 2**	**Assignment 3**	**Assignment 4**	**Assignment 5**	**Assignment 6**	**Quiz 1**	**Quiz 2**	**Quiz 3**	**Final Exam**	**Final Grade**
4													
5	Price	Bob	90	90	95	91	91	96	90	98	78	75	89.4
6	Begoode	Johnny	90	90	99	93	70	95	76	80	83	95	87.1
7	Cyrus	Jacuie	90	90	88	78	78	90	80	80	95	80	84.9
8	Hugue	James	89	90	78	65	65	80	88	90	100	90	83.5
9	Poter	Allison	84	80	80	87	84	86	90	85	70	85	83.1
10	Mackay	Dawn	80	85	85	85	85	85	80	80	84	80	82.9
11	Grant	Michael	72	70	88	86	81	84	85	80	80	90	81.6
12	Ridly	Scott	70	75	90	90	75	92	85	65	85	85	81.2
13	Maushak	Nancy	85	80	70	60	93	50	80	94	97	95	80.4
14	Simth	John	80	85	75	91	70	95	84	70	72	80	80.2
15	Presley	Elvis	70	60	77	88	88	56	95	82	95	85	79.6
16	Little	Richard	67	85	80	75	60	70	75	80	82	95	76.9
17	Dmino	Fats	89	89	80	70	80	30	88	80	67	80	75.3
18	Cheon	Jongpil	78	80	70	67	67	45	87	80	83	85	74.2
19	Crooks	Steve	80	70	88	67	67	90	80	87	100	85	81.4
20													
21	Class Average		80.9	81.3	82.9	79.5	76.9	76.3	84.2	82.1	84.7	85.7	81.4
22	Highest Grade		90	90	99	93	93	96	95	98	100	95	89.4
23	Lowest Grade		67										

Figure 5.30: A Completed Grade Book

Assignment 2: Create a Personal Budget Spreadsheet

Open *MS Excel* and click on the *Windows* button and select *New* and *Blank Workbook* to start with an empty workbook. Name the new workbook *Budget* and save it. Your budget will cover a period of 3 months. The data that you enter may be fictitious. Follow these steps to complete your budget. Save your file after each step.

1. In cell A1, enter *Personal Budget for <your name>*.
2. In cell A2, enter the current date by **Ctrl + ;** (control key plus semicolon key).
3. Since we will be working only with dollar figures for this spreadsheet, select rows 4 through 25 and then click on *Currency* from the *Number* pane in the *Home* menu to set the number format to currency form. (Labels are not affected by currency formatting.)

4. Skip a row and enter the label: *Income* in cell A4. Format the *Income* label to bold by clicking on the **B** (for bold) tool in the *Font* pane of the *Home* menu.
5. In cells B5 through D5, enter the labels: *January, February,* and *March.*
6. In A6 and A7, enter labels for 2 or more income sources such as *Work, Loan, Mom & Dad,* etc.
7. In the cells in columns B, C, and D enter a number indicating the dollar amounts that you plan to receive from each of these sources for each of the 3 months. Some of your income can remain the same from month to month, but you will probably only get a student loan once in a semester.
8. Skip a row and enter the label: *Total Income* in row A.
9. In Row B, next to the *Total Income* label, use the **AutoSum** *function* to add all of your income sources together.
10. Fill the sum formula into the cells for February and March by selecting the two cells to the right of the function you placed in Row B and clicking on the *Fill* icon in the *Editing* pane of the *Home* menu to copy the total income formula to columns C and D.
11. *Skip* a row and now enter the label: *Expenses*. Format the ***Expenses*** label to bold.
12. In the rows below *Expenses* in column A, enter labels for at least 6 expenses such as *Rent, Food, Car payment, Gas, Recreation, Tuition, etc.*
13. In the cells to the right of the expenses, in column B, C, and D enter dollar amounts that you plan to budget for each of these items.
14. Skip a row and enter the label *Total Expenses.*
15. Use the **AutoSum** function as described previously to add all of your expenses in column B.
16. Use the *Fill* command as previously described to copy the expense total formula to columns C and D for February and March.
17. Skip a row and enter the label *Savings.* Format the *Savings* label to bold.
18. In column B, next to *Savings*, enter the formula to subtract your total expenses from your total income and copy the formula to columns C and D. These procedures were described previously.

19. Create a bar chart showing your expenses for your first month. To do this, follow these steps:
    - Select all of your expense labels and amounts in columns A and B by clicking and dragging the mouse.
    - Choose one of the *2-D Pie* using the *Chart* tools in the *Chart* pane of the *Insert* menu as previously described.
    - Click and drag the chart to a location to the right of the data in your worksheet.

Your completed budget should look similar to the one shown in the following figure except that your budget should have a bar graph instead of a pie chart. First, print your budget with the formulas displayed. Second, print your budget showing the values.

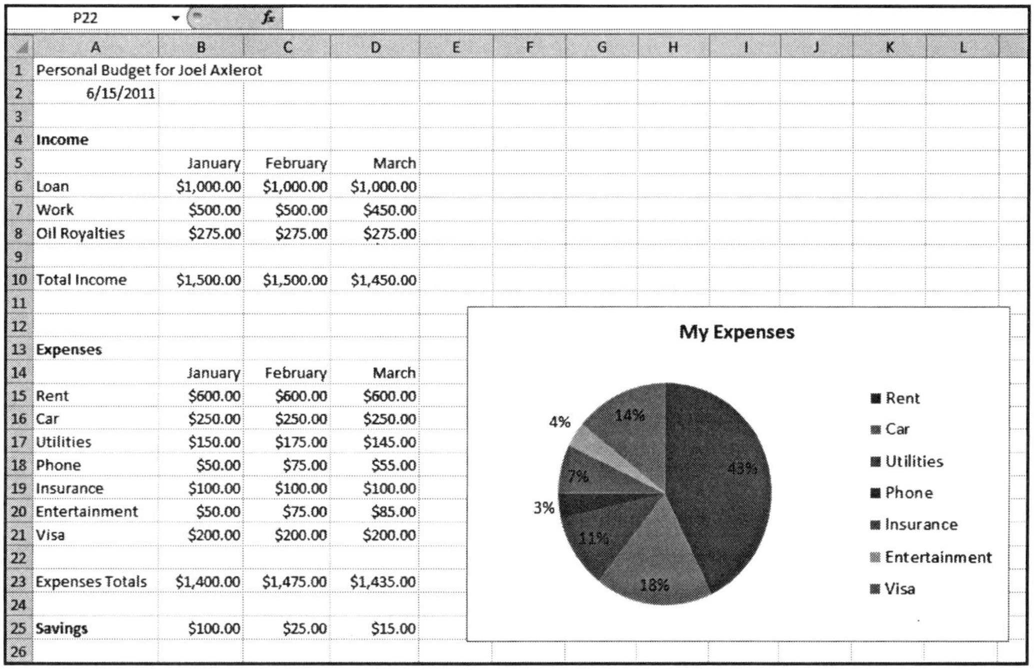

Figure 5.30: A Completed Budget

Assignment 3: Spreadsheet Questionnaire

Answer the following questions and remove this questionnaire from the book to turn it in to your instructor as part of your Module assignment.

1. How is an electronic spreadsheet different from a manual spreadsheet?

2. List and briefly describe the three kinds of data recognized by *MS Excel.*

3. List and describe 3 common functions or formulas that are frequently used when working with an electronic spreadsheet.

4. List several ways that spreadsheets can be used in the classroom or in the office.

5. How can understanding and knowing how to use an electronic spreadsheet assist you in your future career?

You may tear out this page and turn it in with Assignments 1 and 2. You may write on the back if necessary.

Use this page if you need additional space to complete your answers.

MODULE 6

Presentation Graphics

Presentation Graphics

In this module, you will learn about **presentation graphics** and you will learn to use the most popular presentation graphics program, *Microsoft PowerPoint*. Designing effective and motivational presentations that can communicate clearly and hold the viewer's attention is not intuitive. In this module, you will learn how to design effective and professional presentations.

Module Objectives

When you have completed this module, you should be able to:

- Define and describe presentation graphics software and its application;
- Apply the basic rules of layout and design for computer slide presentations to produce an original presentation; and
- Evaluate *PowerPoint* presentations.

Materials Needed to Complete This Module

- This book
- *Microsoft PowerPoint 2010* or later
- A flash drive to store your work on.

How to Proceed

1. Read this module.
2. Review the *Key Terms* located near the end of this module.
3. Complete the *Module Review Questions* located near the end of this module.
4. Complete the *Module Computer Assignments* to turn in to your instructor.
5. Take the *Module* 6 Test.

***Note:* Instructions and assignments given in this module are for *PowerPoint 2010*.**

Presentation Graphics

Microsoft PowerPoint is a user friendly and powerful tool. According to *Microsoft*, some 30 million presentations are made with *PowerPoint* every day. In this module, you will learn to use this prevelant persuasion tool effectively.

The *PowerPoint* 2010 icon.

6.1 Using PowerPoint 2010

Locate *Microsoft PowerPoint* 2010 in the *Programs* folder of your computer and open it. Your initial opening screen should look similar to the one shown in Figure 6.1. Next, we take a look at how *PowerPoint* works.

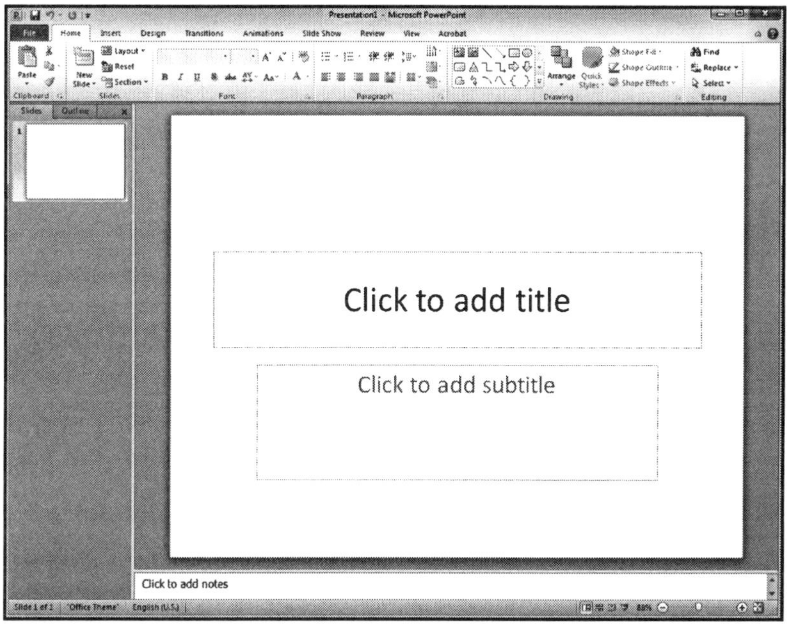

Figure 6.1: The *MS PowerPoint* Normal View Start Up Window

Take a look at the *Home* tab at the top of the screen. Much of it should look familiar by now. The *Font, Paragraph, Editing, Drawing,* and *Editing* panels are much the same as in *MS Word* so we will not go over them again here.

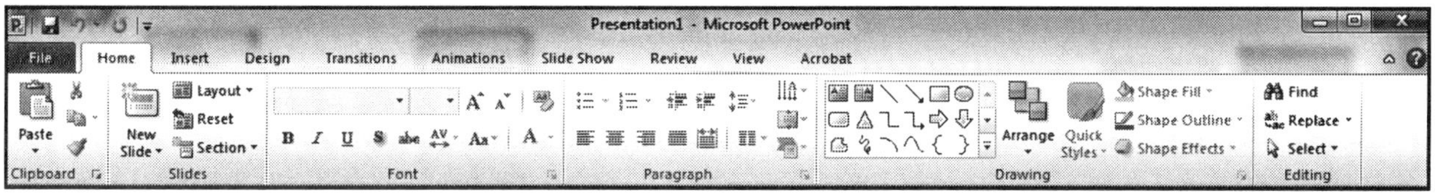

Figure 6.2: The *PowerPoint* Home Menu

There are 2 new panels on the *Home* tab. They are the *Slides* and *Clipboard* panels. The *Slides* tools are used to insert new slides, delete slides, and reset (change the layout) of slides. The ***Clipboard*** **tools** are used to add, delete, and copy slide elements to and from slides.

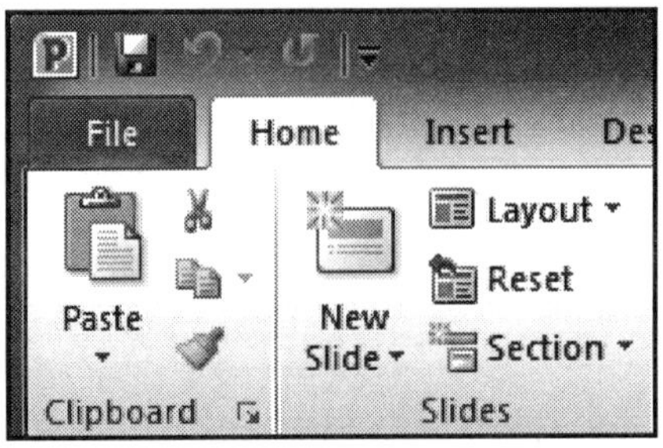

Figure 6.3: The *PowerPoint Slides* and *Clipboard* Panels

The left column of the window shows a miniature version of the slide show or alternatively a text outline of the slide show. The current slide is shown in the main window.

The *Insert* tab provides tools for adding clip art, word art, movies, pictures, sounds, shapes, and other elements to your slides. Pictures or short movies housed on your computer may be included in a presentation. *MS Office* comes with a set of clip art which is shared among programs. Much more clip art may be downloaded from the Microsoft web site or other sites on the Web.

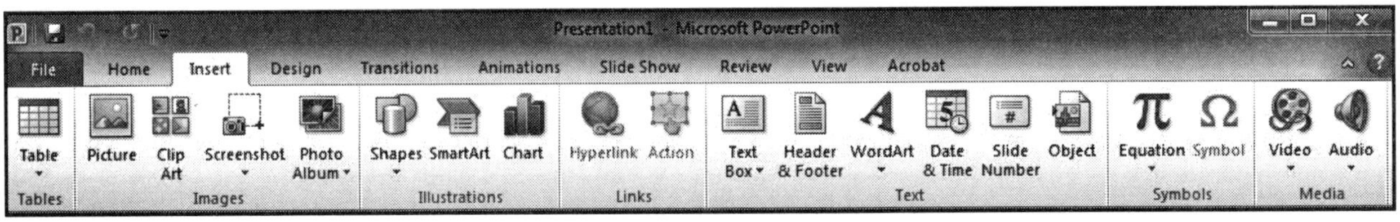

Figure 6.4: The *PowerPoint Insert* Tab

The *Design* tab provides a set of **themes** that may be applied to a presentation. Themes are the *PowerPoint* design templates. Passing the cursor over one of the themes will allow you to preview it on your slide presentation. Selecting and clicking on a template will apply it to the current slide presentation. Each theme can be altered by using the tools for background, color scheme, font, etc. from the *Design* tab. In addition to the themes that come preinstalled with *PowerPoint*, many other themes may be downloaded from the *Microsoft.com* web site.

> *PowerPoint's* ease of use can save a lot of time for people who otherwise would have used other types of visual aids such as hand-drawn or mechanically typeset slides, blackboards or whiteboards, or overhead projections.

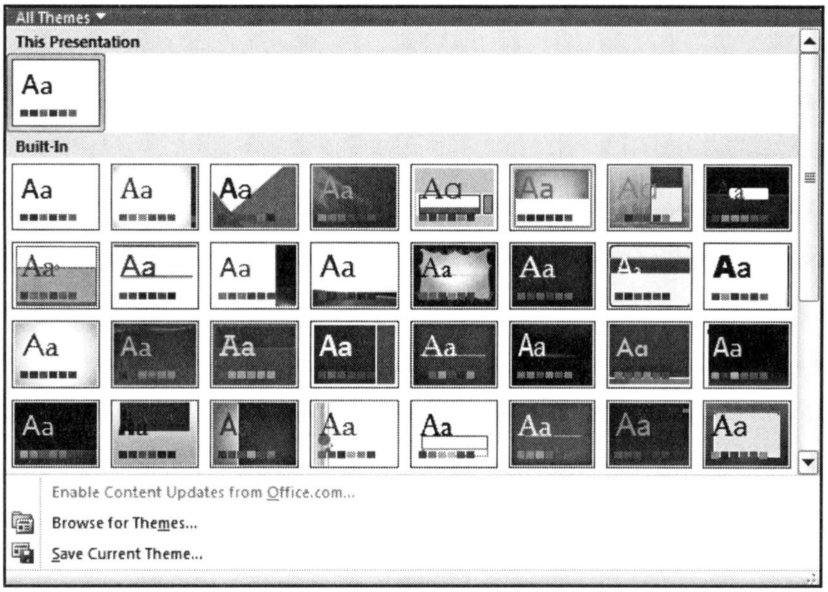

Figure 6.5: *PowerPoint Themes*

> *PowerPoint* is widely used by business people, educators, students, and trainers and is among the most prevalent forms of persuasion technology.

The new *Transitions* tab contains various **transition settings** that allow you to specifically adjust transitions to each slide. These are applied when the user changes slides. Clicking on a transition previews it. Transitions include cuts, fade throughs, dissolves, and others. Sounds may be applied to transitions as well. Built in transition sounds include clicks, bells, whooshes, laser sounds, and many others. These may be previewed by passing the pointer over them. *Transition* animations and sounds are a good way to renew your audience's attention during a slide presentation. The *Transition* tab also allows presenters to move from slide to slide either on a mouse click or through a timer. Timers are generally not used in face-to-face presentations but may be useful in displays and unattended events where a presenter is not presenting to an audience.

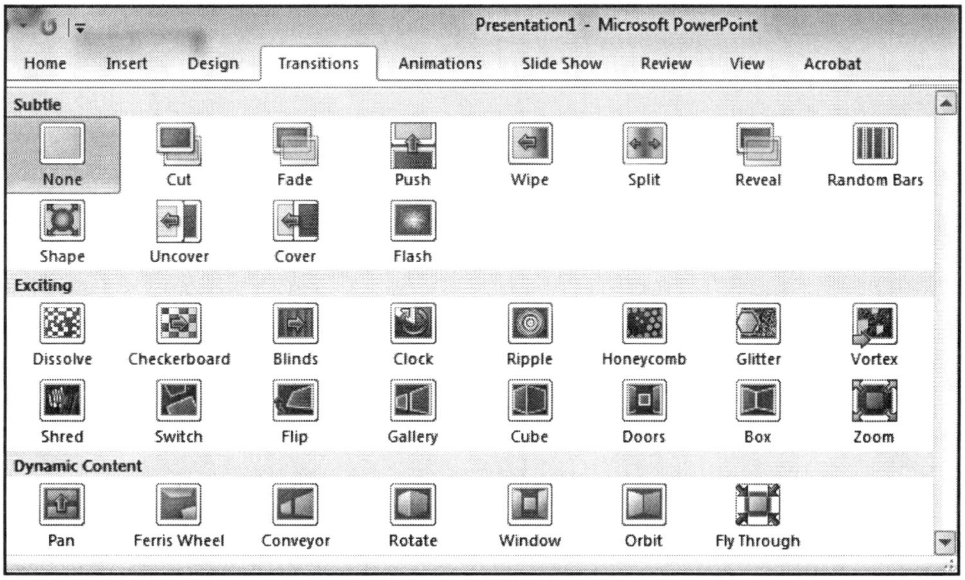

Figure 6.6: *PowerPoint Transitions Tab*

The *Animation* tab contains everything you need to create custom animations without having to open extra windows. You can add an animation to any object or text by selecting it and then selecting the desired animation from the *Animations* ribbon. You can also preview animations by hovering the pointer over specific options on the *Animations* ribbon. Animations include Appear, Fade, Fly In, Float In, and many others. *Triggers* can also be used to designate a specific object as the "trigger" for an animation. When a trigger has been applied to an object, you must click on that object to begin the animation. Finally, options to control the timing and order of any animated sequence are available on the *Animations* ribbon.

The *Slide Show* tab allows presenters to practice their presentation and set parameters such as hiding some slides, or showing only part of a presentation, and to set the screen resolution desired. One of the more useful features of the *Slide Show* menu is the ***Record Slide Show*** tool. This feature allows users to record narration for a presentation while reviewing the presentation. This is useful for presentations which will be used when the presenter is not present such as in distance education or exhibits. To record narration, a microphone must be connected to the Mic input jack of the computer.

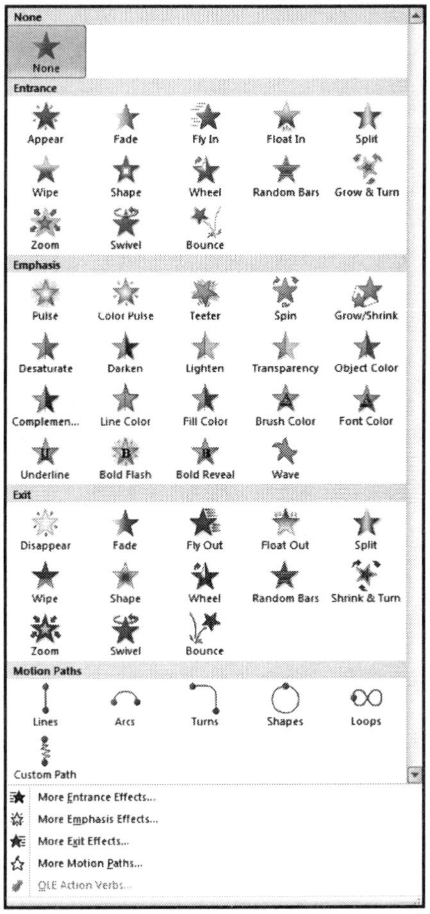

Figure 6.7:
The *PowerPoint Animation* Tab

Figure 6.8: The *PowerPoint Slide Show* Tab

The *Review* menu allows presenters to check spelling and grammar. This should always be done as the last step before finalizing a presentation. Other *Review* features include the ability to translate the presentation into other languages, consult a thesaurus, or to lock the presentation to protect it from accidental change or deletion.

The *View* menu is another useful tool. The ***Normal View*** is the default view shown in figure 6.1. Other views include a ***Slide Sorter*** which shows miniature views of all slides. The *Slide Sorter* allows users to rearrange the order of slides by clicking and dragging them. *Notes* view allows the presenter to make notes for each slide. These may be printed as an aide for the presenter. The ***Slide Show*** view allows the user to review the slide show as it will appear when presented.

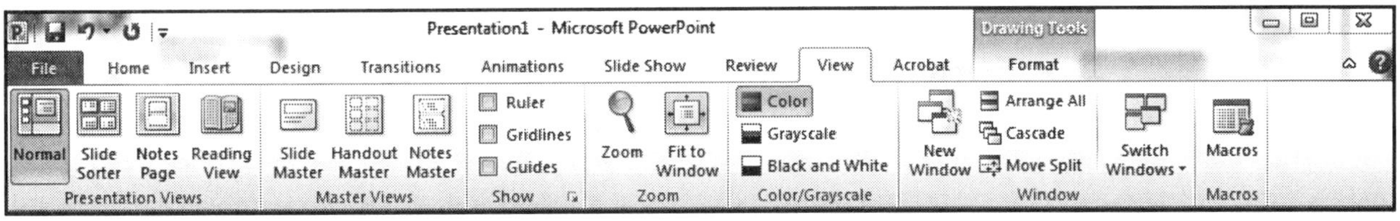

Figure 6.9: The *PowerPoint View* Tab

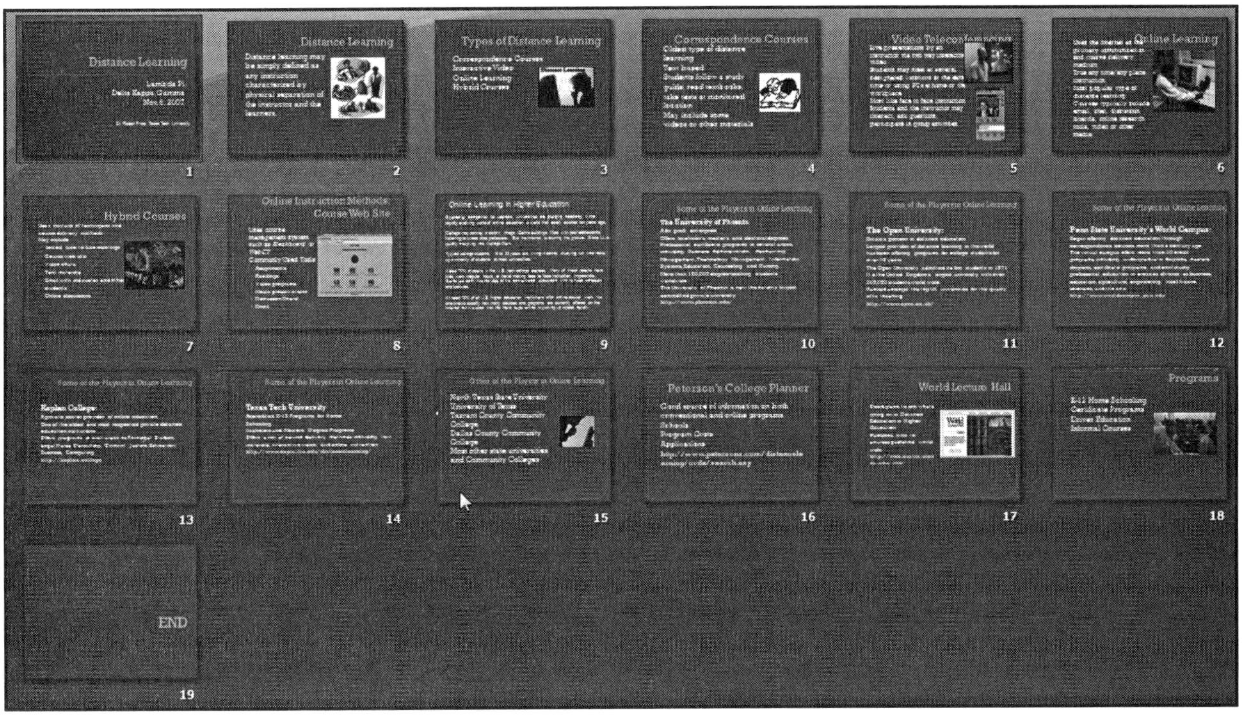

Figure 6.10: The *Slide Sorter*

Another useful feature of *PowerPoint* is the ability to prepare printed **handouts** for an audience. Several slides may be printed on a single page. Handouts with space for audience notes may also be made.

6.2 Message Design

Here are some basic design principles that can be applied to any *MS PowerPoint* presentation:

1. The first slide should be a blank slide. This is so you can add a sound and/or a visual effect on the transition to the title slide.
2. A **title slide** will be next and should be followed by additional slides that indicate who the presenters arc, and who or what organization is responsible for the presentation.
3. The content of the **introduction** will vary depending on the type of presentation. State the intended audience for the presentation, define important terms, introduce any characters or basic precepts, provide history or background for the topic, and state the need for or reason behind the presentation.
4. The next part of the presentation is the **main body**. It should explain the topic of the presentation logically and sequentially. Points should be made clearly. Explanations about how the design is to be carried out, the objectives to be reached, or the hypothesis to be tested should be given. Details about the steps involved should be given as needed.
5. The **conclusion** will summarize the main points, draw conclusions, re-emphasize the importance of the topic, or state what action is required of the audience, as appropriate.

PowerPoint presentations consist of a number of individual pages or "slides". The "slide" analogy is a reference to the slide projector, a device that has become somewhat obsolete due to the use of PowerPoint and other presentation software.

6.3 Aesthetic Appeal

1. Use fonts that are easy to read and large enough to be seen.
2. Use font colors that contrast sharply with the background colors. **Value** refers to the degree to which a color is dark or light; do not use font or background colors that are medium in value because it is impossible to get high contrast. Instead, use a font color with a low value color (such as black or dark blue) on a background with a high value color (such as white or a bright or pastel color,) or the reverse (light font on dark background.)
3. Never use more than 1-2 fonts in the same presentation.
4. Keep background colors consistent throughout a presentation.
5. Vary font color to help illustrate content. A good presentation design includes elements that indicate both unity and variety.

6. Use appropriate sound and transitions. Experiment with the transitions and sound effects to see what works well. Do not use sound effects on very many slides throughout the presentation, just one now and then for effect. If possible, match sound effects to content. Also, do not use too many flashy transitions between slides; you do not want to distract from the presentation itself.
7. Follow the **7 X 7 rule**: no more than 7 lines on a slide and no more than 7 words on a line. Cluttered slides are hard to read.
8. When using bulleted lists, make each bullet on the bulleted list appear on the slide one line at a time. Its effect is similar to uncovering a list on an overhead projector one line at a time; it helps maintain interest. If you introduce 5 or 6 bullets at once, people will read ahead of you and tune you out. Use bullets wherever they are appropriate.

6.4 Nine Tips for Creating Effective PowerPoint Presentations

An alternative to *PowerPoint*?

Some people are born presenters. They just love getting up in front of a crowd. They do not sweat if they drop their note cards at the last minute; they do not stress about not having the audio-visual equipment they need. If you are one of those people, count yourself fortunate. If you are not one of those people, you need *PowerPoint*. It helps you prepare presentations that are easy, smooth, and professional, whether you are a seasoned show person or a novice quaking in your boots. Here are 8 fast and practical tips you can use as you create great presentations with *PowerPoint*.

1. Start with an end in mind.

The expression "Death by *PowerPoint*" has become popular for describing poor presentations. "Death by PowerPoint" does not necessarily mean that the presentation itself is boring. The problem could lie with the presenter.

What do you want to accomplish with your presentation? Are you giving the presentation to educate the sales staff about a new product, to inform stockholders about fluctuations in pricing, to conduct a class, or to inspire people to volunteer for your cause? Do you need a short, simple presentation that leaves the viewer wanting to know more, or an involved, longer presentation that teaches audience members how to do a specific task? Think through the practical issues—where and how you will be delivering the presentation. Know the room in which you will be presenting, how big your audience might be, what kind of handouts you will need, and so on. Thinking your presentation through before you begin will help you make the right choices as you pull everything together.

2. If you are not sure of the presentation design that you want, use a theme.

If you are unsure of your design abilities, choose a look from the design themes available. Themes in *PowerPoint* range from smooth professional to bright casual. Whether you are presenting to your sales staff or a national convention of herb gardeners, you are likely to find a look that fits.

PowerPoint presentations are often used with a projector for large audiences.

3. Use the Outline View to write content.

Sometimes tackling both the look and the content at once is a bit overwhelming. Why not try getting your thoughts down in the *Outline* View quickly and then build from there? In the left panel of the *PowerPoint* window, click the *Outline Tab*. Begin typing a thought and press ENTER and it becomes a new slide title. You can continue creating slides and entering slide titles by typing information and pressing ENTER. If you want to add content to a slide, press TAB (instead of ENTER) and *PowerPoint* records the text as a bullet point. To add a bullet within a bullet point, press TAB again. You can create several levels of bullets, but usually one or two levels works best.

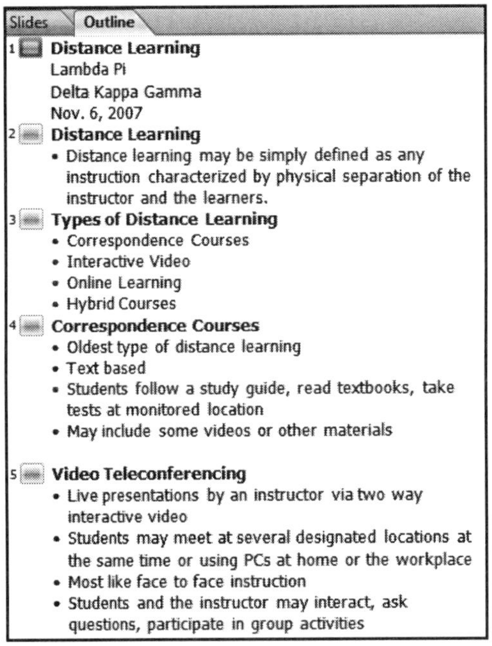

Figure 6.11: The *PowerPoint Outline View*

4. Use pictures and clip art to add visual interest to your presentations.

Not all presentations need a lot of images. In fact, some of the most effective presentations use images and other special effects (music, video, and more) sparingly, but a picture is worth more than a thousand words when it really drives your message home.

5. Use a chart to present data.

You will really enjoy the wide range of easy-to-apply choices you have with *PowerPoint* charts. Not only can you apply literally dozens of different chart types (in both two-dimensional and three-dimensional views), but you can also create flowcharts and more using the diagramming features in *PowerPoint*.

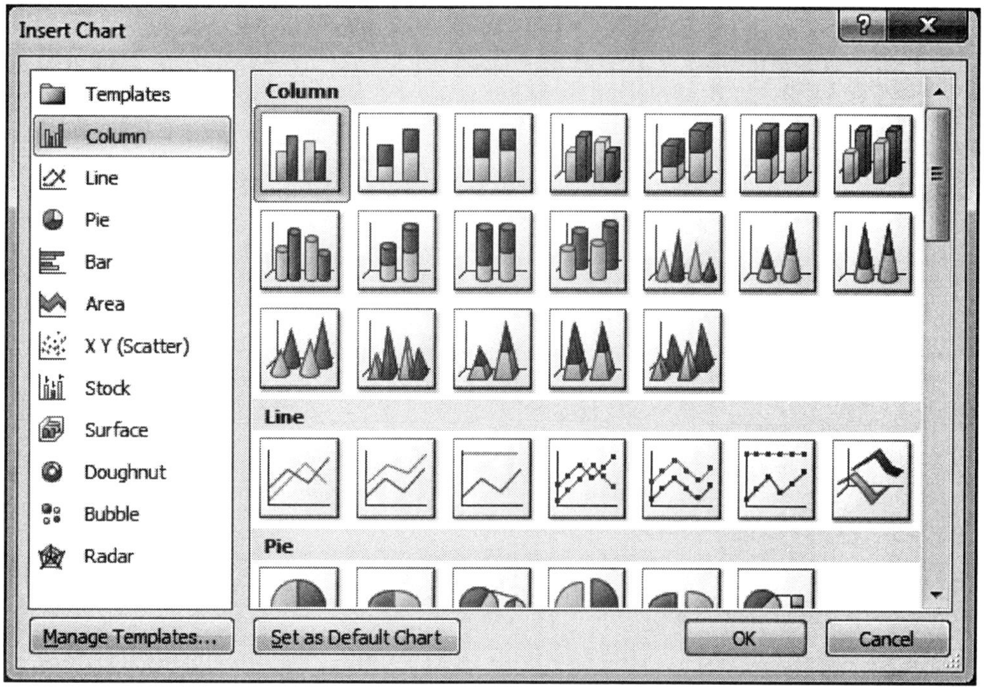

Figure 6.12: PowerPoint Chart Tools

The next figure is an example of one of the many types of charts that you can construct for *PowerPoint* presentations.

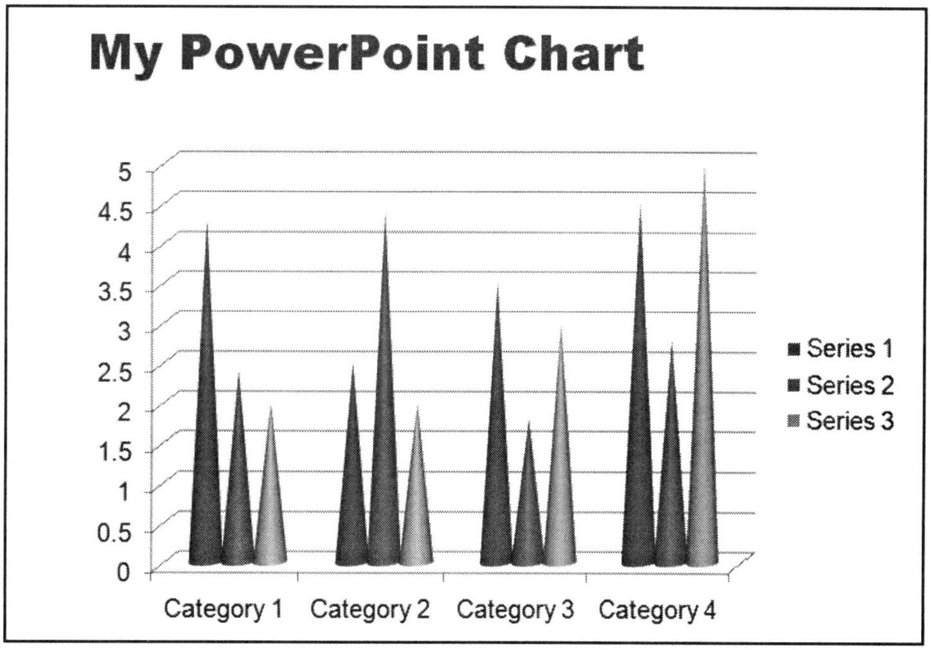

Figure 6.13: A PowerPoint Chart

6. Create your own templates for repeat presentations.

If you are creating the same presentation over and over again—or at least updating one that you use regularly—you can turn your presentation into a **custom template** that you or others can use quickly. A template saves all the settings you have selected—background images, color scheme, font selections, and so on—and ensures that the presentations you create based on that template all have the same elements in common. This is great if you have a look that you want to adhere to. To turn a presentation into a template, just choose *Save As...* from the *Office Button* and choose *PowerPoint Template* from the options in the dialog box.

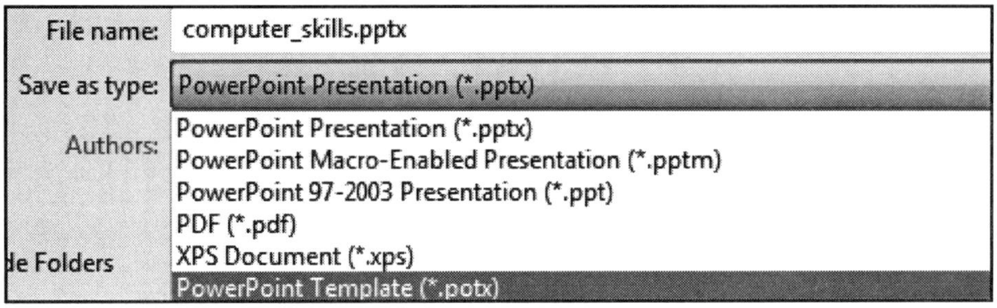

Figure 6.14: Saving a Presentation as a Template

Another extra that can really help: add instructions about special formats, font choices, or video clips in the *Notes* area under each slide, if others will be using your template or as a reminder to yourself.

7. Color coordinate your materials.

Print handouts, cards, slides, and other collateral materials in the same font and colors on complementary paper or stock. Better yet, if your budget allows, put it all together in a folder that matches the basic colors of your presentation. When someone goes to reach for your materials later they will find what they need easily—and notice how well prepared you are.

> By using two monitors, you can run your *PowerPoint* 2010 presentation from one monitor (at a podium, for example) while your audience views it on the second monitor.

8. Practice and use Rehearse Timings.

PowerPoint is a great help for those pre-presentation jitters. By relying on the program's professional look, the content prompts, and the help it gives you along the way, you can create an impressive presentation even if it is your first time out. And who knows? Pretty soon you may love presenting so much you will be looking for excuses to get up in front of a crowd.

Figure 6.15:
PowerPoint Audio Files

6.5 Advanced PowerPoint Techniques

Once you have mastered the basics, *PowerPoint* provides several options that can make your presentations really stand out as attention grabbers. A few of them are described in this section.

1. Add sound to your presentations.

Computers today are multimedia devices. Most have built in speakers and most also have output jacks that can be hooked up to larger room speakers. *PowerPoint* comes with a variety of music and **sound clips**. To use clips from *PowerPoint*'s collection, click on **Audio** from the Insert tab. A few sounds are included in the clip art collection. You can record your own sound files through a microphone or from the Web or from a CD. You can hear the sounds by clicking on the *Preview* option. You can also play an audio CD during your presentation and control it with *PowerPoint.*

2. Add video to your presentations.

Short video clips can be added to your slide shows in a similiar manner to adding sounds. The movies included with the clip art gallery are really just animated clip art. You can download video clips from *Microsoft* to use in your presentations from **Microsoft Video** at: **http://preview.microsoft.com/video**. Movie files that you create yourself can also be incorporated into your presentations or they can be downloaded from other sites on the Web. Some videos available from Microsoft are shown in the following figure.

Figure 6.16: PowerPoint Video Tab

3. Add Custom Animation to Your Presentation.

Both text and graphics can be animated to spin, fly in, dissolve, or fade in or out. To animate objects, select the *Animations* tab. Select an object, such as a title or clip art, and then click the button on the *Animations* ribbon that represents the animation effect you desire to create (e.g., Wipe). With a little experimentation, you can create lively animated slides.

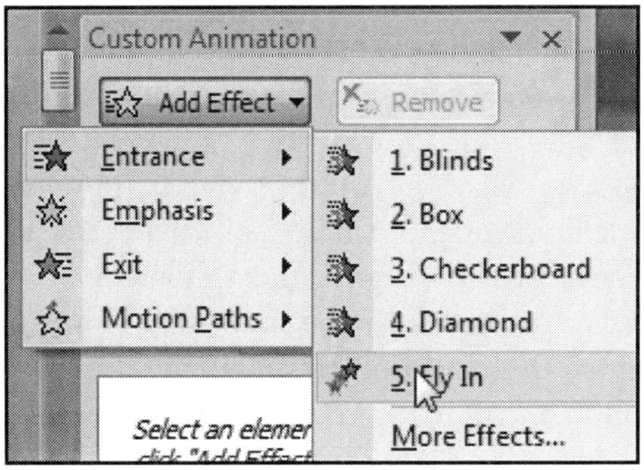

Figure 6.17: Adding Animation to *PowerPoint* Presentations

6.6 Saving PowerPoint Presentations

Before you share a final version of your presentation with other people, you can use the **Mark As Final** command to make the presentation read-only.

To save your *PowerPoint* presentation, select **Save** or **Save As...** from the **File Menu**. Normally, you will save your finished product as a **presentation (PPT),** which is indicated with the ***.ppt*** appendix to the file name. Presentations created with *PowerPoint* will work only when opened with versions of *PowerPoint* that are the same as or higher than the one used to create it. You cannot open a *PowerPoint* file created with *PowerPoint 2007* using *PowerPoint XP* unless you save it as a *PowerPoint 97-2003* file.

To save a completed presentation for viewing only, you can save your presentation as a ***PowerPoint* Show (PPS).** These are self-running packaged presentations and are indicated with the appendix ***.pps*** to the file name. PPS files can be shown on computer systems that do not have *PowerPoint* installed or those that have a different version of *PowerPoint.*

You can also save *PowerPoint* Presentations as Web pages and in other formats, which are beyond the scope of this discussion. Your presentations can also be saved as a **Rich Text Format (RTF)** file, which is designated with the ***.rtf*** appendix added to the file name. *PowerPoint* presentations tend to be large files because they contain so many graphics. In cases where file storage space is a problem, you can save the essentials of your presentation as an *.rtf* file. This format does not save the graphics or backgrounds, but it does preserve the text and text formatting of the presentation. Sending *PowerPoint* presentations through E-mail can be slow since they are usually very large files. They may also take up more space than some Internet servers allow for. *PowerPoint* presentations

The official home of *MS PowerPoint* is located online at this URL: http://office.microsoft.com/en-us/powerpoint/

stored on web sites will run very slowly for users who use POT systems. In this case, you might want to save your *PowerPoint* presentation as an RTF files instead of in the *.ppt* or *.pps* format.

You can also save your slides as JPEG files, which are designated with the ***.jpeg*** appendix to the file name. These are graphic files that may be used on web sites or as titles or graphics for video presentations. PowerPoint allows you to save individual frames or an entire presentation as graphics.

<u>DO NOT forget to spell check your presentation before saving</u>. Even the most polished presentations lose much of their credibility when spelling errors are shown to an audience.

6.7 Conclusion

This module has provided you with the guidelines needed to create effective presentations using *PowerPoint.* Creating effective presentations is a skill you can use in many ways to help you communicate your ideas effectively in a variety of situations.

Key Terms

Animations
Chart tool
Clipboard Panel
Custom Template
Death by PowerPoint
Microsoft Video
Normal View
Outline View
PPS
PPT
Presentation Graphics
PowerPoint
Record Slide Show Tool
RTF
Slide Sorter
Sound clip
Start Up Window
Template
Themes
Transitions
XML File
7 X 7 rule

Computer Application Assignments

There are 2 computer application assignments for this module: 1. Creating and evaluating your own *PowerPoint* presentation and 2. Evaluating a *PowerPoint* presentation created by someone else.

Assignment 1: Create a PowerPoint Presentation

1. Create a *PowerPoint* presentation consisting of about 12 slides that illustrates or teaches a subject that is of interest to you. This should be a presentation that you could use for a class or present to a club, at a business meeting, or at some other group function. Refer to the design principles and tips for *PowerPoint* presentations given in sections 6.2, 6.3 and 6.4 of this module when designing your presentation. Be sure to include the following elements in your presentation:

   - a title page
   - several images (clip art or pictures)
   - one or more slides containing a graph or chart
   - overall layout and design that follows the guidelines presented in this module

   After you complete your presentation, save it to your disk or flash drive.

   Print a slide handout using the 6 slides per page format to turn in to your instructor. To do this, follow these steps:

   - Select *Print* from the *File Menu.*
   - Select the drop-down menu next to *Full Page Slides.*
   - Select *Six Slides Horizontal.* See below. Do not print individual slides on separate pages.

2. Evaluate your own presentation using one of the two ***PowerPoint Presentation Evaluation Forms*** that are included on the next page. Remove the evaluation forms from this book to turn in to your instructor with the other assignments for this module.

Assignment 2: Evaluate a PowerPoint Presentation

Many presentations are available on the World Wide Web. Several Web sites that provide *PowerPoint* presentations are given below. Most of these provide presentations that can be viewed online or downloaded. To locate more presentations, you could search for "*Power Point* presentations" using your favorite search engine.

Evaluate a presentation of your choice by completing one of the evaluation forms on the next page as you view the presentation. You may remove the evaluation forms from this book to turn in to your instructor.

Select a *PowerPoint* presentation of your choice. Some sources of *PowerPoint* presentations are given below:

http://office.microsoft.com/en-us/FX010857971033.aspx

http://www.pppst.com/

http://www.tlccreative.com/ppt_examples.htm

http://school.discovery.com/

PowerPoint Presentation Evaluation Form

Title of Presentation: ____

Evaluator: ____

Current Date: ____

Place a check mark to indicate your rating for each item.

	Excellent	Good	Fair	Poor
1. First slide is blank.	_____	_____	_____	_____
2. Title slide is included.	_____	_____	_____	_____
3. Appropriate introduction	_____	_____	_____	_____
4. Logical and clear presentation	_____	_____	_____	_____
5. Appropriate conclusion	_____	_____	_____	_____
6. Easy to read fonts used.	_____	_____	_____	_____
7. Font colors contrast with background.	_____	_____	_____	_____
8. No more than 2 fonts used.	_____	_____	_____	_____
9. Background is consistent.	_____	_____	_____	_____
10. Appropriate sound and transitions	_____	_____	_____	_____
11. 7 X 7 rule is followed.	_____	_____	_____	_____
12. Bulleted items appear 1 at a time.	_____	_____	_____	_____
13. Appropriate use of images	_____	_____	_____	_____
14. Overall visual appeal of presentation	_____	_____	_____	_____
15. Free from spelling & language errors	_____	_____	_____	_____
16. Overall rating	_____	_____	_____	_____

Comments and suggestions for improvement:

Use this page for additional comments on the *PowerPoint* presentation.

PowerPoint Presentation Evaluation Form

Title of Presentation: ____

Evaluator: ____

Current Date: ____

Place a check mark to indicate your rating for each item.

	Excellent	Good	Fair	Poor
1. First slide is blank.	_____	_____	_____	_____
2. Title slide is included.	_____	_____	_____	_____
3. Appropriate introduction	_____	_____	_____	_____
4. Logical and clear presentation	_____	_____	_____	_____
5. Appropriate conclusion	_____	_____	_____	_____
6. Easy to read fonts used.	_____	_____	_____	_____
7. Font colors contrast with background.	_____	_____	_____	_____
8. No more than 2 fonts used.	_____	_____	_____	_____
9. Background is consistent.	_____	_____	_____	_____
10. Appropriate sound and transitions	_____	_____	_____	_____
11. 7 X 7 rule is followed.	_____	_____	_____	_____
12. Bulleted items appear 1 at a time.	_____	_____	_____	_____
13. Appropriate use of images	_____	_____	_____	_____
14. Overall visual appeal of presentation	_____	_____	_____	_____
15. Free from spelling & language errors	_____	_____	_____	_____
16. Overall rating	_____	_____	_____	_____

Comments and suggestions for improvement:

Use this page for additional comments on the *PowerPoint* presentation.

MODULE 7

Database Management & Desktop Publishing

Database Management & Desktop Publishing

Database management concepts and terminology are included in this module. While use of a database management program is beyond the scope of this book, some database basics are included here.

Desktop publishing goes beyond word processing and includes **page layout.** Desktop publishing applications include newsletters, brochures, signs, and catalogs.

Module Objectives

When you have completed this module, you should be able to:

- identify functions and terminology associated with database management programs;
- differentiate between a field, a record, and a file in a database;
- recognize advantages and applications of using an electronic database;
- list several advantages of page layout and desktop publishing software; and
- produce an original page layout document using *Microsoft Publisher.*

Note:* Instructions and assignments given in this module are for *Office 2010.

Materials Needed to Complete This Module

- This book
- *Microsoft Word 2010*
- *Microsoft Publisher*
- Flash drive on which store your work.

How to Proceed

1. Read this module.
2. Review the *Key Terms* at the end of the module.
3. Complete the *Module 7 Review Questions* at the end of the module.
4. Complete the *Module 7 Computer Application Assignments.* In the computer application assignments for this module, you will create a newsletter. Specific instructions for these assignments are provided later in this module.
5. Take the Module 7 test.

7.1 Database Management Systems

A **database management system (DBMS)** is a valuable electronic record keeping system. A DBMS may be thought of as an electronic filing cabinet, permitting the storage of information that can be recalled, organized, and managed according to individual or organizational needs. Many bundled software packages and integrated software programs include a database application program. You have seen that *MS Word* includes a small database application which is used mainly for the storage of mailing lists and other information that may be used with form letters and reports. Other stand-alone database management programs are much more powerful and sophisticated than the database application included with *MS Word.* Some important database concepts will be covered in this module.

> Originally, DBMSs were found only in large organizations with the computer hardware needed to support large data sets.

A **database management program** is not a word processor. Although some of the commands are the same, the purposes are much different. The purpose of a word processing program is to help the user to produce written text efficiently, while the purpose of a database program is to store, sort, and retrieve information.

A **database** is an organized body of information that can be manipulated. Libraries are huge databases - all the information in a library is organized according to some system. Various pieces of information (books, magazines, etc.) can be shuffled, sorted, and searched according to that system of organization. We can think of the whole library as a database. We can also think of the library catalog as a database. Actually the catalog is just an encapsulated version of the entire library. The library catalog database provides an efficient method of searching the contents of a library.

A filing cabinet full of file folders is also a database with which we are familiar. A filing cabinet contains an organized body of information that can be shuffled, sorted, and searched. Other everyday examples of databases are phone books and address books.

7.2 Database Management

If a **database** is an organized body of information that can be manipulated, then it is obvious that an electronic database is an organized body of information that is stored and manipulated electronically. ***Microsoft Office Access*** is the most commonly used DBMS. However, *Access* is a sophisticated application. It does not come with all versions of *Microsoft Office* and its use is beyond the scope of this book. However, it is appropriate that we include some general concepts and information on database systems.

Electronic databases are sometimes referred to as electronic filing cabinets. Sometimes the term electronic database is used; sometimes the term **DBMS,** for **database management system,** is used. A DBMS makes it possible to create an electronic database as well as search and sort a large amount of information in a very short time.

Another application of a DBMS is that it can be used as an inquiry tool that allows a user to gather and organize information, and then formulate hypotheses and conclusions based on the organized records.

You have now had some experience using a word processor. You should have gained an appreciation for the fact that a word processor is a tool that can manage text much more efficiently than a typewriter or a pen. In a previous module, you worked with an electronic spreadsheet. A spreadsheet is a number-manipulating tool. With an electronic spreadsheet, you can organize and manipulate numbers much more efficiently than you could with a ledger and a pencil. A database management system is a tool that can manage information more efficiently than a filing cabinet. While the word processor is a writing tool and the spreadsheet is a number tool, the database management system is a filing tool. It is a tool that allows us to manage information efficiently.

7.3 Using a DBMS

A database management system allows you to organize information and store it in electronic memory or on disk. When the organization is carefully thought out, the information can then be sorted very quickly. For example, if a business had a database consisting of names, addresses, and personal information of all the customers, it would be easy to find all customers who meet specific criteria quickly. For example, if a business owner wished to know the ages of the customers and what products they purchased, a DBMS could sort customers by age and produce reports stating which products they purchased. Another example of how a DMBS can be used is locating all customers who live in a particular ZIP Code area.

> A Data Base Management System is a complex set of software programs that controls the organization, storage, management, and retrieval of data in a database.

Another use of a DBMS is to search for information on a particular customer. Even if the customer's name is not known, the customer record could be located by using the phone number or address. With a DBMS, the computer retrieves the information so fast that it seems instantaneous.

Suppose a teacher wants to reorganize a student DBMS so that, instead of filing students alphabetically by name, they are filed by student number. The student with the lowest number will appear first and the student with the highest number will appear last. Doing this with an old-fashioned filing system would take a great deal of time. With a DBMS, you could reorganize the whole system within seconds.

Just as with the word processor, you can print the information you desire using a DBMS. In fact, the DBMS allows you to process or reorganize information so that it can be printed out in various report styles.

A DBMS supplies users with information needed to operate a business or organization and allows users to make better informed decisions.

> Often it is desirable to limit who can see or change which attributes or groups of attributes. This may be managed directly by individual, or by the assignment of individuals and privileges to groups.

7.4 Database Management Software

In addition to *MS Office Access*, there are other popular database management programs. Some of them are: *FileMaker Pro*, *Lotus Approach*, and *dBase V*. Database programs are also included in *Microsoft Works*. These programs are relatively simple to learn and to use, but they are not as powerful or sophisticated as other multi-user database management software packages used in the business environment, such as *Oracle* and *Microsoft SQL Server*.

7.5 Organizing Database Information

Organization of information in an electronic database is very similar to the organization of a typical filing system. If you were going to develop a filing system for all the students in a school, you would first develop a form or format for organizing the information. You would probably sit down and do some brainstorming about what kind of information you wanted on each student; then, you would design a form so that the information for each student was recorded in the same place and in a similar fashion. Now you know why you have to fill out forms everywhere you go in life; every organization has its own filing system, and they want information about you in a particular format.

If we were starting a database on all the students in a school using a DBMS, we would think of the information for each individual student as a record. A **record** is like a form. It is all of the information on one individual organized in a particular manner. The separate pieces of information within a record, such as name, address, etc., are called categories or **fields**. In a previous section on mail merges, the first name, last name, address 1, address 2, city, state, and zip are all individual fields. The complete set of information on one person is a record.

Once a number of records is entered into the computer, the set of information is saved as a **file**. A file is similar to a filing cabinet; it holds information in a given database. A record is similar to a form or data sheet; it holds information on one person. A field is similar to a single line on a form or data sheet. A single record from a simple database could look like this:

LAST NAME:	SMITH
FIRST NAME:	JOHN
ADDRESS:	2314 BLUE ST.
CITY:	TUCSON
STATE:	AZ
ZIP CODE:	23475
AGE:	19

Each item (Last Name, City, ZIP Code, etc.) in the record is a field name. Fields hold the basic items of information in a database file. Items of information are filed, sorted, and/or searched by field(s). The most important part of setting up an electronic database is deciding how to organize the information.

Unless information is organized correctly, you will be unable to conduct the types of searches and sorts that you desire.

The first step in building a database is to choose the name of the file. The file name should indicate what type of information is contained in the file. Next you need to decide what will constitute a record. For example, if you are building a database that consists of information about a group of people, a record usually represents the information on one person. Finally, you must decide what fields will make up a record. Decisions on what to include as fields will greatly affect how flexible and useful your database will be.

7.6 Advantages of Database Management Systems

Computers have two virtues: they can manipulate symbols rapidly and they are very accurate. When these features are combined in a DBMS, you have a tool that allows searching and sorting of vast quantities of information at a high rate of speed with a high degree of accuracy.

Whether at work or home, everyone works with data. A database management program helps you organize raw data into meaningful information for later analysis, thus saving you valuable time.

A database management system provides the ability for many different users to share data and process resources.

One of the easiest and most common applications of databases as personal tools is the electronic address book. You can keep track of addresses and other pertinent information, such as birthdays, anniversaries, and even clothing sizes. You could print out your greeting card list in a flash! Some DBMS programs will even dial a stored phone number for you from your computer.

Other uses might include a file of your favorite book, videotape, DVD, or music collections. You might keep the title, length, topic, date, and location in a database. You could locate any given program quickly and see all of the pertinent information. Another widespread application is the personal inventory. A file consisting of the major items you own might consist of the name, model number, serial number, cost, date of purchase, etc. Such a file could be invaluable for police or insurance uses in the event of a natural disaster such as a flood, tornado, or fire. Furthermore, wise students often keep a database of persons who may be used for references in future job applications.

> Throughout recent history specialized databases have existed for scientific, geospatial, imaging, document storage and like uses. Functionality drawn from such applications has lately begun appearing in mainstream DBMSs as well.

Have you ever wished that you could recall exactly where you saw some particular story or fact so that you could use it again? Using a database program, would allow you a to keep track of these important references, with issue and volume numbers, dates, titles, and notes that would permit you to locate information quickly and easily.

While electronic databases were originally developed for filing purposes, educators have discovered that they can be used as powerful teaching tools. A DBMS can be used in a variety of ways in the classroom, but it is best used as an inquiry tool. To use a DBMS as an inquiry tool, the teacher could:

1. *Select a topic for study.* Within the regular curriculum there are a wide variety of topics where using a database as an inquiry tool could enhance the teaching-learning process. One example would be in geography. Gaining a perspective of the similarities and differences among countries could be augmented with a database management system.
2. *Design a database.* Designing the database, as we have already pointed out, is the most crucial part of using a DBMS. Involving the learners in the design of the database would force them to think through the entire database. From this experience, they learn to think critically about databases as well as learn how to organize information.
3. *Gather information.* Once the database is designed, the learners should be active in gathering and entering information. Using the example of the geography database, the learners could use encyclopedias, textbooks, maps, and periodical literature to glean pertinent facts about the countries in the study, and then enter this information into the database. This process also provides significant experience on how to search for information.
4. *Formulate hypotheses.* When sufficient information has been gathered to work with, the learner should begin formulating hypotheses or theories relating to similarities and differences among the countries. For example, using the geography database, a student might form the hypothesis that a small percentage of countries in the European Union grow cotton.
5. *Arrive at Conclusions.* Arriving at conclusions and drawing inferences based on the data in the database is the grand finale of the database experience. By formulating many hypotheses and testing these hypotheses, students will gain a mastery of both obvious and subtle relationships among the various countries.

In addition to integrating the database management system into the curriculum as a teaching-learning tool, students could be taught to use it as a personal management tool.

Students could create their own personalized address and phone number list, for example. High school seniors could use a DBMS to create a database containing pertinent information on all of the colleges and universities that they are interested in attending. This database could then be sorted and searched to help each student select the right college or university.

> **Querying is the process of requesting attribute information from various perspectives and combinations of factors. Example: "How many 2-door cars in Texas are green?"**

A database management system is an invaluable tool for most businesses. For example, a company can manage inventory as part of its general account procedures, manage customer accounts, and manage personnel records. Political campaigns often use databases to keep information on campaign contributions and contributors.

7.7 Factors to Consider in Selecting a DBMS

There are, of course, many factors to consider when selecting a database management system. Some of these factors are important in making any software decision and have been described in Modules 2 and 3 of this book. Three factors are especially important when considering a DBMS. These factors are:

1. *Ease of use.* Database management systems differ widely in level of difficulty. Some very sophisticated systems such as *dBase* or *Microsoft Office Access* would be totally inappropriate for use in an elementary school classroom; however, they would be appropriate for use at the high school or university level. *GroveSite's online database,* on the other hand, is in a class of easy-to-use systems that children can use after only brief instruction.
2. *Versatility of output.* Database output occurs in two ways: (1) on the computer screen, and (2) on the printer. When students really start working with databases, they will want to see information both on the screen and on printed copies. The degree of flexibility the user has in displaying information is an important consideration.
3. *Cost.* DBMS programs can be pricey. *MS Office Access* is available in the *Office Professional* version of *MS Office* which retails, for around $499. Other DBMS programs range in price from $200 to more than $600. More basic database management applications cost much less. A general rule about electronic database programs is that you always sacrifice sophistication for ease of use and visa versa. The more powerful the software is, the more difficult it will be to learn and to use. Naturally, the more powerful programs also cost more.

The term "desktop publishing" is attributed to Aldus Corporation founder Paul Brainerd, who sought a marketing catch-phrase to describe the small size and relative affordability of this suite of products in contrast to the expensive commercial phototypesetting equipment of the day.

7.8 Desktop Publishing

Modern computer applications have provided us with the capability of designing professional appearing printed materials with our PCs. Software called **desktop publishing programs (DTP),** also known as **page layout programs,** aid in using the capabilities of the computer to design professional newsletters, signs, greeting cards, business cards, brochures, pamphlets and a host of other materials. These programs, along with high-resolution ink jet and laser printers, enable the average PC user to create and produce documents that are almost as professional in appearance as those produced by professional publishers and printers.

Desktop publishing applications generally require more time to learn than word processing programs due to the many editing features they contain. Features common to desktop publishing applications are text-wrapped graphics, master page layout design capabilities, variable column-width formatting, and accommodation of multiple graphic file formats. Full-featured, professional level desktop publishing applications are often expensive and complex. However, there are less complicated and less expensive desktop publishing applications available that are more suitable for the average end-user such as teachers, students, and small business professionals.

7.9 Desktop Publishing Software

Professional desktop publishing programs such as ***Adobe InDesign*** provide sophisticated page layout capabilities that include the ability to place a variety of types of word processing, outside documents, graphics, and objects into a document. These programs also allow the use of word-wrap around graphics objects. These programs include templates for newsletters, flyers, and other documents that help the designer to remember to include a number of elements, and provide a unified color and font scheme. ***Microsoft Publisher*** is a user-friendly and low-cost page layout program that has many of the features of more expensive programs. However, a major disadvantage of *Publisher* is the inability to produce color separations, which are necessary for professional printing. *MS Word,* while not a full featured desktop publishing program, also has the capability to produce basic page layout products.

A desktop publishing system

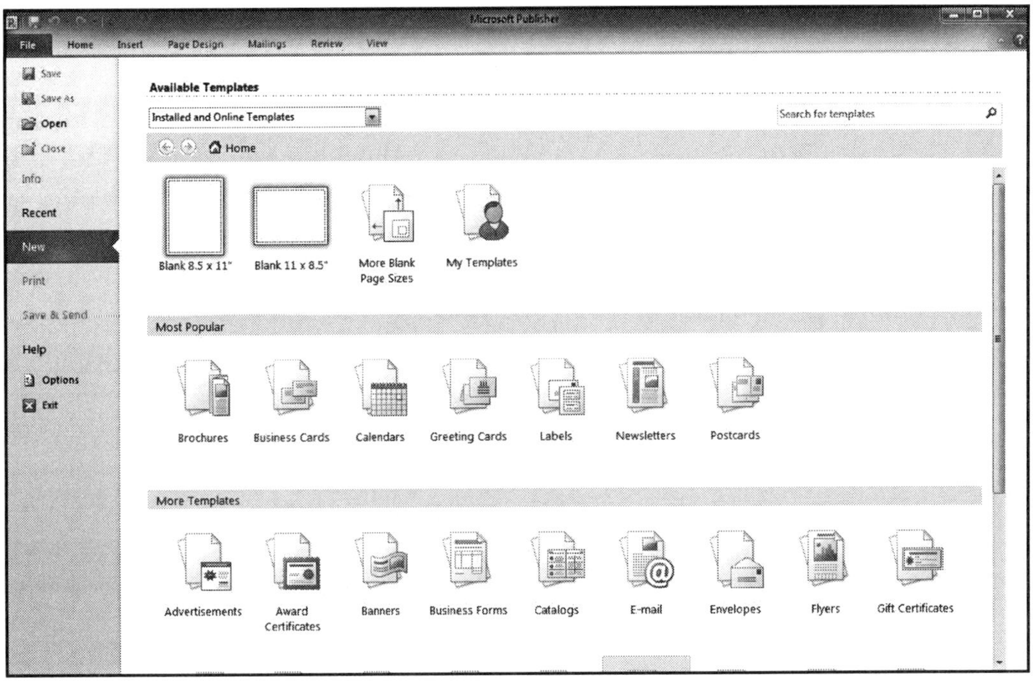

Figure 7.1: The Start Up Screen from *MS Publisher*

7.10 Lettering Guidelines in Desktop Publishing

The following general guidelines can be used when selecting font type, size, and style in a publication produced with a desktop publishing application.

- Select a typeface or font that enhances readability and reveals the expressive quality of your words.

> Desktop publishing began in 1985 with the introduction of *PageMaker* software from Aldus and the LaserWriter printer from Apple Computer.

- Use sans serif typefaces for headlines or titles, and use them sparingly. Sans serif fonts are best used in a large size.
- Use serif fonts for body text to help a reader's eye move from one letter to the next.
- Use ornate text only for visual effects.
- Avoid mixing typefaces or fonts except for a distinct purpose.
- Select a letter size or font size that matches the message and its impact
- Use font style (plain, bold, italics, etc.) for emphasis.
- Allow for blank space around blocks of text to enhance readability.

7.11 The Elements of Design for Printed Materials

Balance, composition, harmony, unity, variety, and interest are the elements of good design. Remember that all of these terms refer to qualities that are subjective in nature.

While desktop publishing software provides extensive features necessary for print publishing, modern word processors now have publishing capabilities beyond those of many older DTP applications, blurring the line between word processing and desktop publishing.

Balance refers to the symmetry achieved on a page. If two pages face each other, their symmetry carries across the middle to balance the entire format area of the pages. In either case, a balance of elements helps achieve a pleasant layout. Text without bold type or other extra weight can be balanced at a one for one ratio; in other words, you should try to balance the amount of text of that type throughout a page. Bold and headline fonts are different; you have to consider the darkness, complexity, and size of a line of heavy type to balance it against a similar line. Graphic elements can balance each other or be used to balance heavy type.

Composition refers to placement of elements on the page in a way that draws the eye from one element to another. Generally, good composition draws the eye into the picture, and bad composition makes the viewer want to look out of the picture. Arrows and arrow-shaped graphics should point in. Faces should look in to the open page, not out. Triangles and circles are solid shapes; when items form loose triangles or circles it helps give the composition stability.

7.2: Sample Publications Created with Desktop Publishing Software

A Partial List of DTP Programs:

- Adobe InDesign
- QuarkXPress
- Adobe PageMaker
- Framemaker
- Impression Publisher
- Microsoft Publisher
- PagePlus SE
- PageStream

Harmony refers to the harmony of elements throughout the composition. Using botanical drawings and highway maps on the same page might not look good. Harmony is a subjective quality, as are all of these terms.

Unity refers to the use of font, borders, capitalization, punctuation, etc. throughout. Consistency is relevant to the overall effectiveness of the work. Using several fonts or several border types is distracting.

Variety is achieved by using daring and innovative approaches to layout. Mixing several sizes of graphics, finding ways to tie all graphics to a theme, and combining images in unexpected ways can help to spice up a dull work. Using variety in your composition is different from using design that lacks unity or harmony.

Interest refers, in this case, to the content of the graphic elements. In some cases a graphic of a spider may be much more effective than one of a butterfly. You have to decide what elements to include based on the ideas you are trying to communicate. Shock value can add to or detract from a composition; you have to develop your own style.

7.12 Planning a Newsletter

Newsletters are one of the most popular and most used DTP applications. Schools, classes, businesses, clubs, churches, and organizations all use newsletters to communicate with their clients. You may have noticed that some of the newsletters that you have seen do not look professional. Some of these are produced by individuals who do not understand how to communicate effectively with printed materials. As a consequence, their products look amateurish. In order to help you better understand how to plan effective documents, the basic elements of a newsletter and some principles for planning an effective newsletter are reviewed here. You can adapt these rules to other types of documents. As in all art-like areas, no rule is set in stone. Creativity is more important than adhering to patterns because the unusual gets more attention than the usual.

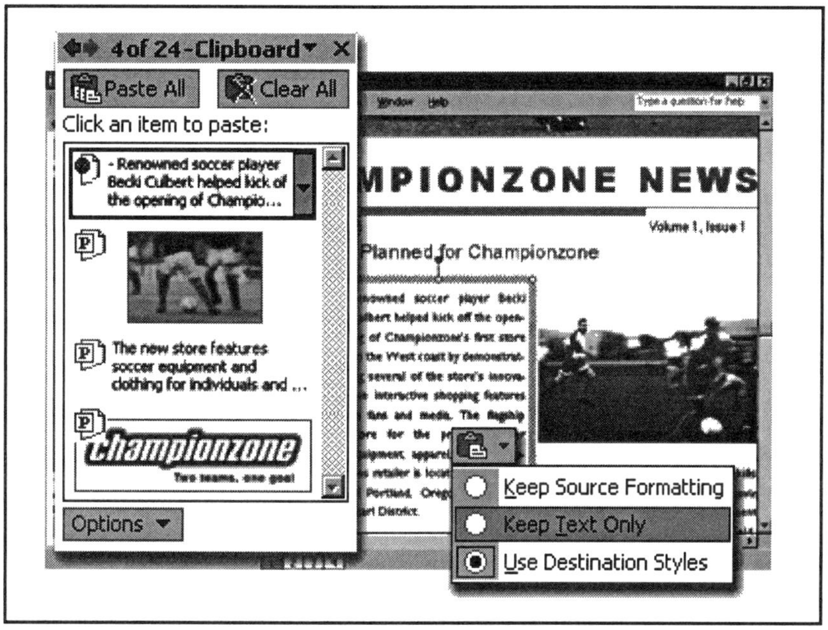

Figure 7.3: Newsletter Creation with *MS Publisher*

Of course, the most important element of any newsletter is selecting information that is interesting and important to the intended readers, and writing articles that communicate effectively. There is no substitute for judgment and good writing. However, writing style and mechanics are beyond the scope of this book. Here we deal with layout and design of newsletters, which may be almost as important as the information that they contain.

Some guidelines for designing newsletters are listed below.

- Newsletters customarily use 2-4 columns per page rather than the single column that we are accustomed to seeing in letters and manuscripts.
- Regular 8 ½ x 11 paper is most often used for newsletters.
- Titles and headlines should be placed in boldfaced type that is 2-4 times larger than the text in the articles.
- The text of the newsletter should use a uniform font size throughout except for headlines. Most newsletters use 10-12 point font for text in articles.
- Short lines of text look better if they are **full justified**, that is, when both left and right margins are flush. This is why newspapers use full justified text. A 3 or 4 column newsletter should use full justified text to improve readability and appearance. If the columns are very narrow, justified text can result in large gaps between words. Left justified text, which is flush on the left with ragged right-hand margins, should be used when the lines of text are longer. This is why letters and manuscripts use left justified text. Two-column newsletters are something of a toss up as to which type of justification is best.

- Placing a vertical line or border between the columns improves readability and appearance.
- Numbering pages, after the first page near the outside bottom or top edge of the page, helps the reader with orientation and also helps to ensure proper printing.
- Use easy to read and attractive fonts. Today, there seems to be a fascination with elaborate and unusual fonts. Avoid these. Some effective fonts for newsletters are Helvetica, Times, Times New Roman, Palatino, and Bookman. Poor choices include Script, Courier, Stencil, Old English, and any font with an ornate design.
- Use only 1-2 fonts when planning newsletters. Overuse of too many fonts makes the newsletter look amateurish and unprofessional.
- Graphics can be placed anywhere in the newsletter, but they should be visually balanced. One graphic on the side of a page looks unbalanced. Two graphics on the same part of a page that contains no other picture elements also looks unbalanced. If there is only one graphic, place it near the center of the page. If there are two, you might place one on the top left and one on the lower right or perhaps put one on each side of the page near the middle. Balance graphics on the first or last page within that individual page. When there are facing pages, achieve balance considering the entire 2-page area.
- In placing graphics, make faces or pointers lead the eye into the page instead of out of it; never point to (or have a face looking at a place off the page).
- Use graphics and pictures to add interest. Too much text looks mundane.
- Avoid hyphenation in a formal newsletter, a sales flyer or an instructional pamphlet.
- Avoid clutter; there is nothing wrong with a little white space here and there. Do not fill the page with graphics and symbols that serve no purpose.
- Be sure to have an even number of pages since the newsletter will be printed on both front and back.

> Publishing is the process of production and dissemination of literature or information – the activity of making information available for public view. In some cases authors may be their own publishers, meaning; originators and developers of content also provide media to deliver and display the content.

- If you plan to mail the newsletter, leave a blank space on the bottom half of the last page for the label. Inside the mail label space, place your return address in the upper left corner.
- On the back page, above the mailing label space, place an announcement or article that is interesting and different. This is the article a person will see first when your newsletter is lying around. The back page is a good place to include a contact name and address for the organization that your newsletter is representing.

7.13 Designing the Front Page of a Newsletter

- The **masthead**, or title of the newsletter, is placed at the top in large text. Many newsletters try to use a catchy, identifiable title. Make the title large and include a graphic logo if appropriate. Separate the masthead from the articles with a horizontal line, graphics, or blank space.
- Place a date, volume, and issue number, if appropriate, in the border between the title and headline.
- Do not list editors and publishers on the front page; place this information in a box on the second or third page.
- Put the most important or interesting articles on the front page. If you have several important articles, start them on the front page and continue them on later pages.
- Also on the front page, place an introductory article such as a word from the editor or something similar. An explanation of whom the newsletter represents or its purpose or objective would also be appropriate.
- Include some graphics or pictures on the front page to capture reader interest.

7.14 Using Microsoft Publisher to Create a Newsletter

The *MS Publisher* opening window provides a variety of templates to choose from. The easiest way to get started using *Publisher* is to select one of the publication templates. In this example, *Newsletters* has been selected and a variety of newsletter templates are shown.

Note that there are also templates available for calendars, certificates, labels, brochures, invitations, and a variety of other materials. After you select a template, you can edit it according to your particular needs. Information can be entered into the newsletter by clicking in the appropriate box and typing. Figure 7.4 shows a sample newsletter template available within *Publisher*.

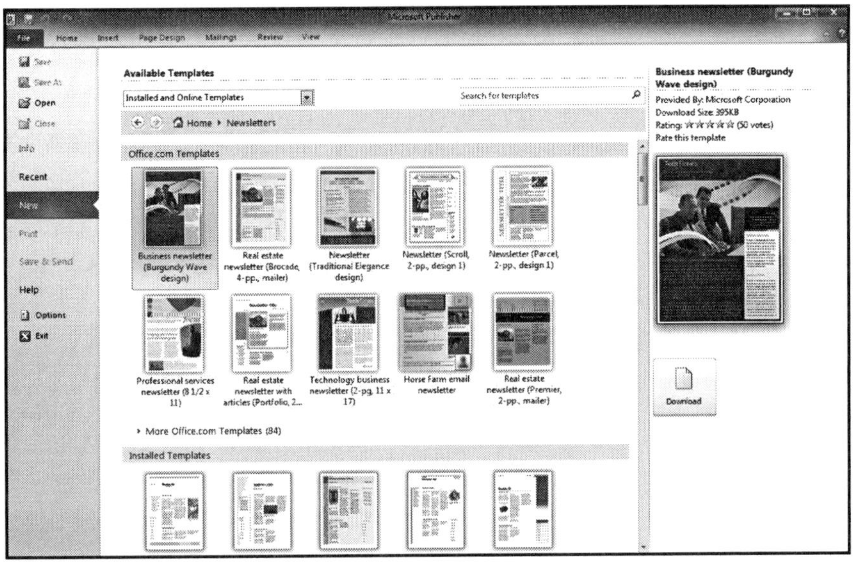

Figure 7.4: *Some MS Publisher* Newsletter Templates

While templates are easy to use, they also limit flexibility. Users are confined to the format provided, and making changes is difficult. The alternative is to start with a blank document. In this case, the user must define all parameters such as column placement and width, graphic placement, etc.

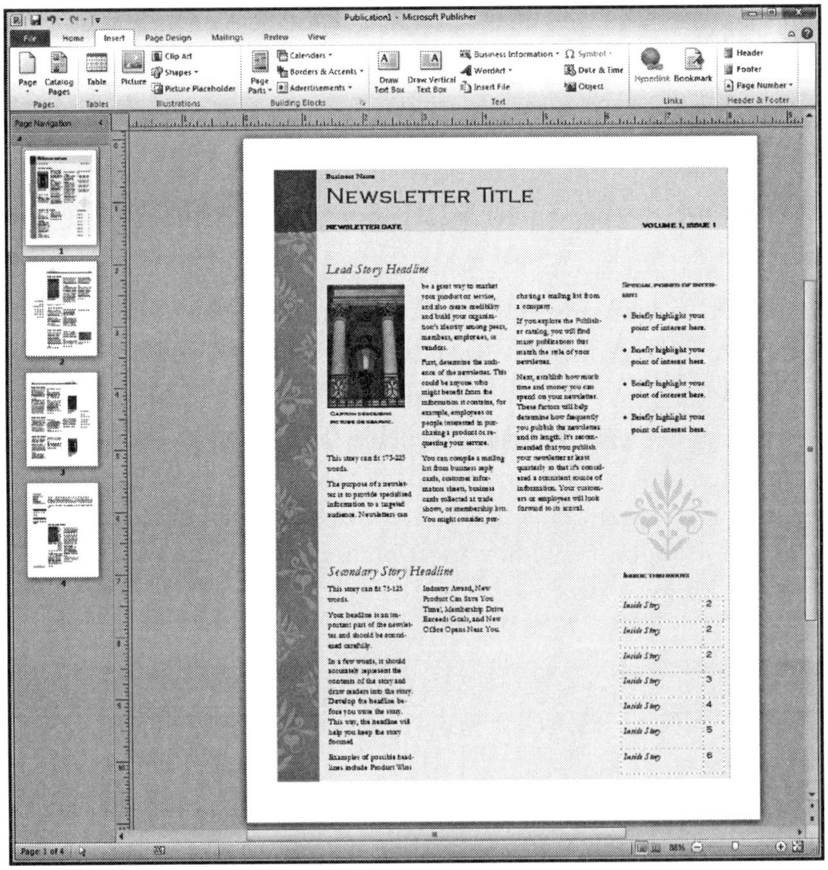

Figure 7.5: *MS Publisher* Newsletter Templates

For beginners, it is best to begin with a template. Type your stories in the spaces provided. The text in the articles provides some tips on newsletter design. This text can be deleted so that users can type their own stories. The graphics in the template are place holders. You can click on one, delete it, and then insert your own picture or graphic by clicking on *Picture* from the *Insert* menu.

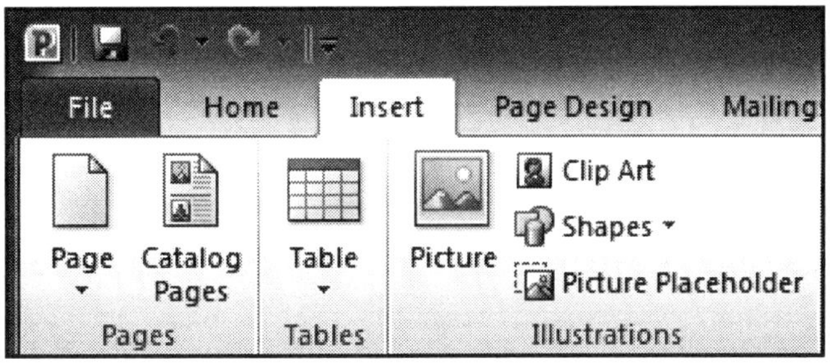

Figure 7.6: Inserting a Picture with *Microsoft Publisher*

If you need help using *Publisher*, help is available in the menu bar. Select the question mark to open the help window. See the following figure.

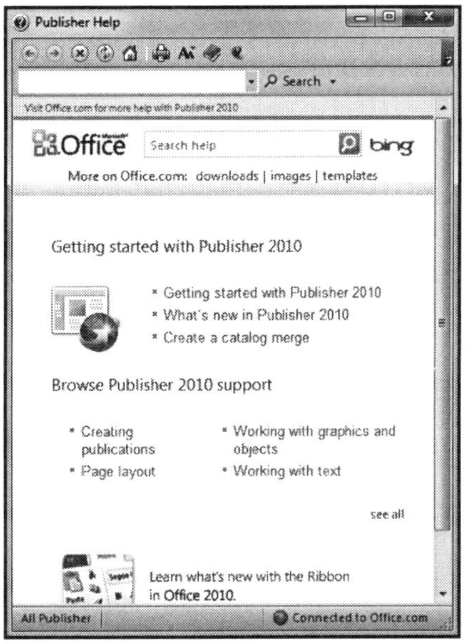

Figure 7.7: The *MS Publisher* Help

7.15 Printing Devices

Output devices are used to move the image out of the computer into a form that people can see and use. There is not as much variety in output devices as there is in input devices. Some computer graphics are intended only to be displayed on the computer screen. In this case, the computer monitor is the only output device needed. However, most computer graphics work is designed to be transferred from the screen to paper with a printer. Just as with input devices, you need to remember that a given printer will only work when the software you are using is designed to support it.

There are 2 types of printers that are commonly used. A brief description of each of these printer types follows:

Ink Jet Printers. Most of the printers used with computers today are ink jet printers. Ink jet printers form letters on the page by spraying tiny droplets of ink in the shape of letters. Ink jet printers are less expensive to purchase than are laser printers, but the expense of ink cartridges results in a high per-page cost. Most ink jet printers produce less sharp images than do laser printers. Ink jet photo printers can produce photographic quality images. There are ink jet printers that can print 4-inch photographic prints and others that can print on 60-inch wide canvas. One new ink jet printer can even print text and graphics directly on blank CDs.

Laser Printers. Laser printers work by using high heat to fuse a powdered toner to the paper. Known for their sharp images and quick printing, laser printers are used for most business and network printing. Laser printers are still more expensive to purchase than are ink jet printers, but laser printers are becoming more affordable for use in small offices and at home. Laser printer toner cartridges are also more expensive than ink jet cartridges; however, thousands of pages can be printed with a single toner cartridge, making the per-page cost of laser printing less expensive. Color laser printers are now available, but their high cost limits their use.

Plotters. Plotters are used almost exclusively for architectural and engineering drawings. Their ability to print on large sheets or rolls of paper makes them well suited for technical drawings. A plotter is basically a robotic arm holding a pen that moves over the surface of a sheet of paper. To change colors the pen must be changed either manually or automatically by the plotting arm. Plotters were never widely used due to high cost and slow speed. Few programs outside of specialized drafting programs will support a plotter.

Figure 7.8: A Graphic Plotter

7.16 Conclusion

This module has provided a foundation of information on database management and desktop publishing. Use of *MS Publisher* has been described. In the application exercises for this module, you will have a chance to use this programs and to practice putting some of the skills and guidelines that have been discussed in the module into practice.

The use of database management software is beyond the scope of this book; however, the brief overview provided here should have familiarized you with the basics of DBMS programs and the ways in which they can help provide users with easily accessible and valuable information.

Key Terms

DBMS

Database

Field

File

San serif fonts

Serif fonts

Templates

TrueType fonts

DTP

Fonts or typefaces

Full Justified

Graphic arts

Input devices

Ink jet printer

Laser printer

Masthead

MS Publisher

Newsletter Template

Output devices

Page Layout Programs

Plotter

Module 7 Review Questions

Choose the BEST answer according to the material provided in Module 7.

1. An electronic database record consists of several
   a. fields.
   b. files.
   c. sections.
   d. folders.

2. One advantage of using an electronic database over using paper filing systems is the:
   a. elimination of the need for data processing personnel.
   b. ease of locating and storing information.
   c. ease of checking for spelling errors.
   d. elimination or reduction of training time needed.

3. All of the information about one student in a student information system database would be considered a:
   a. record.
   b. file.
   c. field.
   d. data bit.

4. A teacher might use a DBMS as a/an ____________ tool.
   a. word processing
   b. calculating
   c. inquiry
   d. grading

5. Field is to record as:
   a. apple is to orange.
   b. apple is to vegetable.
   c. slice is to apple.
   d. knife is to apple.

6. When using a *MS Publisher* template, the graphics and text are ___________ .
   a. unnecessary
   b. place holders
   c. impossible to remove
   d. ready made content

Module 7 Review Questions Continued

7. Which of the following is not a printing device?
   a. Inkjet Printer.
   b. *Microsoft* Printer.
   c. Lazer Printer.
   d. Plotter

8. DTP refers to
   a. Desktop publishing software.
   b. Page layout software.
   c. Database software.
   d. Spreadsheet software.

9. Which of the following is not a common application of database software?
   a. Electronic address book
   b. Gradebook for teachers
   c. Inquiry tool for teachers
   d. Electronic collection of DVDs

10. Balance, composition, harmony, unity, variety, and interest refer to
    a. Elements of writing an essay.
    b. Elements of design for database managment.
    c. Elements of design for print material.
    d. Elements of effective word-processing documents.

Computer Application Assignments

Assignment 1: Database Questionnaire

Answer the following questions and remove this page from your book to turn in to your instructor as part of your Module 4 assignment.

1. What is a database?

2. What is a database management system?

3. Define or describe the following database terms:
   - File
   - Record
   - Field

4. List 3 advantages of using a database over the traditional filing cabinet method of storing information.

5. List 3 applications for a database system.

6. List 3 factors to consider in selecting a DBMS.

7. List 4 guidelines for designing newsletters as given in this module:

   1. ______________________________

   2. ______________________________

   3. ______________________________

   4. ______________________________

Assignment 2: Creating a Newsletter

Create a 2-page newsletter using either *MS Publisher* or *MS Word*. Instructions are given in this module for use of *MS Publisher*. If you choose to use *MS Word*, you will need to use other references for guidance on creating your newsletter. It is recommended that you use a newsletter template. The content of the newsletter are up to you. <u>Refer to the guidelines presented in Section 7.10 and 7.11 for guidance on designing your newslette</u>r.

You will need to write your own original articles.

Include the following elements in your newsletter:

√ A chart, graph, or clip art image that is relevant to one or more of the stories;

√ A masthead title using a sans serif font;

√ Appropriate choice of font, size and style for headlines and body text.

Your completed newsletter should be a professional looking, 2 page document that demonstrates good writing skills and creativity. Save your newsletter as Assignment 2 and print it to submit to your instructor. You can print in color if you wish. Your newsletter should look similiar to the sample below:

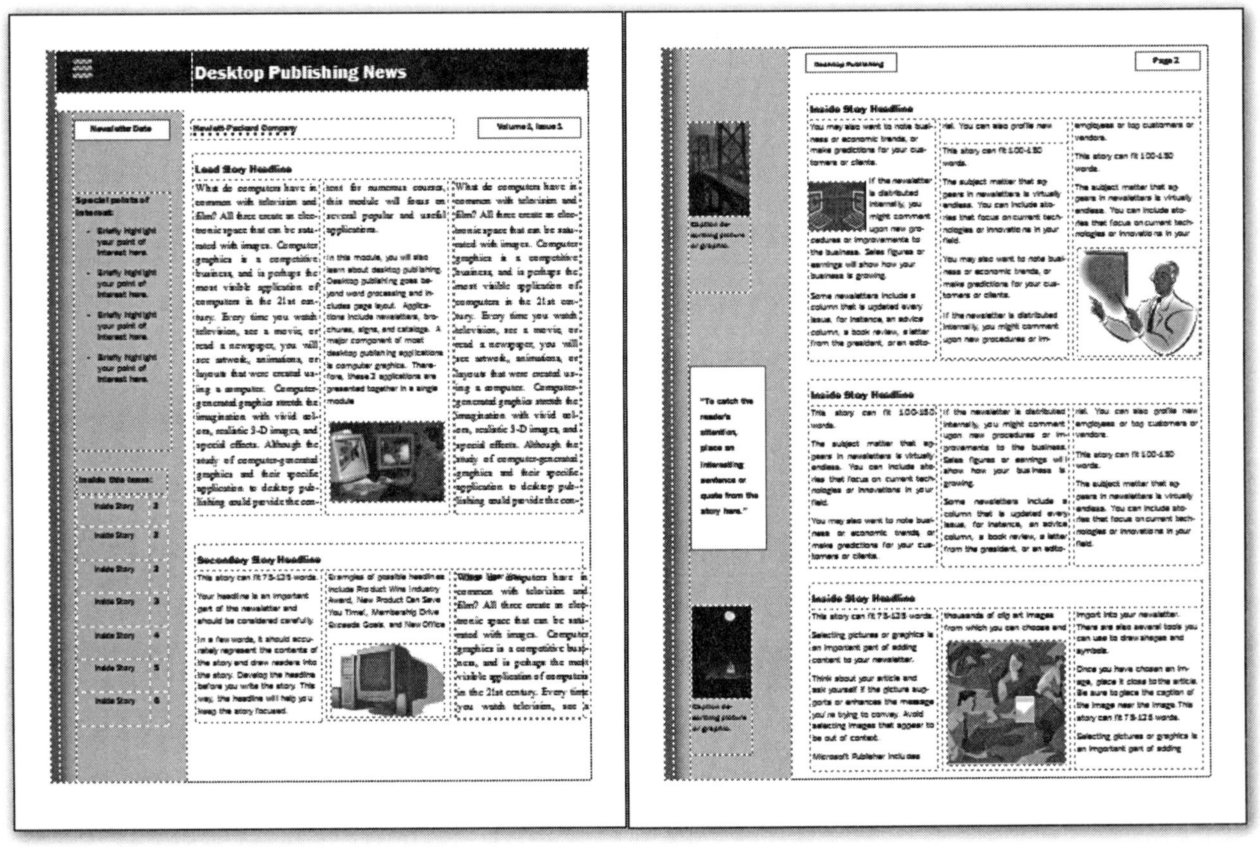

MODULE 8

Computer Graphics & Photohop

Computer Graphics & Photoshop

In this module, you will learn about creating and manipulating photos and graphics with digital editing software. Digital graphics, photos, and illustrations are useful in many personal productivity applications as well as for personal uses. The ability to work with digital images is important for both professional and amateur photographers, web designers, and graphic designers. For any job which includes the production of printed materials, web sites, or photographic images, knowledge of the use of digital images and image editing software is essential. Advanced applications of digital imaging include film and video editing, manufacturing and medical imaging, computer aided design, engineering, and scientific research.

Computer-generated graphics stretch the imagination with vivid colors, realistic 3-D images, and special effects. This module will focus on several popular and useful applications graphics applications.

You will learn to use borh the drawing tools included with *Microsoft Word* and Adobe Photoshop.

Module Objectives

When you have completed this module, you should be able to:

- recognize the advantages of using computer graphics software over traditional graphics production techniques;
- state at least 7 ways that computer graphics can be used;
- describe 4 distinct types of computer graphics software;
- describe 3 ways of producing graphics with a computer;
- discuss important issues of hardware requirements for producing computer graphics;
- describe input devices commonly used in the production of computer graphics;
- demonstrate appropriate use of the Microsoft Word drawing tools;

Materials Needed to Complete this Module

- This book
- *Microsoft Word* software
- *Adobe Photoshop*

How to Proceed

1. Read this module.
2. Review the *Key Terms* located near the end of this module.
3. Complete the *Module 8 Review Questions* located near the end of this module. Check your answers at the end of the book.
4. Complete the *Computer Application Assignments* for this module to turn in to your instructor.
5. Take the Module 8 Test.

8.1 Computer Graphics

A dictionary definition of graphic arts reads as follows: "The fine and applied arts of representation, decoration, and writing or printing on flat surfaces together with the techniques and crafts associated with them." One of the most fascinating ways the computer has been harnessed as a tool has been to turn it into a graphic arts generator.

> Image processing is any form of signal processing for which the input is an image, such as photographs or frames of video.

Computer graphics in the broadest sense encompasses manipulating visual images electronically. There are now a wide variety of computer graphics applications available, ranging from a child drawing a simple picture on the computer screen, or an architect using the computer to design a multimillion dollar building, to a computer game designer creating a 3-D interactive virtual world.

8.2 Using Computer Graphics

As you become acquainted with computer graphics, the first thing you will probably notice is the quality of the finished product that can be obtained. Users with little artistic ability can produce professional looking pictures and charts using a computer and the correct graphics software. Serious graphics work can be performed with computers and you should be aware of the many different levels of computer graphics tools. Graphic software tools range from a level where the computer does most of the work to programs that use the computer screen as simply a blank canvas upon which the artist has total freedom to create.

Figure 8.1:
A Computer Graphics User

In addition to the wide variety of applications and the improved quality of work that children in classrooms can produce, many teachers are finding that computer graphics activities are intrinsically motivating both for their students and for themselves. This should not be surprising. The developmental psychologist, Jean Piaget, identified that young children learn, and are intensely motivated, by manipulating images and objects. Teachers know that school children love to color, paint, and draw, and computers and graphics software tools can give children lots of practice doing what they love to do.

8.3 Advantages of Computer Graphics

There are several different ways that one can put a computer equipped with the appropriate graphics software to work in the classroom, in a business, or in the home. Here are a few examples:

Create visual representations of objects. The computer is a medium for creating visual representations of objects being studied. Examples can range from a teacher creating a map of Europe for a geography class to a scientist studying the three-dimensional nature of a molecule.

It is often thought that the first feature film to use computer graphics was *2001: A Space Odyssey* in 1968, which attempted to show how computers would be much more graphical in the future. However, all the "computer graphic" effects in that film were hand-drawn animation, and the special effects sequences were produced entirely with conventional optical and model effects.

Summarize numerical data into charts and graphs quickly and accurately. This capacity provides the student and the professional with the ability to represent data visually that would otherwise be difficult to understand. Not only can actual data sets be represented but also abstract concepts. Electronic spreadsheet software and graphics programs are often used to create effective presentations.

Develop problem-solving and creative thinking exercises. One of the great challenges of educators is to develop problem-solving and creative thinking abilities in their students. Since the computer has the capacity to represent abstract concepts visually, it becomes a natural tool for creating experiences that will help teachers develop such skills in their students.

Develop learner knowledge and perform skill assessments. Computers have long been used in evaluation or assessment. Adding graphics capabilities to computer assessment systems can make them more effective. In a biology class, for example, students are tested on their mastery of comparative anatomy by taking apart (virtual dissection) and putting back together the anatomical parts of a computer-generated frog. In mathematics, discovering the common elements that comprise a set is an early exercise in teaching set theory. Computer graphics could be utilized effectively to generate activities where students compare two or more sets of one or more attributes.

Stimulate ideas for creative writing. One of the hardest parts of any creative writing project is getting an idea and getting started. Animated visual images could be used to prompt or stimulate ideas in children's minds, allowing them to get started quickly and effectively at the creative writing center.

Reinforce previously learned skills and concepts. As you will see in a later module, the computer makes an excellent drill-and-practice tool. Many skills and concepts can be reinforced by providing students and workers with individualized practice using computer-generated visuals.

Provide a medium for artistic expression. Probably the most simple and straightforward use of computer graphics is to provide students with a new and powerful medium for artistic expression.

8.4 Applications of Computer Graphics

A broad classification of major sub-fields in computer graphics might be:

1. Geometry: study ways to represent and process surfaces
2. Animation: study ways to represent and manipulate motion
3. Rendering: study algorithms to reproduce light transport
4. Imaging: study image acquisition or image editing

Here are a few of the ways that computer-generated graphics can be used:

1. *Signs.* Schools and businesses always have a need for signs. Neatly printed signs are quick, easy, and look more professional and attractive than hand made signs.
2. *Banners.* Large banners, usually the width of the computer paper and of almost any length, can announce sales, meetings, birthdays, and other important happenings.
3. *Letterhead.* It is easy to make specialized, professional looking stationary with computer graphics packages.
4. *Greeting Cards.* Customized greeting cards can give a personal touch to any occasion. Public domain clip art pictures can be purchased and used in a computer graphics program to generate an original personal message.
5. *PowerPoint Presentations.* The same techniques used to create printed materials can be used to create attractive transparencies for presentations and dynamic *PowerPoint* presentations.
6. *Promotional Materials.* Graphics can make handouts, newsletters, memos, workbooks, and other printed material look attractive. Graphics can also help to illustrate difficult concepts. Many of the graphics you see in this book are used to help you understand the concepts being described.
7. *Instructional Computer Programs.* Many computer graphics are intended for use on the computer rather than for printing on paper. They can help illustrate concepts and add interest to instructional software.
8. *Computer-Aided Design (CAD).* Complex designs can be generated and stored for later retrieval. As a drawing and design tool, the computer has revolutionized the work of architects, engineers, and scientists.
9. *Computer Art.* Using complex mathematical algorithms, computers can generate random patterns called fractals (similar to a kaleidoscope), or they can serve as tools in the hands of human artists.

8.5 Computer Graphics Software

As stated earlier, computer graphics encompasses a wide range of applications. For each application, a particular type of software package is required. Computer graphics software can be divided into several general categories. A brief description of each of these categories with examples of commonly used educational and professional software packages follows:

Computer-aided design (CAD) is the use of computer technology to aid in the design and drafting of a part or product.

Print Shop Deluxe type software. A popular computer graphics software package used in schools is *The Print Shop Deluxe*. *The Print Shop Deluxe* is typical of a collection of software packages designed to make it quick and easy to produce professional looking products such as signs, banners, certificates, greeting cards, and stationary letterhead. While the software in this category is quick and easy, it does not allow for much creativity or flexibility on the part of the user. Products are usually created by simply selecting from a menu of figures, patterns, borders, and text fonts that are programmed into the software. Popular software packages in this category include *The Print Shop Deluxe, Certificate Maker,* and *Zoner Draw.*

Drawing or painting software. This category of graphics software allows for more artistic creativity than *Print Shop Deluxe* type software. While the users can choose preprogrammed shapes and figures from this category, they may also create free-hand art work using simulated pencils, paint brushes, or spray cans. Some of the popular software packages in this category are *Paintbrush, Adobe Illustrator,* and *Macromedia Fireworks.*

Animation production software. As the name of this category suggests, it includes software specifically designed to create animated visual productions. Popular software titles in this category are *Microsoft GIF Animator* and *Adobe Flash.*

Adobe Photoshop is the most widely used application for producing professional computer graphics.

Image-editing software. This graphics software is used to edit scanned photos by touch up and cropping, to add special effects to produce digital photo albums and slide shows, and to prepare graphics for placement on web pages. Features include several levels of undo and redo, editable text with character-level formatting, and color management. Some versions of this type of software can also connect to on-line processing services to receive true photo prints. Examples of software applications in this category include *Adobe Photoshop* and *Microsoft Image Composer.*

Chart and graph production software. This computer application is used by business and industry as well as by educators. Numerical data can be summarized into charts and graphs that are easy to understand. This is a process that once was very specialized and expensive. Now it is quick and easy because of the computer. The software does most of the work in this application. All the user has to do, in most cases, is enter the data and make some selections from a menu relating to such things as type and size of graph. Software packages such as *Microsoft Office's Excel* software contain graphing capabilities.

8.6 Creating Graphics

In summarizing the basic techniques for using computer graphics software, 3 different techniques of getting a visual image on the computer screen are reviewed here.

Drawing. This method turns the computer screen into an artistic medium. The screen becomes a sketch pad, a blank canvas, or a block of clay. The artist (user) then creates a graphic by moving a mouse, pressing keys, or using some other device to move the cursor around on the screen. This type of drawing can be done with the drawing tools included with *MS Word*. See the following figure.

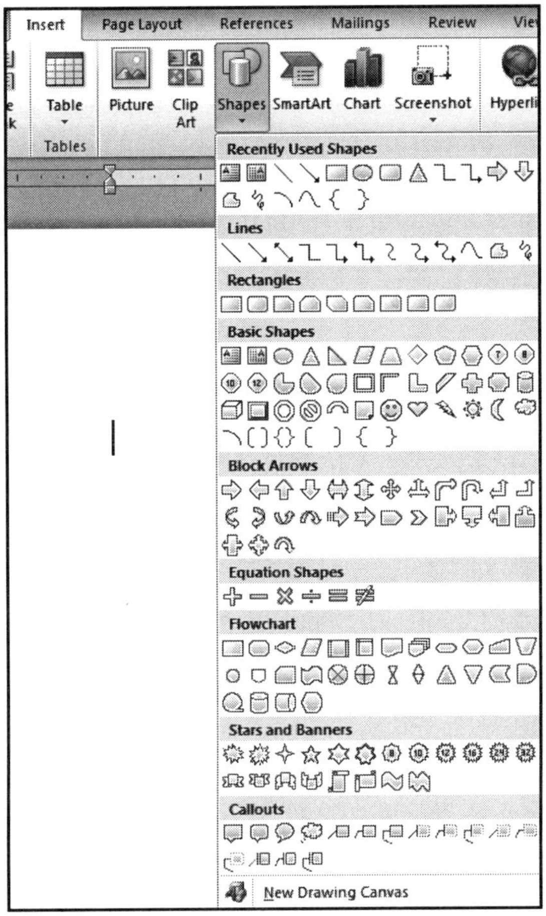

Figure 8.2: Some *MS Word* Drawing Tools

Selecting from professionally drawn items. In this method, someone else has done most of the art work. All the user has to do is select the various combinations of shapes, patterns, type fonts, figures, and borders. The creative part of the process comes about when the user chooses size, location, combination, and text for a production. *Print Shop Deluxe* is an example of this type of software.

Importing visuals. Using this method, graphic items can be chosen from a wide variety of sources. A photograph or drawing may be *scanned* with a computer scanner and then imported into the user's production. Files from digital cameras can also be easily incorporated into your projects. For example, pictures created with other graphics programs can be imported into *Print Shop Deluxe* productions.

8.7 Selecting Computer Graphics Software

When selecting computer graphics software, the most important rule to keep in mind is that the software must be compatible with the available hardware. The best software in the world will be of no value to you if it will not run on your computer. Like many other software applications, graphics software may be specific to only one computer operating system such as *Windows 7* or *Vista.*

Graphics programs also tend to require lots of RAM. Some graphics software will not run on computers with limited memory even if the operating system and computer itself are compatible.

Another consideration is the type of peripherals needed. Many graphics programs need specialized input devices. Typical input devices include a mouse, or an optical scanner. A mouse can be used to literally draw the image into the computer. A scanner is used to photocopy the image off of paper and into the computer. Many printers today are multifunction devices that serve as scanners as well as printers. Digital cameras can also be used as input devices for computer graphics.

When shopping for graphics software, be sure to know the exact specifications of your computer system in order to ensure that the software is compatible with your system. Like all software, graphics software should be powerful enough to do what you want it to do, and be easy to use. Be sure to look at the cost as well. There are many graphics programs on the market and prices vary according to the features supported by the software.

8.8 Considerations for Choosing Data Graphing Software

One of the common uses of graphics software is to summarize numerical data in a chart or graph. The type of software needed to accomplish this differs somewhat from the software used to produce pictures. When selecting a software package for use in creating charts and graphs from numerical data, consider the following ramifications:

Type of graph the software will produce. There are many different types of graphs and charts that can be used to summarize numerical data. You will need to know if the software you are considering will support the type of chart or graph you need.

Ability to save finished products. Once you have created the exact chart or graph desired, you will probably want to save it for future use. You need to be aware that not all graphing software will allow you to do this.

Degree of difficulty in editing. Data graphing software packages differ widely in degree of difficulty associated with editing. Unless you are going to use such a package extensively, you will probably want a package that has a relatively easy-to-use editing feature.

Ability to import data. Some software packages will allow you to work only with data created using that software. Other packages permit you to import data from other sources such as databases and spreadsheets, or to use graphics produced with other programs.

This part of the module has introduced you to computer graphics. As you work with computers more, you will develop a greater awareness of the potential of computer graphics. As with all types of computer applications, you will learn the most from hands-on experience.

8.9 Using The Microsoft Word Drawing Tools

Word 2010 has greatly improved graphics and drawing tools. In this section, we will review these tools. You will get a chance to create a drawing with these tools in the applications exercises for this module.

There are 5 basic types of graphics tools included with *MS Word*. They are:

- Drawing Objects
- SmartArt
- Charts
- Pictures
- Clip Art

Drawings refer to a drawing object or a group of **drawing objects**. Drawing objects include shapes, diagrams, flowcharts, curves, lines, and WordArt. You can change and enhance these objects with colors, patterns, borders, and other effects.

To create a drawing with *MS Word*, follow these steps:

1. Click in your document where you want to create the drawing.
2. On the *Insert* tab, in the *Ilustrations* panel, click *Shapes* and the click *New Drawing Canvas*. A drawing canvas will be inserted into your document.
3. Click on any shape from the *Shapes* tool in the *Illustrations* pane.
4. Click on a location within your drawing canvas and the selected shape will appear.
5. With the new shape selected, you may size the shape by clicking and dragging or add fill color, shadow effects, or change the outline color or pattern by making choices from the *Drawing Tools*.

Figure 8.3: A New Drawing Canvas

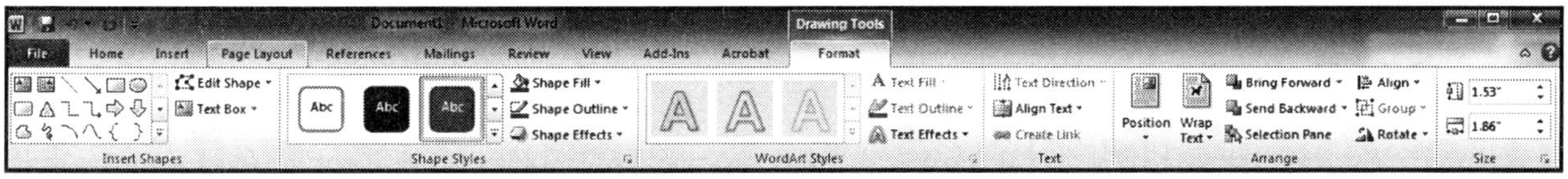

Figure 8.4: *MS Word* Drawing Tools

6. By clicking anywhere in the drawing canvas, you can change the color, border or style of the drawing canvas.
7. To add a text box to a drawing, click on the ***Text Box*** icon, located in the *Shapes* panel and then click and drag within the drawing canvas.
8. To alter an object or the entire drawing canvas, double click on it and select from the drawing tools.

By using the drawing tools, you can create flow charts, banners, simple cartoons, drawings, and charts. *Word*'s *Preview* feature allows you to see the effect of changes before you apply them.

You can also add clip art and pictures to the drawing canvas by clicking on the clip art or picture tool from the *Illustrations* pane of the *Insert* menu. The following figure shows a simple flowchart created with the *Word* drawing tools. The flowchart summarizes the process of creating a drawing. A clip art figure has been added to the drawing.

8.10 Digital imaging

Digital images may include photographs, drawings, graphs, and other types of illustrations. **Digital imaging** is the creation of digital images including the processing, compression, storage, printing, and display of images using a computer or other digital device such as a digital camera.

Digital images may be created directly from a scene by a digital camera or from another image in an analog medium, such as photographs, photographic film, or printed paper, by a scanner or similar device.

Image editing encompasses the processes of altering images, whether they are digital photographs or traditional **analog photographs** or illustrations. Before digital scanners and cameras became mainstream, traditional analog image editing was known as **photo retouching**, using tools such as an airbrush to modify photographs, or editing illustrations with any traditional art medium. However, since the advent of digital images, analog image editing has become largely obsolete. **Graphic software programs** are the primary tools with which a user may manipulate, enhance, and transform images. Many image editing programs are also used to create **computer art** from scratch.

Before digital scanners and cameras, traditional analog image editing was known as photo retouching, using tools such as an airbrush to modify photographs, or editing illustrations with any traditional art medium.

Due to the popularity of digital cameras, image editing programs are readily available. Minimal programs, that perform such operations as rotating and cropping are often provided within the digital camera itself. Other, more elaborate programs, are often sent free to the user on a CD when images are processed. More powerful editing programs contain more features to perform a large variety of advanced image manipulations. Popular raster-based digital image editors include *Adobe Photoshop, Corel Paint Shop Photo Pro, Visualizer Photo Studio, Pixel image editor, PixBuilder Studio,* and others.

Digital Images may be stored in a variety of file formats. Many image file formats use **data compression** to reduce file size and save storage space. Digital compression of images will take place in the camera and can be done in the computer with the image editor software. When images are stored in **JPG** format, compression has already taken place. Both cameras and computer programs allow the user to set the level of compression.

With the JPG file format, the greater the compression, the more information is lost, ultimately reducing image quality or detail. JPG uses knowledge of the way the brain and eyes perceive color to make this loss of detail less noticeable.

8.11 Features of Digital Imaging Software

Listed below are some of the most used capabilities of the better graphic manipulation programs. The list is by no means all inclusive. There are also a myriad of choices associated with most of these features.

Selection

One of the prerequisites for many of the applications mentioned below is a method of selecting part(s) of an image, thus applying a change selectively without affecting the entire picture. Most graphics programs have several means of accomplishing this, such as a marquee tool, lasso, vector-based pen tools as well as more advanced facilities such as edge detection, masking, alpha compositing, and color and channel-based extraction.

Layers

Another feature common to many graphics applications is that of **layers**, which are analogous to sheets of transparent acetate (each containing separate elements that make up a combined picture), stacked on top of each other, each capable of being individually positioned, altered and blended with the layers below, without affecting any of the elements on the other layers. This is a fundamental workflow which has become the norm for the majority of programs on the market today, and enables maximum flexibility for the user whilst maintaining **non-destructive editing** and ease of use.

Layers are analogous to sheets of transparent acetate, each containing separate elements that make up a combined picture, stacked on top of each other, each capable of being individually positioned, altered and blended with the layers below, without affecting any of the elements on the other layers.

Figure 8.5: Editing an Image with Layers

Image Size Alteration

Image editors can resize images in a process often called **image scaling**, making them larger, or smaller. **Digital cameras** produce large images which are often reduced in both physical size and image resolution for printing or for Internet use. Image editor programs use a mathematical process called resampling to calculate new pixel values whose spacing is larger or smaller than the original pixel values.

Cropping

Digital editors can be used to **crop** images. Cropping creates a new image by removing a desired rectangular portion from the image being cropped. The unwanted part of the image is discarded. Image cropping does not reduce the resolution of the area cropped. Best results are obtained when the original image has a high resolution. The primary reason for cropping is to improve the image composition. In the figure below, an uncropped and a cropped image are shown.

Figure 8.6: Cropping an Image

Noise Removal

Image editing software can add or remove **noise** in an image. Dust and scratches can be removed and an image can be **despeckled**. Noise tends to invade images when pictures are taken in low light settings. Adding noise can also be used to create special effects. For example, a new picture can be given an antiquated effect by adding uniform monochrome noise.

Removal of unwanted elements

Most image editors can be used to remove unwanted picture elements such as people, branches, etc, using a "clone" tool. Removing these distracting elements draws focus to the subject, improving overall composition. In the following picture, a group of people is shown walking in front of the fire station in the unedited picture. In the second picture, they have been removed.

Figure 8.7: Removing Unwanted Picture Elements

Selective color change

Some image editors have color swapping abilities to selectively change the color of specific items in an image, given that the selected items are within a specific color range. For example, it is possible to change the color of a car, a dress, or someone's hair.

Image Orientation

Image editors are capable of rotating an image in any direction and to any degree. Mirror images can be created and images can be horizontally or vertically flipped. A small rotation of several degrees is often enough to level the horizon or correct verticality of a building, for example.

Figure 8.8: Flipping an Image

Perspective Correction

Some image editors allow the user to change the shape of an image. While this might also be useful for special effects, it is most commonly used to correct **perspective distortion** which results from photographs being taken at an oblique angle to a rectilinear subject. The effect mimics the use of a perspective correction lens, which achieves a similar correction in the camera without loss of definition. In the following figure, the first photograph shows a photograph in which the building is distorted due to the angle of the camera. In the second picture, the distortion has been corrected with imaging software.

Image editors have functions to correct images for various lens distortions including pincushion, fisheye and barrel distortions.

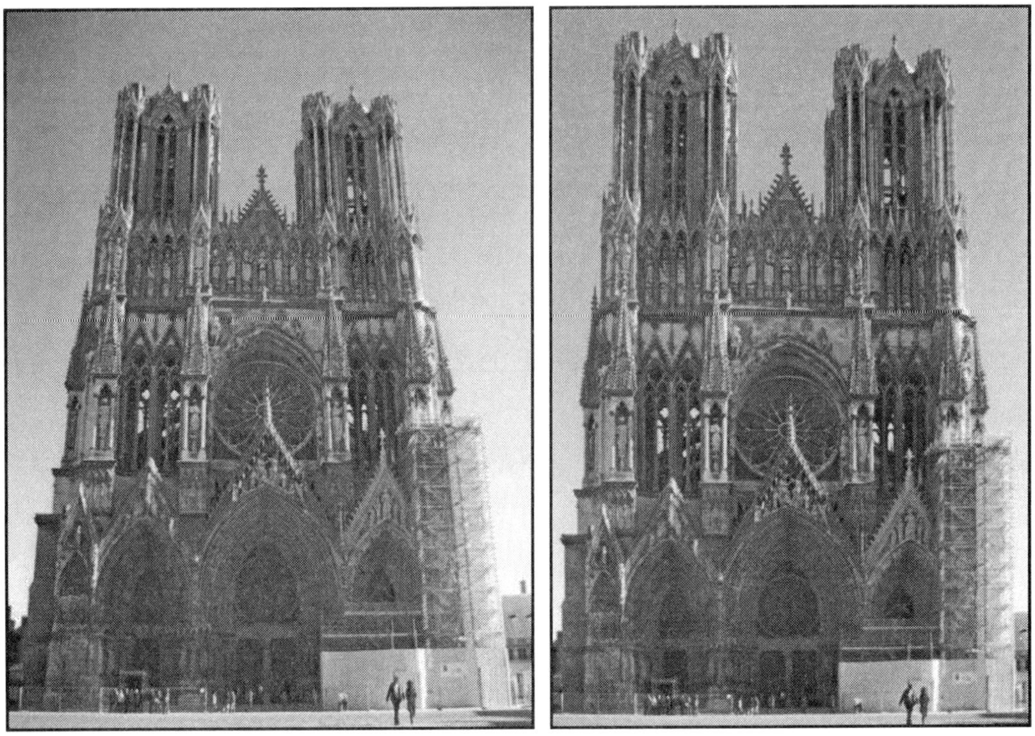

Figure 8.9: Perspective Correction

Special Effects

Image editors usually have variety of **special effects** that can create unusual results. Images may be skewed and distorted in various ways. Several special effects can be applied to an image which might include various forms of distortion, artistic effects, geometric and texture effects, and combinations thereof.

Scores of special effects can be applied to an image. These include various forms of distortion, artistic effects, geometric and texture effects, and combinations thereof.

Figure 8.10: A Photograph Enhanced With Special Effects

Many an underexposed image can be improved by using the contrast and brightness control.

Contrast and Brightness Adjustment

Image editors have provisions to change the contrast of images and brighten or darken the image. Many an underexposed image can be improved by using this feature. Recent advances have allowed more intelligent exposure correction whereby only pixels below a particular luminosity threshold are brightened, thereby brightening underexposed shadows without affecting the rest of the image. In the bear scene in the next figure, the image on the left is the original photo while the image on the right has been improved with greater contrast and brightness.

Figure 8.11: Contrast and Brightness Adjustment

Color Adjustments

The color of images can be altered in a variety of ways. Colors can be faded in and out, and tones can be changed. The color balance can be improved. Special effects, like sepia and gray scale can be added to an image. In addition, more complicated procedures such as the mixing of color channels are possible using more advanced graphics editors.

Image Filters

All good image editing programs will include a variety of **filter effects**. Chief among these are the **sharpening and blurring filters**. Portraits often appear more pleasing when softened particularly the background, to make the subject stand out more. This is an example of shallow depth of field. By selecting the background portion of an image, and then blurring it, people in the portrait appear to stand out more.. Photographs also can be sharpened to make the images appear sharper and clearer.

The **anti red eye filter** can eliminate the **red-eye effect**, which occurs when flash photos are taken when the pupil is too widely open, thus reflecting back the color of the blood-rich retina.

The **haze filter** is commonly used to color balance the blue tint that often occurs in landscape scenes with a great depth of field. By lessening the amount of blue in a photo and increasing the yellow, haze filters make can make the photograph more pleasing. In the images which follow, both a haze filter and a sharpening filter have been applied to the image on the right.

Figure 8.12: Image Filtering

8.12 Printing Images

Controlling the print size and quality of digital images requires an understanding of the **pixels-per-inch (ppi)** variable that is stored in the image file and sometimes used to control the size of the printed image. Within the *Image Size Dialog Box*, the image editor allows the user to manipulate both pixel dimensions and the size of the image on the printed document. These parameters work together to produce a printed image of the desired size and quality. Pixels per inch of the image, pixel per inch of the computer monitor, and dots per inch on the printed document are related, but in use are very different. The *Image Size Dialog Box* can be used as an image calculator of sorts. For example, a 1600 x 1200 image with a ppi of 200 will produce a printed image of 8 x 6 inches. The same image with a ppi of 400 will produce a printed image of 4 x 3 inches. Change the ppi to 800, and the same image now prints out at 2 x 1.5 inches. All three printed images contain the same data (1600 x 1200 pixels) but the pixels are closer together on the smaller prints, so the smaller images will potentially look sharp when the larger ones do not. The quality of the image will also depend on the capability of the printer.

8. 13 Images for Internet Use.

Images for Internet use should be kept small because the download speed of web pages is greatly affected by the file size of the images that they contain. Also, video monitors are only capable of much lower resolution that photographic prints. Therefore, images that are higher resolution than the video monitor's capability serve no purpose and only serve to consume more storage space and require more download time. As a rule of thumb, JPG images of 5" x 7" or smaller with medium resolution are good bets for Internet graphics. A high resolution image from a digital camera could have a resolution of 72 pixels per inch and dimensions of 2048 x 1536 pixels. An image of this type would be about 28.5" x 21.5" in physical size and would have a file size of 684 KB. (Ultra high resolution cameras produce even higher resolution images.) The same image reduced in size to 5"x 7" at medium resolution would have a file size of about 320 KB. When shown on a video monitor, there would be no noticeable difference in the appearance of the two pictures.

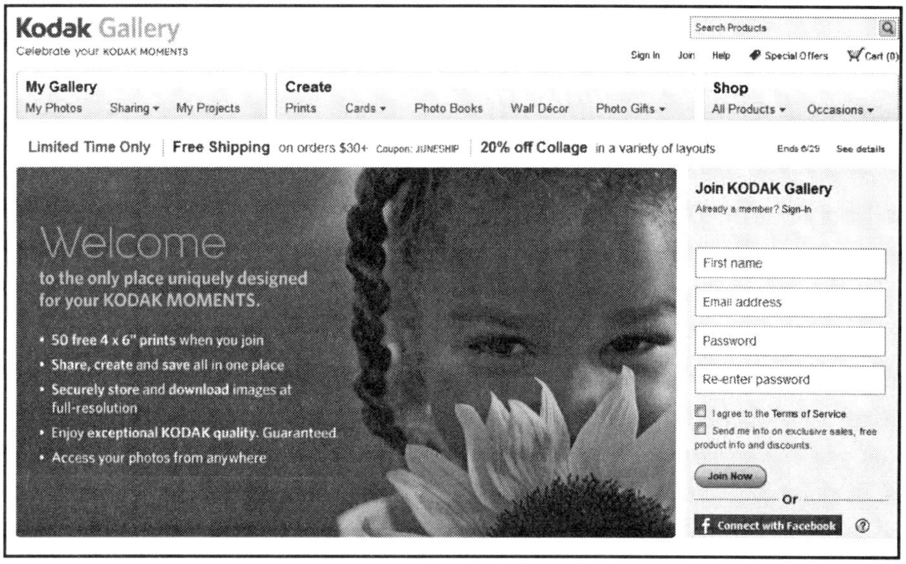

Figure 8.13: A Web Page with Graphics

8.14 Adobe Photoshop

Adobe Photoshop, or simply *Photoshop*, is a **graphics editor** developed and published by **Adobe Systems**. It is the current market leader for commercial image manipulation, and is the flagship product of Adobe Systems. It has been described as the industry standard for graphics professionals. Although originally designed to edit images for paper-based printing, *Photoshop* can also be used for a wide range of other professional and amateur purposes.

Thomas Knoll

In 1987, **Thomas Knoll**, then a PhD student at the University of Michigan, wrote a program on his Macintosh to display images on a **monochrome display**. He called his program ***Display***. His program caught the attention of his brother John Knoll, who was an employee of Industrial Light & Magic. He convinced Thomas to turn his program into a full-fledged image editing program. Thomas took a six month break from his studies in 1988 to collaborate with his brother on the program, which they renamed *ImagePro*. In 1988, Thomas renamed his program *Photoshop* and worked out a short-term deal with a scanner manufacturer to distribute copies of the program with their scanners. About this time, John traveled to Silicon Valley and gave a demonstration of the program to engineers at **Apple Computer Inc.** and **Adobe Inc.** Both showings were successful, and Adobe decided to purchase the license to distribute *Photoshop* in September 1988. *Photoshop* 1.0 was released in 1990 for the Macintosh exclusively, and fit on one 1.44 MB floppy disk. Continual revisions were made to the program and new versions were released in the following years. In 2003, the program was renamed *Adobe Photoshop CS*. The name uses the abbreviation CS for products in ***Adobe Creative Suite***. CS5 includes several programs, including *Dreamweaver, Flash,* and *Fireworks* that were developed by *Macromedia*, a former rival acquired by *Adobe* in 2005. Use of programs other than *Photoshop*, contained in the CS3 suite are beyond the scope of this book.

The most current version of *Photoshop*, was released in April 2010 and is marketed as **Photoshop CS5**. The *CS* reflects its integration with other software products in the *Creative Suite.*

Figure 8.14: *Photoshop CS5*

While *Photoshop* is the industry standard image editing program for professional raster graphics, its relatively high suggested retail price is too much for the amateur market. Competition with other products, led Adobe to introduce ***Photoshop Elements***, a version of *Photoshop* with some of the professional features removed. *Photoshop Elements* is aimed at the general consumer market but is less desirable for professional work.

To complete the exercises in this book, users who do not have *Photoshop* available to them can download a free 30 day trial version of *Photoshop* from Adobe. A free trial (or Tryout) version of *Photoshop Elements* may be downloaded from Adobe at the URL below:

http://www.adobe.com/products/photoshopelwin/tryout.html

8.15 Working with Photoshop

Photoshop is a sophisticated tool and it is not the intended purpose here to provide a comprehensive review of everything that *Photoshop* can do. However, this section does provide sufficient information for you to get started using *Photoshop* and to complete the module assignments.

When you open *Photoshop*, you will see a screen similar to one in the following figure. Pull down menus are shown across the top of the screen and the main picture tools are on the left hand side of the screen.

Figure 8.15: *Photoshop*

To get started working with an existing picture, select *Open* from the *File Menu. Photoshop* will open all of the common types of visual formats such as PICT, JPEG, GIF, and BMP files.

The *File Menu*, which is shown at left provides the means of opening and closing files, importing and exporting visuals to various file formats, printing, and other functions.

To create a new visual from scratch, select *New*. The *Browse* tool helps you locate the picture files on your computer that you want to work with. The *Import* and *Export* options allow users to import frames from video and to export *Photoshop* files to other Adobe applications. The *Page Setup* and *Print* commands provide a means of printing your pictures.

Once a visual is opened, it appears in the main window. The menu options across the top of the window and the tools on the right side are used to edit the picture. The desert picture is one of the sample pictures that come with *Photoshop*. Open the butterfly picture or another picture of your choice to practice with.

Cropping an Image

Select the **crop tool** (the broken line rectangle) from the tools on the left side of the screen. Click and drag the + to enclose a part of the image. To make the cut, select *Crop* from the *EDIT* menu. See the figures which follow.

Figure 8.16: Cropping with *Photoshop*

Rotating the Image

Select *Rotate Canvas* from the *Image* drop down menu and experiment with rotating the picture in various ways. Save the cropped and rotated image as *Butterfly2* on your computer.

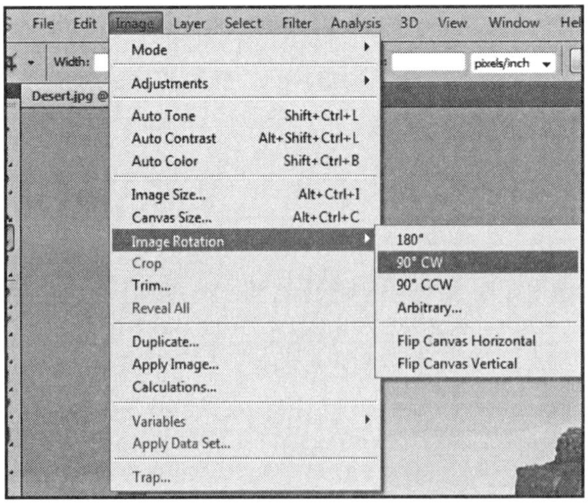

Figure 8.17: Rotating an Image

Photoshop Magazine

> Photoshop has strong ties with other Adobe software for media editing, animation and authoring. Files in Photoshop's native format, .PSD, can be exported to and from Adobe ImageReady, Adobe Premiere Pro, After Effects and Adobe Encore DVD.

Adjusting the Contrast and Brightness

Select *Adjustments* from the *Image* drop down menu as shown in the following figure. Then select *Brightness/Contrast.* Using the sliders in the dialog window, adjust the brightness and contrast. The results will be shown on the image preview as you move the sliders.

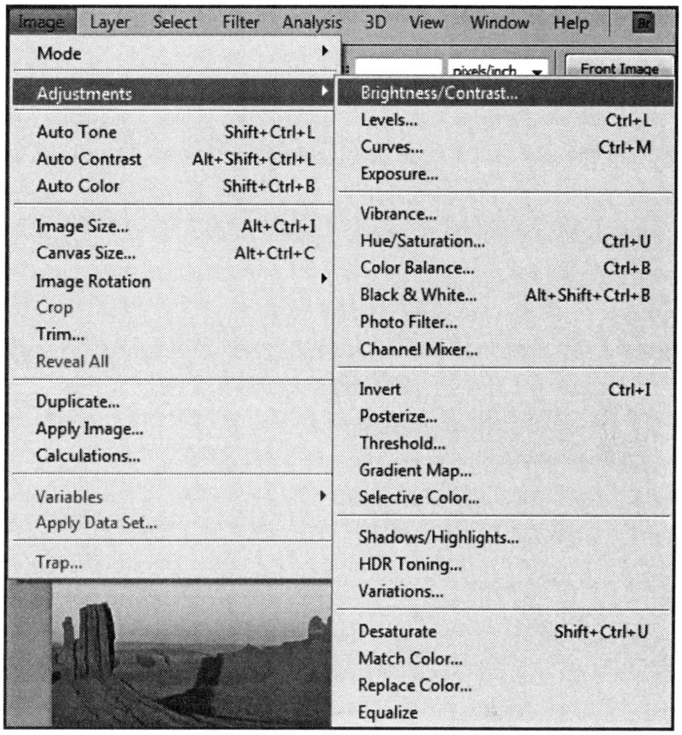

Figure 8.18: Image Adjustments

Other Image Adjustments

For practice, try adjusting the **color balance.** This is done in a similar manner as adjusting the contrast and brightness. Experiment with some of the other adjustments on the *Adjustments* drop down menu.

Another useful adjustment is **Auto Levels**. Many photographs can be improved by simply applying the auto levels adjustment. Auto levels automatically adjust color balance, brightness, and contrast and frequently lead to a better picture.

Change the image size by choosing *Image Size* from the *Image* menu. After choosing *Image Size*, the physical size of the image is shown in the *Image Size* dialog window. Often, this is larger than the image that you see on the screen. The image is automatically reduced to fit on the monitor. You can change the size of the image by entering different values for either the *Pixel Dimensions* or *Document Size*. For practice, change the document width to 7" in the width. The width and height of the image are linked to preserve proportions. Altering either will change both.

The image resolution in pixels per square inch is also shown in the *Image Size* dialog. The higher the number shown, the higher the image resolution. This can also be changed. For practice, change the image resolution to a lower number and save it to your computer with a different name. You can see the file size of the image when the image is saved.

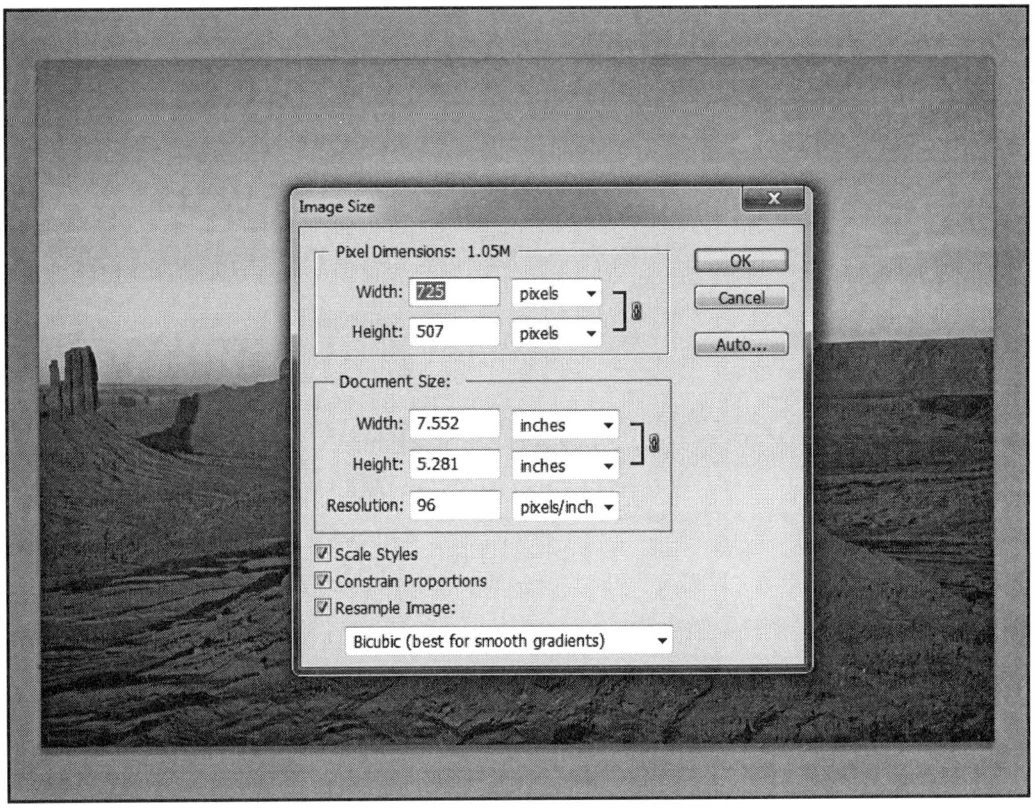

Figure 8.19: Altering the Image Size

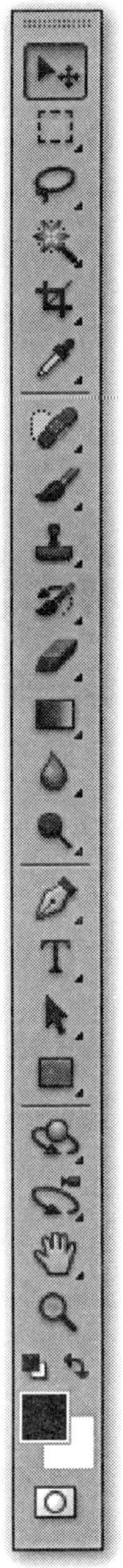

Photoshop toolbar

If the image partially disappears when the image size is altered, don't be alarmed. To view the complete image, open the *View Menu* and choose *Fit on Screen*. You can also experiment with *Zoom In, Zoom Out*, and *View-Actual Pixels*. The image window can be changed by clicking and dragging a corner.

Adding Text

Titles, labels, and other text can be added to pictures with *Photoshop*. To add a title to a picture, select the **text tool** which is the **T** in the toolbar. Place the text cursor at the desired location over the picture and type the desired text.

The font, color, size, and style of the text can be manipulated with the **text tool bar** which appears at the top of the window when the text tool is selected. To change any text attribute, select the text by clicking and dragging over it, while the text tool is selected, and then choose the desired font, style, color, or other attribute desired. To move or change the size of the text box, select the **Move Tool** (the arrow with the cross next to it) which is located near the top of the toolbar. Then click on the text box to move or enlarge it.

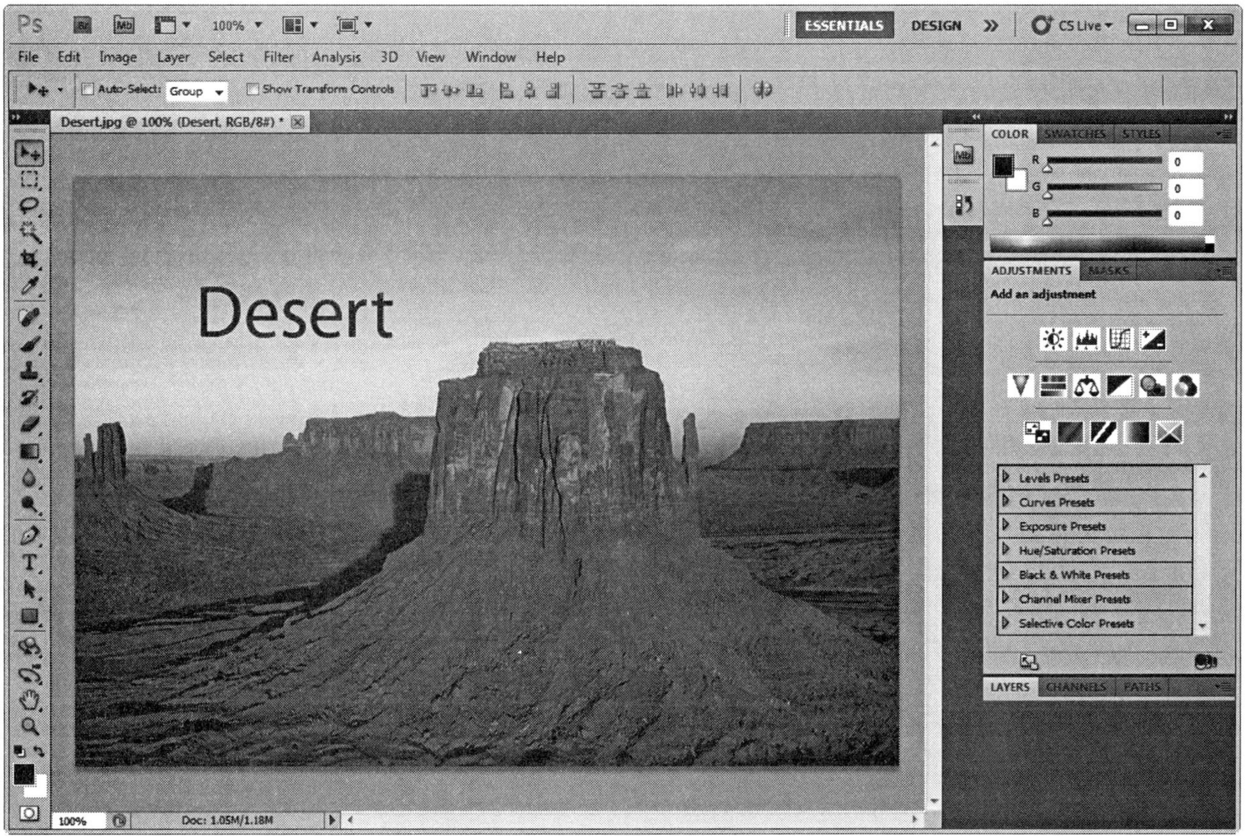

Figure 8.20: Adding Text with *Photoshop*

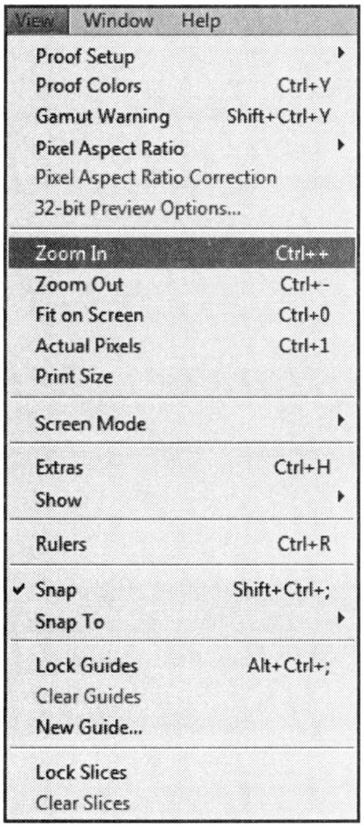

Figure 8.21: The View Menu

Note that when the text tool is selected a new layer automatically appears. Layers can be added or deleted by selecting the **Layer** drop down menu and then *Add Layer* or *Delete Layer*. Layers also appear automatically when text or drawings are added to a photograph. To work with any given layer, be sure to select it from the layer window.

Viewing or Hiding Windows

Most of the tools and windows available in *Photoshop* can be shown or hidden as desired. If something that you need isn't on the screen, such as the *layer window, brush pallet*, or *style menu*, or *toolbar*, open the **Window** drop down menu and select the window that you wish to display. *Photoshop* has so many tools and windows available that the screen would get very cluttered if all of them were visible all the time.

Adding, Changing, or Deleting Picture Elements

One of the most important editing capabilities of *Photoshop* is the ability to add, change, and delete picture elements. For example, you might wish to add a tree, duplicate a flower, delete a telephone pole that's in the wrong place, remove a traffic sign, or add a person to a picture. There are a variety of techniques for editing picture elements that are beyond the scope of this book.

8.16 Saving Files

By default, *Photoshop* saves files in its own file type, called **PSD**, for **Photoshop Document**. Saving files in this format, preserves all of the layers independently so that you can work with the illustration again at a later time. However, when you have finished editing a document, it is best to save it in a common interchange format such as JPG so that it can be easily inserted in a document or web page. To save a file as a JPEG, just select File>Save as… and JPG. Saving an illustration as a JPG file combines all of the layers so that they can no longer be edited independently. It is best to save each image in both formats if you think that there is a possibility that you may wish to edit it for another purpose in the future.

When saving a file as a JPG document, you have a choice of resolution and image size. If you wish to print a photograph on paper, a high resolution image is desirable, especially if a large size print is to be made. However, high res images are larger files and require more storage space and download time. For web graphics and images to be emailed, a smaller file size is desirable.

8.17 Creating New Graphics

To this point, we have discussed working with photographs with *Photoshop*. However, *Photoshop* may also be used to create original graphics.

To start a new graphic, follow these steps.

1. Close all open images.
2. Select the **Background Color** from the *Tools* by clicking on the foreground square.
3. Using the **Color pallet** which will appear, select a blue background color.

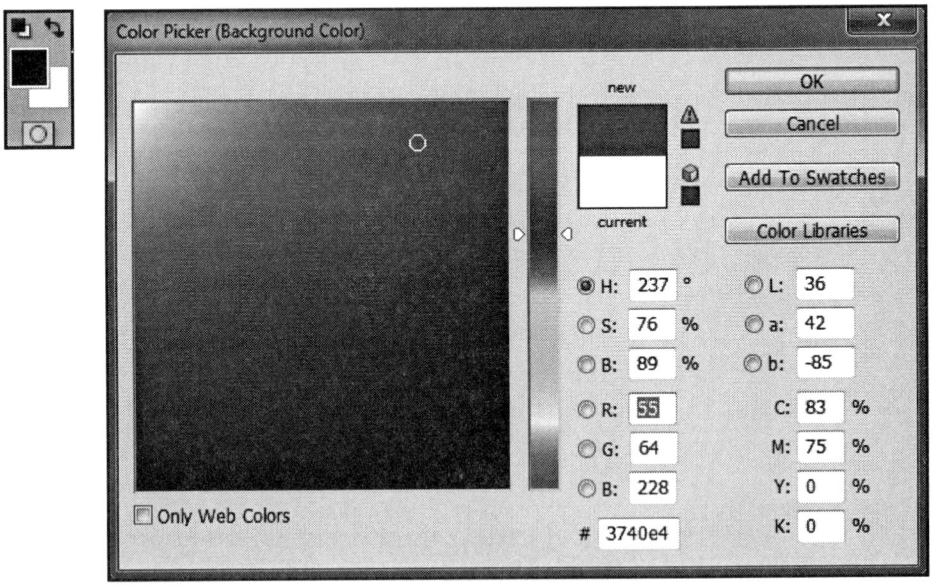

Figure 8.22: *Photoshop Foreground/Background Color Tool* and *Color Picker*

4. Choose *File>New.*
5. In the dialog window that will appear, set the width and height to 500 pixels.
6. Choose *Background Color in Background* Contents option.

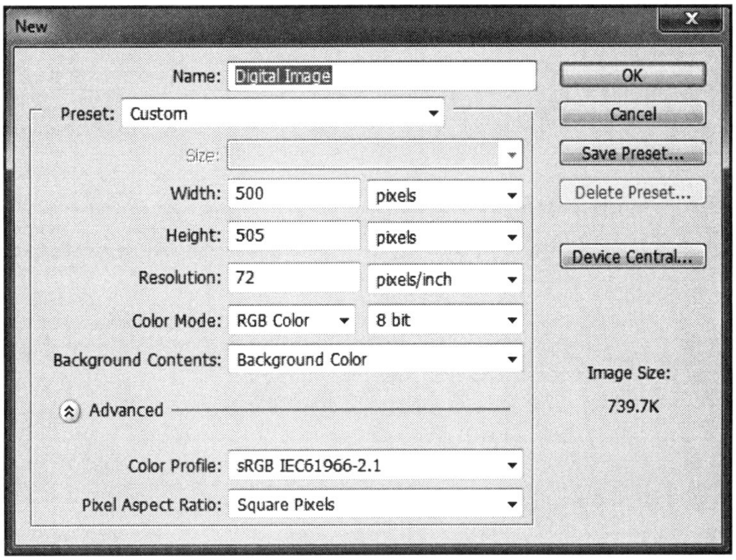

Figure 8.23: *New file*

7. Select the *Text Tool.*
8. From the *Text Options* that appear at the top of the frame, choose a text color that contrasts with the background color.

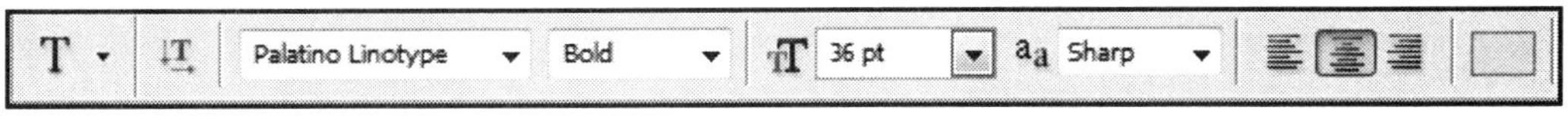

Figure 8.24: *Photoshop* Text Options

9. From the *Text Options*, choose a text size of 36 points.
10. Choose a font and style from the *Text Options.*
11. Type the following text: "Digital Imaging by <Your Name>" and the current date.
12. Save and close your original graphic.

Your original graphic should look similar to the one in the following figure.

Figure 8.25: A *Photoshop* Original Graphic

This graphic is pretty basic. However, sophisticated original illustrations can be constructed by importing clip art or photographs and working with other *Photoshop* tools.

8.18 Learning More about Photoshop and Digital Imaging

This module has provided an introduction to digital imaging and *Photoshop*. However, *Photoshop* is a sophisticated program and there are many aspects of it that have not been covered here. There are several ways to learn more.

- Use and practice with *Photoshop*. Experiment with the different tools and options.
- Use the ***Help*** feature to find information online. *Adobe* has provided www.adobe.com.
- Get one of the many books on *Photoshop*. Read and practice with the program as you go.

Use this page for additional explanation if needed.

MODULE 9

The Internet

The Internet

You have probably used the Internet for school or at home. The Internet reaches millions of people in every country on the planet. The Internet has been described as a network of networks. Advances in hardware and software have expanded the potential of the personal computer tremendously in recent years, enabling users to communicate around the world. Personal computers routinely send and receive E-mail and search the Internet for all types of information. In this module, you will become acquainted with practical uses of the Internet and other types of telecommunications.

Module Objectives

When you have completed this module, you should be able to:

- define telecommunications and Internet-related terms;
- identify major uses of telecommunications and the Internet;
- identify components of a computer telecommunications system and their functions;
- describe types of services available from commercial information services;
- use Boolean logic to design and conduct an online search for information;
- identify important considerations for selecting an internet service provider, web browser, or web-filtering software;
- identify strengths and weaknesses of WWW search engines;
- identify and explain the meaning of common WWW error messages;
- identify and explain major societal, ethical, and legal issues concerning the Internet and WWW;
- describe copyright issues and fair use guidelines related to the Internet; and
- demonstrate appropriate use of WWW search engines.

Materials Needed to Complete This Module

- This book
- Access to the Internet
- *Microsoft Internet Explorer* or another web browser
- Disks or other storage media to store your work on. (These may be the same disks you used for previous modules).

How to Proceed

1. Read this module.
2. Review the *Key Terms* near the end of this module.
3. Complete the *Module Review Questions* at the end of the module. Check your answers at the end of the book.
4. Complete the *Module Computer Application Assignments* and turn in to your instructor.
5. Take the Module 9 Test.

The Internet

This module introduces networking and telecommunications concepts with an emphasis on the Internet.

9.1 Telecommunication Concepts

The term **telecommunications** simply means communicating across distances using common carriers such as the telephone, television, and radio, as well as satellites and computers. Data communications is the electronic exchange and processing of data or information, which includes text, graphics, sound, and video information that is digitally coded. This module will focus primarily on data communications or communicating via computers.

Telecommunications ties consumers, businesses, governmental agencies, individuals, and organizations together via multidimensional networks. Most big businesses have their own networks, called **Intranets**, linking offices and businesses across the country or around the world.

Businesses rely on telecommunications for managing distributed operations, enterprise resource planning (ERP), and E-commerce.

Personal and educational applications of computer telecommunications are growing rapidly. In the educational community, data communications facilitate the sharing of research and other academic information. Some of the common applications of telecommunications networks are:

- Sending and receiving **E-mail** (electronic mail) from people throughout the world (saving time, postage, and paper),
- Participating in discussions through electronic bulletin boards, newsgroups, or listservs on a wide range of topics,
- Accessing electronic databases containing information on everything from the weather to online registration and college loan programs,
- Performing library research using bibliographic databases, and
- Sharing files of information through networks.

9.2 The Communication Process

Two types of signals are carried by telecommunications systems: **analog** and **digital**. **Analog signals** can be represented by a wave having amplitude (peaks and valleys) and frequency (number of waves over a certain interval). See Figure 9.1.

Figure 9.1: Analog Signal (Left) Vs. Digital Signal (Right)

Using the example of analog sound signals, the higher the wave (amplitude) of an analog signal, the louder the sound. The closer together the sound waves are (higher frequency), the higher the pitch. Radio and telephone transmission uses analog technology.

Digital signals use "on-off" electronic pulses. Digital electronics is the way that computers process information. Digital signals are less affected by interference (usually called noise) than are analog signals.

The public telephone network using an analog system was the first environment of the Internet. Now the shift is to wireless and digital technologies.

9.3 Internet Access Methods

The public telephone network, called **POTS** for "plain old telephone service," is an analog signal system. When computers communicate over networks involving POTS, the computer's digital signal must be converted to an analog signal. The conversion of the digital signal to analog signal is termed **modulation**, and is performed by the piece of telecommunications hardware known as a **modem**. The modem on the sending computer modulates the digital signal to analog. The modem on the receiving computer **demodulates** the analog signal to a digital signal. The name modem is derived from this *mo*dulating/*dem*odulating process.

The speed at which data is transferred across phone lines is measured in bits per second (bps). Common bps rates are 28.8K, 33.6K, and 56K bps. A 28,800 bps modem sends and receives information at about 28,800 bits per second. A 56K modem is approximately twice as fast. Most modems today are also equipped to send and receive faxes as well as handle voice mail.

There are two commonly used higher speed alternatives to POTS systems: **cable Internet service** and **digital subscriber line** (**DSL**). Cable Internet service is provided by cable television companies. With cable-based Internet service, a special **cable modem** is employed and telephone lines are not used. Motion video, 3-D effects, and audio can be transmitted in real time. The cost of cable Internet service is about $30-$50 per month.

Many locations such as motels, coffee houses, and even campgrounds now provide **WI-FI** service. WI-FI provides a wireless signal broadcast from a wireless router connected to the hosts DSL or cable internet service. The signal is short range. Users with wireless modems and laptop computers may use the host internet service.

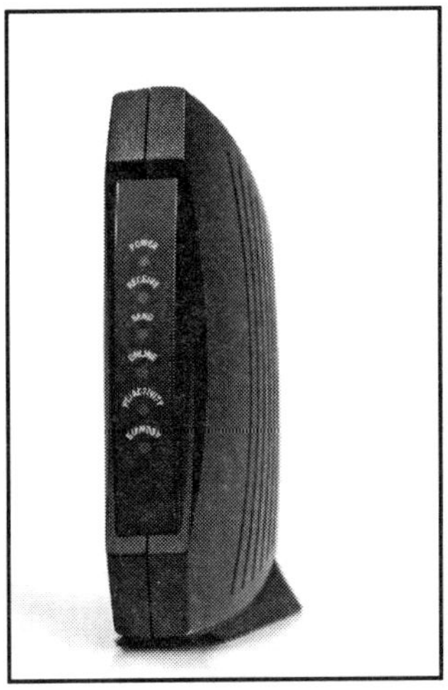

Figure 9.2: A Cable Modem

DSL is offered through telephone companies to provide home users a transmission rate of around 1.544 Mbps per second. The cost is about the same for both cable Internet service and DSL. The problem for many small office/home office PC users is that cable Internet service and DSL lines are not available in their areas, which means they are limited to POTS systems.

Recently, Americans have signed up for high-speed Internet access through DSL and cable in record numbers, lured by price wars among service providers. Overall, 42 percent, or about 84 million, adult Americans had broadband service by mid 2006. This is up dramatically from just 30 percent in the previous year.

Fiber optic technology increases the quality and quantity of data transmission over twisted cable and coaxial cable media.

9.4 Communication Channels

Electronic signals must be carried from one location to another by way of communication channels, also known as communication media. Some common examples of communications media are:

Cable Technology. At one time telephone cable was twisted copper wires. Insulated copper wire technology was developed (coaxial cable) that was less prone to electrical interference, which enabled it to carry more data.

Fiber-optic Technology. Fiber-optic technology was a major advance in data transmission. Information travels through glass fibers in the form of light (laser) waves. Data transmission can reach the speed of light and carry more data. A glass fiber the size of a hair can carry 30,000 simultaneous telephone calls (or over five times the volume of a coaxial cable).

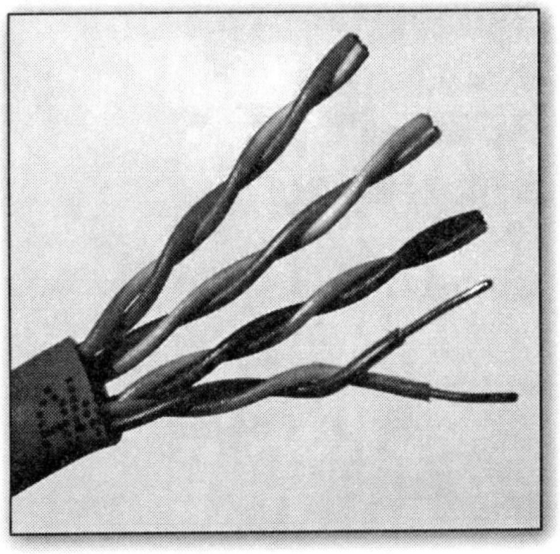

Wireless Technology. Wireless communication channels include data transmission over cellular telephones, microwave transmissions, and PDAs (personal digital assistants). Microwaves can transmit large volumes of data, but they require line-of-sight transmission (transmissions where one relay is in a

As of March 31, 2011, 2.095 billion people use the Internet according to Internet World Stats.

The prevalent language for communication on the Internet is English.

direct line with another). Cellular radio technology takes advantage of the Federal Communication Commission (FCC) having divided service areas into hexagonal *cells* (honeycomb appearance). At the center of each cell is a *transceiver* that can boost the digital signal along to another cell or connect the signal to the wired network, POTS. In 1999 the Wireless Application Protocol (WAP) allowed the Internet to interface with the cellular network. Now wireless technology users are able to access the Web.

Satellite Communications. Satellite communications are digital transmissions that are also line-of-sight, but the altitude at which a satellite operates results in a large line-of-sight area, called a "footprint." Several disadvantages with satellite transmissions include cost, lack of privacy (anyone over a large area can capture any signal), and a delay of one-forth second in transmissions due to distance, which can make the signal unusable for some applications.

WI-FI. A Wi-Fi enabled device such as a PC, game consoles, cell phones, MP3 players, or PDAs can connect to the Internet when within range of a **wireless network** connected to the Internet. The coverage of one or more interconnected access points—called a **hotspot**—can comprise an area as small as a single room with wireless-opaque walls or as large as many square miles covered by overlapping access points.

9.5 The Internet

Figure 9.3: A Conceptual Computer Network

The Internet began with the birth of the **ARPAnet,** which was commissioned by the U.S. Department of Defense in 1969. The motivation for ARPAnet was a communications network that allowed computers at distant locations to "talk" with each other in order to exchange military and national security data in case the Cold War turned hot.

By the 1980s, networking was quickly evolving into an established tool of the scientific research community. In order to expand information access, the National Science Foundation (NSF) established five supercomputer centers (called *nodes*) around the country. These powerful, expensive supercomputers had the advantage of increasing the amount of data processed, but there was one drawback. The main nodes that form the backbone of the Internet are connected by a fiber-optic network, which is primarily operated by MCI, a telecommunications company.

No central agency operates the Internet. A key to the rapid growth of the Internet has been the free and open access to information, as well as the development of protocols such as TCP/IP. Rules and procedures needed to be developed before computers of different types could communicate with each other. TCP/IP technology could package the electronic data from one computer into small units called *packets*, which could then be transmitted over the Internet. There is a family of TCP/IP protocols. One member is Telnet, which allows the user to access another computer and to transfer or download files, text, or software.

Over subsequent years, additional networks spread to general scientific and academic use. Universities and research groups began to develop in-house networks known as **Local Area Networks** (**LANs**). A LAN would connect one computer in an office or department with all other computers within the building or same geographical location. A LAN with IP software could connect with other LANs. These networked LANs formed a **Wide Area Network** (**WAN**), which connect computers in different geographical locations.

While the Internet is not owned by a single entity, it is governed by a voluntary international collective of researchers, academics, and users who determine the future of the network (known as the ISOC). Within the ISOC is the *Internet Architecture Board* (the IAB) whose main function is to maintain the Internet by creating and enforcing international networking standards, as well as making sure that no two users have the same IP address.

For a monthly fee, anyone with a computer, a telephone line, and a modem can connect to the Internet. Commercial services called **Internet Service Providers** (**ISPs**) include national ISPs like America On-Line (AOL) or MSN (Microsoft Network), or local ISP, such as The Door (www.door.net) in the Lubbock, TX area. Services provided by ISPs include access to the World Wide Web, E-mail, and instant messaging, with more services being added to make their services more competitive. ISPs provide users with access to the Internet via **gateways**.

A gateway is a network point that acts as an entrance to another network. On the Internet, the network consists of gateway nodes and host nodes. The computers that serve network users and the computers that serve content (such as Web pages) are **host** nodes. The computers that control traffic within a university's network or at your local ISP are gateway nodes.

By continent, 44% of the world's Internet users are based in Asia, 23% in Europe, 13% in North America, and 10% in Latin America and the Caribbean.

9.6 The World Wide Web

The **World Wide Web** originated in 1991 with developers **Tim Berners-Lee** and others at the European Laboratory for Particle Physics, also known as *Conseil Europeen pour la Recherche Nucleaire* (CERN). The developers at CERN created the protocol based on hypertext that enables users to connect content on the Web with hyperlinks. **Hypertext markup language (HTML)** is a specification for making hypertext documents. Hypertext is a concept that allows one piece of text to cross-reference other pieces of text, either in the same document or in other documents on a computer network. According to Berners-Lee, "the dream behind the Web is of a common information space in which we communicate by sharing information. Its universality is essential: the fact that a hypertext link can point to anything, be it personal, local, or global, be it draft or highly polished." A single authority does not control the WWW. Virtually anyone who has access to a computer and the Internet can use web authoring tools to create a Website. **The World Wide Web Consortium (W3C)** oversees the development of Web technology and promotes the Web by developing common protocols for transmitting information over the Internet. The major commercial networks intersect at four main network access points (NAPs) near New York, Washington, D.C., Chicago, and San Francisco. The commercial backbone of the Internet is overseen primarily by MCI.

Many people use the terms *Internet* and *World Wide Web* (or just the *Web*) interchangeably, but, as discussed in this module, the two terms are not synonymous.

```
<html>
<head>
<meta http-equiv="Content-Type" content="text/html;
charset=iso-8859-1">
<title>Computer Network Diagram Stock</title>
<meta name="distribution" content="global">
</head>
<body>
Computer Network Diagram as shown in Figure 1
</body>
</html>
```

Figure 9.4: An Example of An HTML Document

Web sites may be maintained by companies, organizations, or individuals. Web sites are written in **hypertext markup language** or **HTML**. HTML is written in the form of tags, surrounded by angle brackets. HTML can also describe, to some degree, the appearance and semantics of a document, and can include embedded scripting language code.

9.7 Web Authoring Software

While it is possible to create html web pages with any text editor by using html tags, the task of creating web pages is best done with programs called **web editors**, also known as **html editors** or **web authoring software**. Various software programs allow the publishers of web sites to create web pages consisting of formatted text, graphics, video, pictures, and hyperlinks. These programs have a user friendly interface that allow users to create sophisticated web sites by use of templates and by clicking and dragging page elements.

Many programs may be used as web authoring tools including *MS Word* and *PowerPoint*. However, these tools have limited power and flexibility. Serious web authors prefer dedicated web authoring programs. There are various web authoring programs on the market today. Microsoft's web authoring tool is *Microsoft Expression Web*. Other popular web authoring program is *Adobe DreamWeaver.*

9.8 Internet Domains

An **Internet domain** is a collection of network addresses that are organized in levels. Top-level domains are generally classified by geographical location or purpose. For example, each non-U.S. domain has a two-letter top-level domain that represents the host's country. For example, the following domain name is registered to The Sydney Regional Scientific Visualization Laboratory (Australia). You will notice that the two-letter top-level domain name is ".au."

http://www.vislab.usyd.edu.au

Domain Name System (**DNS**) is the way Internet domain names are located and translated to IP addresses. The domain name for Microsoft Corporation is www.microsoft.com. When you type in this **uniform resource locator (URL)**, DNS translates this domain name into an IP address such as 129.118.56.50 so that the computer can communicate via the TCP/IP protocol.

In general, the Internet domain naming system is divided into categories according to the type of organization. The following shows how second-level domains are organized:

.com	-	commercial enterprises
.org	-	nonprofit organizations
.net	-	networks
.edu	-	educational institutions
.gov	-	government organizations
.mil	-	military services
.int	-	organizations established by international treaty

Due to the explosive growth in the Internet, additional domain names have been developed and made available recently.

9.9 Web Browsers

A **web browser** is a software program which enables a user to display and interact with text, images, videos, music and other information located on a Web page at a website on the World Wide Web. Text and images on a Web page can contain hyperlinks to other Web pages at the same or different websites. Web browsers allow a user to quickly and easily access information provided on many Web pages at many websites by traversing these links. Web browsers are pretty simple programs. Their task is basically to download and display web pages. Most web browsers today are enhanced with content filtering options to block obscene or fraudulent web sites. Search tools designed to help the user locate information are also included with most web browsers.

The most popular web browsers in use today are ***Microsoft Internet Explorer, Mozilla Firefox, and Google Chrome.***

9.10 What's on the Internet?

Consider the following examples. Which applications of telecommunications could be useful to you?

Example 1: You are sipping your morning coffee and paying your monthly bills, not using pen and checkbook, but rather using a computer and a modem. Using on-line banking, you quickly make your phone, mortgage, and credit card payments without a trip to the mailbox. Your checkbook is automatically balanced for you.

Example 2: You need a gift for Mother's Day. You use one of several on-line (Web) shopping services and buy Mom a bottle of perfume and some gourmet cheeses. Your gifts are sent directly to Mom, and charged to your credit card.

Example 3: You are planning a vacation to Disney World. You log in to Disney World's WWW home page. You are able to print out a listing of the area attractions including their location, hours of operation, and cost. Next, using the on-line airline guide available through a variety of commercial services, you check the schedules and fare rates for all airlines to and from your destination. With this information, you are able to choose the flights with the best price that best fit your schedule. Ticketless purchases are charged to your credit card, and when you arrive at the airport your boarding pass is printed when you check in. While on your three-hour flight to Florida, you use your laptop computer to type a few business letters. When you arrive, you use your pocket modem with the phone in your hotel room to send your letters back to the office for the secretary to mail.

Using the Web, it is easier than ever before for individuals and organizations to publish ideas and information to an extremely large audience. Anyone can find ways to publish a web page or build a website for very little initial cost.

All of these examples of applications are available now. Millions of people use telecommunications regularly. In the future, it will certainly become an even more important means of making us more productive by providing us with timely information, and allowing us to send and receive data easily.

The Internet is comprised of several components that are reviewed below:

Web sites reside on computers called ***web servers.*** When you type in a URL, the web browser communicates with the server using the TCP/IP protocol and requests the server to send a copy of the web page you want. You may have noticed advertisements in magazines that show the WWW address of the advertiser. Each web site consists of pages that might have a combination of text, graphics, sound, and even video. Most technology companies and many commercial companies as well as millions of individuals have web pages. Web pages typically have links to other pages on the same web site or pages on other web sites. These links are often underlined words or sentences are known as **hyperlinks**.

Discussion groups, listservs, and newsgroups are some of the most famous and infamous sites on the Internet. These groups cover thousands of topics from social issues, computers, job searches, sexual issues, politics, and many others. Some groups are not regulated and have harsh language or controversial contents such as pornographic photographs or recipes for making bombs. Other groups are *moderated,* meaning the messages are reviewed by a moderator prior to being posted to the group. Most of the commercial service providers have adopted standards for members of such groups. Internet messaging and bulletin boards are a distributed teleconferencing system that can function in real (*synchronous*) time.

9.11 Electronic Mail (E-mail)

E-mail is the most popular Internet service. You may already be an experienced E-mail user, but you should be familiar with all aspects of E-mail as it is an important part of this module.

E-mail has many advantages over **"snail" mail** as listed below.

95% of E-mail is delivered within 5 minutes.

- *It's fast.* E-mail can travel almost any distance in just a few minutes. A recent article reported that 95% of E-mail reaches its destination within five minutes or less. However, occasionally it may take hours or even longer if there is an unusual problem. Conventional mail, of course, takes days or perhaps weeks.
- *It's cheap.* Usually, no additional fee is charged for sending E-mail messages. E-mail service is included with any basic Internet provider service.
- *It's convenient.* If you are a computer user, it is easy to send and receive your messages on the computer. Your mail can easily be deleted, filed, or forwarded much more quickly, conveniently, and ecologically than can paper messages.
- *It's reliable.* While E-mail may not be 100% foolproof, it certainly beats the U.S. Postal Service. E-mail has become so universal among computer network users that almost all of them support it fully.

On the negative side, E-mail can only be used with other computer users. The recipient of your message is not guaranteed to read your message promptly, either. Some people wait days or even weeks to check their E-mail.

Most business workers today spend from one to two hours of their working day on email.

9.12 Basic Components of E-mail

E-mail consists of both the message itself and the software that creates and sends it. The actual message is usually a simple text (ASCII) file, but sending HTML files (Hypertext Markup Language is the programming language read by web browsers) via E-mail is becoming increasingly popular.

Most E-mail users have E-mail software that resides on their own PC. Almost all ISPs provide a **POP** (Post Office Protocol) server that your E-mail software can automatically access to check and download your personal E-mail, and quickly log off once the E-mail has been transferred to your PC. Sending messages works the same way using only very short connect times.

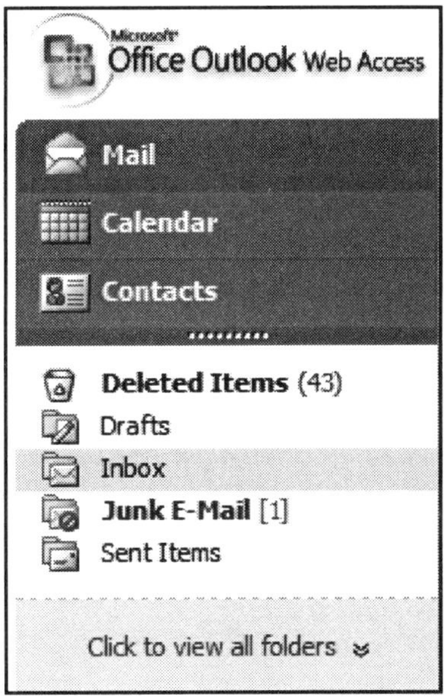

Figure 9.5: An E-mail boxes

Some people prefer to use an E-mail program that is separate from their web browser program. Several good ones are available including *Microsoft Outlook* and *Windows Live Mail.* Different E-mail programs may contain more mail management features, have more editing features, have a better user guide, or be easier to use. Some E-mail software can be obtained free from your ISP or come packaged with your modem. Others are available either as shareware (free or available for a minor fee) or purchased as a commercial version. Most serious E-mail users eventually buy a commercial version of E-mail software for the management features.

The exact appearance of the message on your computer screen will depend on the E-mail software you are using. All E-mail software will display a header and the body of the message. The header generally consists of the date (which is supplied by the computer from the built-in system clock), the user ID of the sender (sometimes the real name of the sender is also included), the address of the recipient, and a subject line. It is always a good idea to include a subject.

Most E-mail systems will display the date, sender, and subject of all messages in a list of your incoming mail, and if no subject is entered in the message, the recipient will not know the nature of the message. Busy people who get a lot of E-mail might choose to read important messages first; normally, they will postpone reading a message that contains no clue in the subject line as to what information is included.

The body of the message is pretty self-explanatory. When typing in the message section, use both upper case and lower case letters and proper punctuation in your message. Do not use all upper case type. On the Internet, all upper case typed messages represent SHOUTING at your recipient. Spell-check your message for typing errors. Basically, just use the same degree of care that you would use if you were writing a business letter or memo. Some E-mail users ignore all rules of grammar and punctuation. This is a bad idea. It tells the recipient that the sender is either unconcerned about the appearance of their messages or ignorant about the rules for language use.

Handheld devices, such as a smart phone, make it easy to check email.

Most E-mail messages are short and most people read them rather quickly and send a reply if appropriate. Long, involved messages are sometimes bypassed for later action. However, senders may send large text files as attachments to E-mail messages. Any type of file may be sent as an E-mail attachment. However, the recipient must have the appropriate software program in order to read your file. A potential problem with sending attachments is the file size. For example, *PowerPoint* presentations often make extensive use of graphics and can be so large that they consume all of the space allocated to the recipient's E-mail account, resulting in return messages such as "Message not delivered. User disk space quota exceeded." Do not send large files via E-mail unless you are certain that your recipient wants to get them, has adequate space available to store them, and has the necessary software to read them.

9.13 Transmitting E-mail

Your E-mail software will determine the exact command for sending a message after you have composed it. Once you have issued the appropriate command to send a message, you will usually see a message to confirm your sent E-mail.

Once you have confirmed the send command, the message will be sent on its way. If there is a problem, the message will be returned to the sender, usually with an error message attached. These messages may be rather long with a lot of extraneous information included. Look for the key messages that they include. The most common error messages for undelivered mail are shown below.

- **Host unkown**: This means that the host name is incorrect or is not registered on the Internet.
- **No such user:** The user name is incorrect, or no account for this user exists.
- **No response for <domain name>:** The computer system to which the message was addressed is not responding and is probably "off-line" due to technical problems.

If you get an error message, recheck your E-mail address carefully. Common mistakes include substituting the capital letter "O" for "0" (zero) and the lowercase letter "l" for the number "1," typing blank spaces within the address, omitting periods or substituting commas for them, or omitting or mistyping the @ symbol. E-mail addresses must be typed exactly or the message will not reach its destination. Since E-mail addresses are rather awkward to enter each time a message is sent, an electronic address book is provided with most E-mail programs so that a user need only click on the name of the intended recipient.

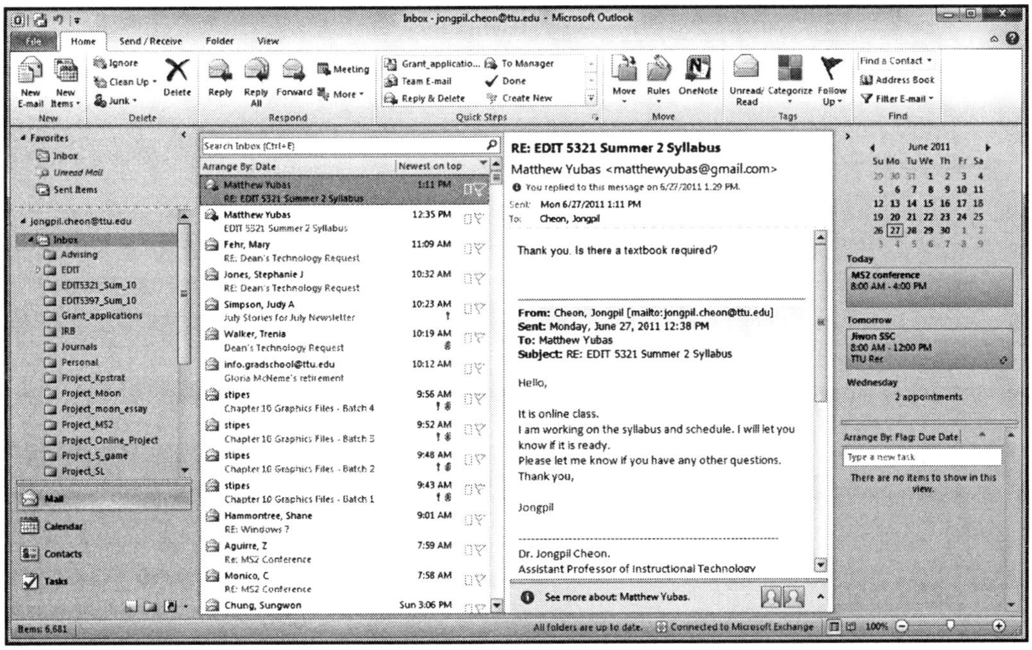

Figure 9.6: An E-mail Inbox

To read a message, you generally select it and press the Return/Enter key or double-click on its icon with the mouse button. Messages do not go away after you have read them. If you do not wish to keep the message, delete it. If you wish to answer the message, enter the "reply" command that your E-mail software supports. The reply command will automatically set the return address. If you wish to forward the message you received to someone else, enter the "forward" command; most E-mail software allows you to type a brief message to accompany forwarded mail. Most E-mail software also allows you to file mail for long-term retention. Networks usually retain E-mail (both messages sent and those received) for a limited period of time (perhaps one month) and then ask for your permission to delete them.

9.14 Choosing an Internet Service Provider

Choosing an **Internet Service Provider** (**ISP**) can be a bit confusing. Consider the following general guidelines when choosing an ISP:

- *Dialing in.* Does the ISP offer service through a local telephone number? Can you get local or toll-free access numbers when traveling?
- *Access.* Can you always get online when dialing in or are all lines frequently busy? The ISP representative is not necessarily the best person to ask! Try calling the connection number at different times of the day to see if you can get through.
- *Technical support and customer service.* Does the ISP have knowledgeable and friendly technical support and customer service staff available when you need them? Is the call toll free? Can you get technical support on-line?
- *E-mail.* What kind of E-mail services does the ISP provide? Can you access your account through another ISP if you are traveling outside your ISP's area?
- *Web pages.* Does the ISP provide for personal web pages? If so, how much space can you get and will you be charged per the amount of traffic that your page generates? Does the ISP offer on-line support for creating web pages?
- *Performance.* How fast do you get your E-mail? How long does it take for Web pages to download? How often are there network failures?
- *Price.* This is where you really have to do your homework. ISPs often have different plans with varying levels of services. Basic service is usually the least expensive, but often involves extra charges for hourly usage. For a modest additional cost, you should be able to obtain unlimited access (i.e., no charges for hourly usage). In addition, many ISPs require that monthly charges be automatically billed to your credit card.

Many newcomers to the Internet and WWW find it easier to purchase the turn-key services of an ISP such as AOL or MSN. These full-service ISPs are the most effective way to explore the types of information available on the WWW, as well as interacting with the varied communities of users. However, they typically are also more expensive than a local ISP.

9.15 Electronic Research Strategies

Online libraries and databases are now the preferred research tools. Searching through card catalogs and dusty rows of stacks for books and articles may soon go the way of the dinosaur. Online libraries contain databases of electronic materials that can be downloaded to your computer and printed or read online. Printed materials can also be located more easily through online searching. The *Magazine Index*, for example, indexes popular magazines from 1959 to the present. The **ERIC** database contains citations and abstracts of over 400,000 online documents and journal articles on all aspects of education. The Texas Education Agency (TEA) database contains information on all Texas schools including names, addresses, salaries, tax information, and curriculum materials. Many other electronic databases are available through database services such as **First Search**.

9.16 Finding Information on the Web

The World Wide Web is a vast and ever-expanding collection of websites. Finding the exact information that you want on the web can be a mind-numbing challenge. To help with the challenge, several **search engines** have been established. Descriptions of the most popular search engines are given below. All allow the use of Boolean logic to help you locate information.

Searching for information on the web is much less precise than searching in a sophisticated electronic database such as ERIC or *Magazine Index*. The designers of the WWW never envisioned the huge number of sites that the Internet has today. The HTML code that is used to construct websites does not lend itself to precise searching. Web searches on just about any topic typically result in a huge number of hits, most of which are not relevant to the searcher's intent. Typically, a user may define a fairly specific search strategy and find that it returns 20,000 or more hits. This phenomenon is not completely preventable and is not due to poor operation of the search engine or poor search techniques on the part of the user. It is a typical characteristic of Internet searches. However, expert use of good search techniques and the use of Internet search engines can help.

All Web search engines work in roughly the same way. They contain databases of information from web sites. Automated programs called robots construct these databases. Robots continually explore all the Internet links they can find, indexing the URL, title, and text into a searchable database. The search strategies used by these robots and frequency of updating affect the accuracy of the search engine database. These robot programs can be supplemented by human searches as well. Most search engine interfaces are very similar. They all use search terms and Boolean logic, and the results are usually reported in order of relevance to the search strategy. Some search engines contain several databases of different types or sources of information and let you specify which database to search. Other search engines let you specify whether search terms must appear together or be an exact phrase match.

As stated previously, searching the web is imprecise. The most common problems are:

- *Too many hits.* A hit list citing thousands of hits is hardly helpful. Try to narrow your search.
- *Not enough results.* This is the other side of the coin. If you narrow your search too much, the search engine may not find any matches at all.
- *Inaccessible links.* This is an unfortunate by-product of large databases that are not frequently updated. It is easier for robot programs to locate information than it is to find and eliminate web sites that are no longer or available or that have changed URLs. Also, some web sites have limited access.
- *Results do not match what you are looking for.* Results that do not match your search criteria are mainly caused by use of a search strategy that is too broad. Try to be as specific as possible in your search strategy.

To improve the likelihood of getting the results you want, follow these hints:

- *Know what you are looking for.* If you just want to browse or look for general information on a broad subject, use a subject index instead of a search engine.
- *Decide which search engine to use.* Most people have one or two favorites. If one search engine does not give you the results that you are looking for, try another.
- *Use the Help feature.* Use Help to phrase your search strategy. It is well worth your time.
- *Structure your search strategy carefully.* For example, to find Social Studies lesson plans, do not simply enter *lesson plans* or *social studies.* Both search terms are too broad and will return a huge number of hits. You might try *social studies lesson plans,* or better yet, look for a specific unit such as *geography lesson plans* or *Civil War lesson plans.* Also, search only the relevant categories such as K-12. This will make your search much faster and more precise.
- *Visit some of the sites.* Visit sites on your list of results for ideas on refining your search and then restructure your search as needed.
- *Use Advanced Search.* Most search engines provide an advanced search feature. It allows more precision in your search strategy.
- *Be careful.* Take care in spelling and typing search terms correctly and using Boolean operators and limiters.

Many use the Internet to access and download music, movies and other works for their enjoyment and relaxation.

9.17 Search Engines

A **Web search engine** is designed to search for information on the World Wide Web. Information may consist of web pages, images and other types of files.

Next is a brief review of some of the more popular search engines, but like all reviews of this nature, this is just a snapshot in time. New sites come on-line and improvements are made frequently. Also, you should know that there are dozens or perhaps hundreds of search engines on the WWW. Some are very specialized. To get the most current information on search engines, check out a few and find one or two that best suit your needs.

Yahoo! (www.yahoo.com) - Besides providing maps, yellow pages, E-mail service, and the ability to create personalized web pages, *Yahoo!* also provides a search engine and allows searching by categories such as Arts & Humanities, Education, Science, Regional, News and Media, and Entertainment using Boolean logic. *Yahoo!* supports basic Boolean searching with AND and OR. Limiters available include Usenet, E-mail addresses, and a person's name, and currency (the date that the web site was produced or updated). Exact phrase match searching is available. Hits are normally displayed 20 at a time, but the user can change this setting. A brief two-line description is given for each hit. *Yahoo!* is good for finding information on popular topics but might not be the best choice for more serious researchers.

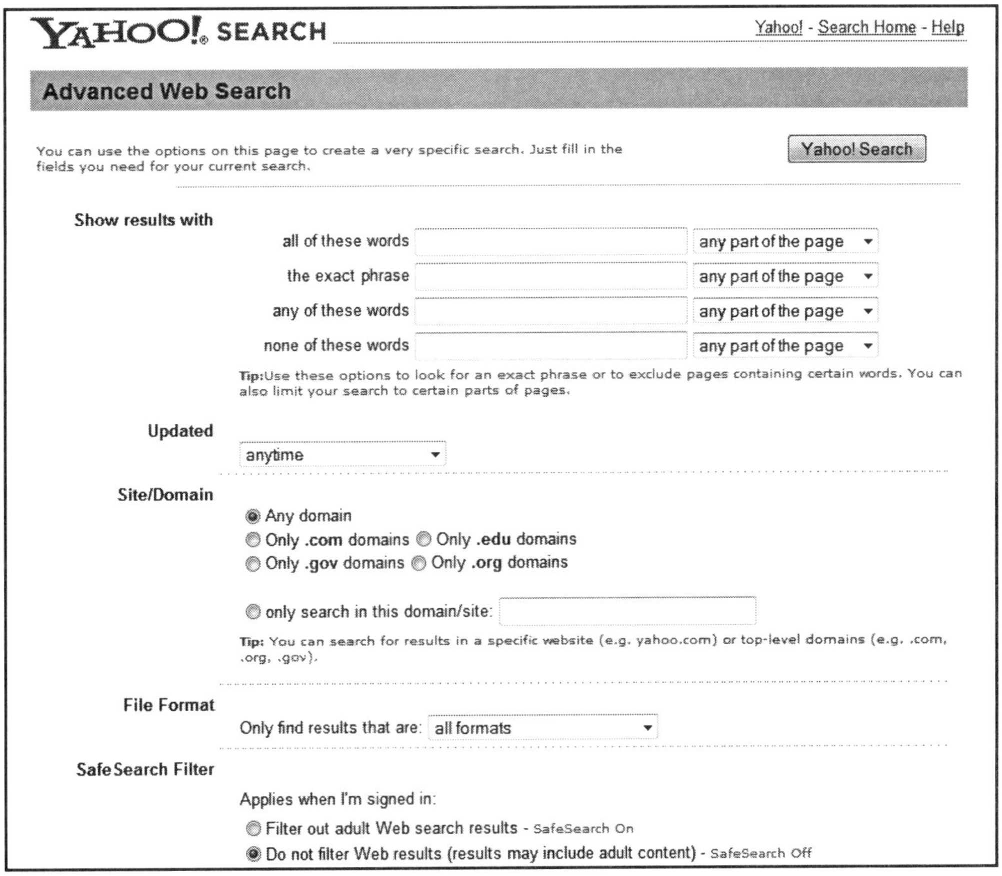

Figure 9.7: The *Yahoo!* Advanced Search Window

Google (http://www.google.com) currently provides the most popular Internet search engine. Google earns revenues from advertising related to its Internet search, web-based e-mail, online mapping, office productivity, social networking, and video sharing. As of March 31, 2010 the company had 20,621 full-time employees and was the largest American company that is not part of the Dow Jones Industrial Average.

Figure 9.8: Google Search

AltaVista (www.altavista.com) supports full Boolean searching with the operators AND, OR, and NOT. Searching can be nested using parentheses, and operators can be in lower or upper case. In both *Basic* and *Advanced Search* modes, the truncation symbol, an asterisk (*), can be used as a *wildcard* for internal or end truncation of 0-5 extra characters. An example of truncation is a search for topics that are relevant to education programs directed to elementary grades about AIDS. One keyword for the search could be *education,* but *education* might appear in the forms "educating, education, educate, educating". The wildcard keyword would be "educat*", which should return forms of the word associated with the other keywords, for example, *elementary, children, AIDS.* A minimum of three characters before the truncation symbol is required. Also, the wild card matches only lower-case characters, not upper-case letters or numbers. Limits can be created by the use of Boolean operators and field searches. For example, *Harvard* and *url: edu* will limit the search for records to sites in the .edu domain of the Internet. In the *Basic Search,* results are automatically ranked by relevance. In the *Advanced Search,* results are not sorted unless one or more terms are included in the Ranking criteria box. Location of the terms (such as in the title), proximity of multiple search terms to each other, and the frequency of the terms determine relevance. Due to the advanced features, *AltaVista* is a good search engine for the average user.

Excite (www.excite.com) - *Excite* is one of the largest search engines. *Excite's Channels* is a subject directory. Its *News* section provides

Some governments, such as those of Cuba, Iran, North Korea, Myanmar, the People's Republic of China, and Saudi Arabia, restrict what people in their countries can access on the Internet, especially political and religious content. This is accomplished through software that filters domains and content so that they may not be easily accessed or obtained without elaborate circumvention.

> The low cost and nearly instantaneous sharing of ideas, knowledge, and skills has made collaborative work dramatically easier.

important access to web versions of newspapers and magazines, with over 60,000 records. Others are known as *meta-search engines.* These are search engines that search other search engines. Examples include www.dogpile.com, www.mamma.com, and www.search.com. Probably the best feature of www.search.com is its access to very specialized search engines. For example, if you want information about employment, legal issues, grant programs, etc., you are likely to get more specific results. The reviews are relatively brief, averaging about four lines in length. Reviews are written in a popular, journalistic style. *Excite* searches can use the "+ -" syntax. However, *Excite* also supports full Boolean searching, and searching can be nested using parentheses. Boolean operators must be in upper case. In their Power Search, neither the "+ -" system nor Boolean operators can be used. Instead, functions must be chosen from the drop-down menus. Phrase searching can be designated by double quotes (" ") around a search phrase. However, *Excite* does not always process a phrase search exactly as expected. It will ignore stop words within a phrase. For example, an *Excite* search on the search term *difference principle* will also find documents that contain "difference in principle." No truncation is available. *Excite* also has an option to sort by site, but this only works for the top 40 hits. There is no option for sorting alphabetically or by date. There is an option to do a follow-up search by selecting the *More Like This* button that creates a new search looking for records similar to the one chosen. *Excite* displays 10 records at a time, except when results are sorted by site. In that case, *Excite* displays the top 40 (those with the highest relevance scores). Excite is a good choice for serious searches, but it might take more time and work to use than some other search engines.

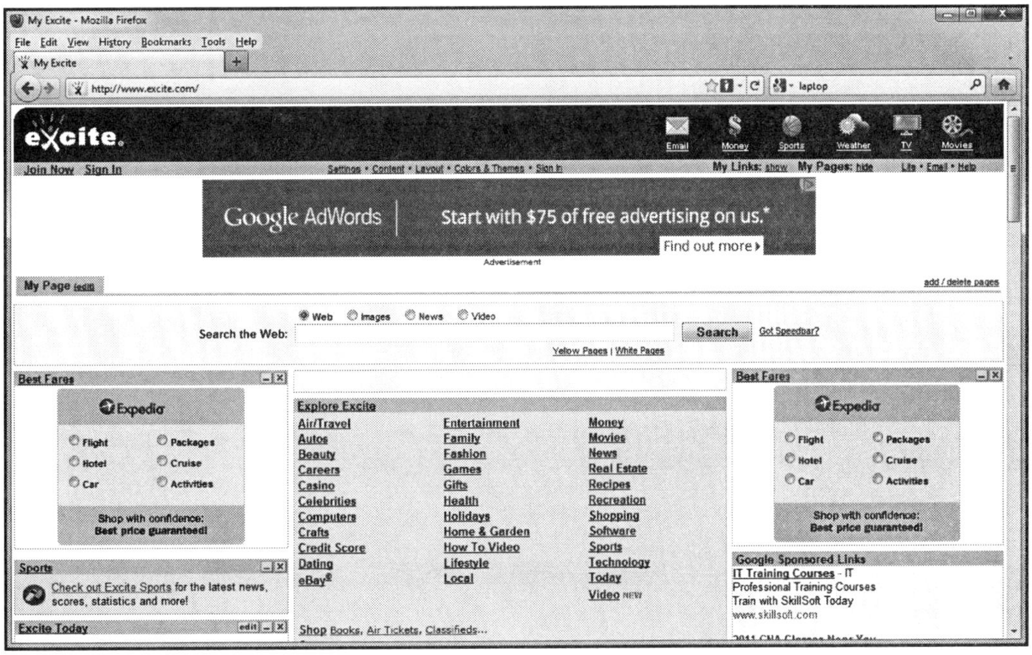

Figure 9.11: The *Excite* Search Window

Hotbot (www.hotbot.com) *Hotbot* is sponsored by *Wired* magazine and is based on the Inktomi search technology created at the University of California Berkeley. The idea of this is that computer systems should be *scalable* ,or able to grow as the need arises.

Hotbot provides an interface to create some of the most complicated searches that you can perform on the web, including limiting the search by date, document types, and even smileys. *Modify* and *Expert* buttons on the search page allow the user to refine a search strategy. *Hotbot* is a good choice for serious researchers.

9.18 Other Search Engines

Below are other search engines you might want to try:

- Lycos http://www.lycos.com
- Dogpile http://www.dogpile.com
- Webcrawler http://www.webcrawler.com

9.19 Copyright and Fair Use

Generally, copying all or a portion of a copyrighted work without the owner's permission is in violation of federal copyright laws. In addition, taking a work and altering or disguising it is also considered copyright infringement. If you take a piece of digital art and alter it, the original work and the altered work are both the property of the original owner and permission must be given to legally use the work.

Fair use is a legal provision of U.S. Copyright Law that allows partial or limited reproduction of a copyrighted work. The following guidelines should be used when applying the fair use doctrine with regard to copyrighted material:

1. Consider the purpose of the work;
2. Consider the nature of the work (i.e., the intended audience);
3. With regard to determining how much of the work to reproduce, consider: (a.) the proportion used in comparison to the whole work, and (b.) whether the portion used comprises the most important part of the work.
4. Will your use affect the potential usability/marketability of the work?

> Since the Internet is widely accessible to hundreds of millions of people in many parts of the world and can provide practically instant information on most topics, it is having a profound impact on the way in which ideas are formed and knowledge is created.

9.20 Netiquette

Nettiquette is Internet etiquette. Problems in etiquette on the Internet are similar to etiquette in face-to-face communication, but sometimes exaggerated. For example, research indicates that some people find it is easier to be brash in telephone conversations than in face-to-face conversations. This type of scenario is compounded over the Internet, where typically there is no sound to go along with the words.

Hear are some basic guidelines for e-mail etiquette:

- Addressing E-mail. With only three choices for addressing an e-mail, i.e. the 'To', 'Cc' and 'Bcc' fields, you would think addressing would be trouble free. Unfortunately, that's not the case. First, there are the users who have no idea that the 'Cc' exists. Every address is listed in the 'To' even if the e-mail is only directed to one person. In cases such as this, the receivers have no clue as to who should take action so either they all do something or they all do nothing. Secondly, there are users who feel that every single e-mail should be copied to their entire address book whether it's relevant to those receiving it or not. These are the 'cry for attention' crowd. So here's a guide on how to use the address fields:

- The addresses in the 'To' are for the people you are directly addressing.
- The addresses in the 'Cc' are for the people you are indirectly addressing. They are the FYI-ers or CYA-ers. Don't over do it here. Copy only those who need to be copied; not your entire universe of contacts.
- The addresses in the 'Bcc' are like 'Cc' except that the addresses in 'To' and 'Cc' do not know that the addresses in the 'Bcc' are included in the conversation. The 'To' and 'Cc' addresses are blind to the 'Bcc' addresses. As you can imagine, use of the 'Bcc' is somewhat unethical and therefore its use is discouraged.
- The 'Reply to All' button is just a button, but it can generate tons of unnecessary e-mails. For example, if I send a dozen people an e-mail asking if they are available at a certain time for a meeting, you should get a dozen replies and that's it. However, if each person hits the "Reply to All' button not only do I get a dozen replies, but so does everyone else for a total of 144 messages! The 'Reply to All' button should be used with care.
- Don't be a novelist. Messages should be concise and to the point. Think of it as a telephone conversation, except you are typing instead of speaking. Nobody has ever won a Pulitzer Prize for a telephone conversation nor will they win one for an e-mail message. It's also important to remember that some people receive hundreds of e-mail messages a day (yes, there are such people), so the last thing they want to see is a message from someone who thinks he/she is the next Dickens.
- Don't get caught up in grammar and punctuation, especially excessive punctuation. You'll see lots of e-mail messages where people put a dozen exclamation points at the end of a sentence for added emphasis. Exclamation points (called "bangs" in computer circles) are just another form of ending a sentence. If something is important it should be reflected in your text, not in your punctuation.
- Plain text is best in email. Using HTML to format messages so that they have fancy fonts, colors or whatever is asking for trouble. There are lots of e-mail clients (and some servers) which cannot handle messages in these formats. The message will come in as utter gibberish or in the worst case, crash the e-mail client.
- Use abbreviations sparingly. In the quest to save keystrokes, users have traded clarity for confusion. Use only abbreviations that are common to the English language, such as 'FYI' and 'BTW'. Beyond that, you run the risk of confusing your recipient.

The following is a list of some of the more common guidelines associated with netiquette on chats and bulletin boards.

Netiquette is a catch-all term for the conventions of politeness recognized on message boards, mailing lists, and email.

- The most important rule of netiquette is, "Think before you post". If what you intend to post will not make a positive contribution to a group and be of interest to several readers, do not post it! Personal messages to one or two individuals should be posted to private email, not to a group.
- Quoting should be interspersed, with your response following the relevant quoted material. The result should read like a conversation, with quotes indented to aid in skimming. A common mistake is to put all new text above the quoted material, without trimming any irrelevant text. This results in a message that is much harder to follow and much less clear context.
- Re-read and edit your posting carefully before you post. Check the spelling, grammar, and capitalization. Typing in all capital letters usually denotes screaming or yelling. Keep your lines to fewer than 70 characters.
- When posting humorous or sarcastic comments, it is conventional to append an emoticon, but do not overuse them.
- Try to post in plain text, not HTML. Most readers use a text-only utility, so any HTML will be lost, anyway.
- Before asking a question, read the messages already in the group and read the group's *Frequently Asked Questions* if it has one.
- Be proud of your postings, but do not post just to see your name in pixels. Remember: your future employer may be reading.

There is also a netiquette rule for how to deal with someone who has violated one of the rules of netiquette:

- If you believe someone has violated netiquette, send him or her a message by *private e-mail*; do not post a follow-up to the offending post. Be polite. The author may not have realized his or her mistake, may be a beginner, or may not even have been responsible for the "crime"—his or her account may have been used by someone else, or the address may have been forged. Furthermore, a person who breaks netiquette over and over may be doing it intentionally to disrupt the group in which case public flaming over the violation would amount to what is termed *feeding the troll.*

9.21 Security on the Internet

As discussed previously, when you send or request information on the Internet, it travels in **packets** that might be routed through several computers before it reaches its final destination. This can pose a security problem. A computer hacker could get access

to credit card and personal information you submit when making a purchase from an unsecured site. Secure sites use security protocols that prevent unauthorized people from seeing data that is being sent to or from these sites. To check a site's security status, look in the URL address window. If you see "**https**," the site is secure. The Federal Trade Commission is increasing its surveillance of Internet fraud as more users conduct on-line commerce. You can report Internet Fraud to the National Consumers League: http://www.fraud.org/ifw.htm.

Security certificates are statements that guarantee the identity of the organization or the security of the web site. Personal certificates are a guarantee that you are who you say you are, and are used when you send personal information over the Internet to a web site that requires a certificate to verify your identity. A web site certificate states that the web site is secure and genuine and ensures that no other web site can assume the identity of the original secure site. Many people have stated misgivings about giving out credit card information over the Internet. However, giving your credit card to a waiter in a restaurant is probably a greater security risk than charging items on-line provided that you use a *secure* web site. In addition, some sites work with your browser to encrypt (encode) your transaction information so that it cannot be read if it is intercepted. On-line banks and investment services use encryption to protect information in transactions. There are generally two levels of encryption. Servers and web browsers use 40-bit or 128-bit encryption. Forty-bit encryption provides billions of possible "keys" to unlock the code for a unique transmission. One hundred twenty-eight-bit encryption provides 300 billion trillion times as many possible keys as 40-bit encryption.

A computer virus is a computer program that can copy itself and infect a computer without permission or knowledge of the owner. While viruses can be intentionally destructive, for example, by destroying data, many other viruses are fairly benign or merely annoying.

9.22 Viruses

In general it is a good idea not to download files from sources that you cannot be sure are safe. Viruses can be attached to executable files such as special-action web files, video files, and E-mail attachments. Several viruses hidden in e-mail have spread globally during the past few years causing millions of dollars loss to businesses. An example was the e-mail attachment entitled "I love you". When opened, the virus would copy itself and send itself to everyone in your E-mail address book. The temptation to open an attachment titled "I love you" from the boss (or someone else) was apparently too great for many people. Good safeguards against viruses are anti-virus programs that scan your computer for viruses, inoculate against known viruses, and sometimes repair damage done by a virus. The following are examples of commercially available anti-virus programs:

Symantec Anti-virus	www.symantec.com
Norton Anti-virus	www.symantec.com/nav
McAfee Virus Scan	www.nai.com

9.23 Cookies

Cookies are small amounts of information that are stored on your computer by a Web site, so that your Web browser returns the information back to the site if you ever visit it again. Cookies are usually harmless; however, they can be used to create a profile of your interests based on the sites you visit in order to customize advertisements to match your interests. The latest commercially available web browsers generally provide an alert before cookies are accepted. This might require that you configure your browser in a particular way. In addition, it is possible to manually delete cookies from your hard drive.

9.24 Spamming

Spam is unsolicited mail on the Internet. Advertisers often send it like bulk mail. Spam is a problem for E-mail account holders just as *junk mail* is a problem in the snail mail world. Span is often fraudlant. Much of it is sent from locations out of the country and thus out of the jurisdiction of U.S. law enforcement. Spam often seeks to defraud the gullible by stealing personal information, false appeals for charitible contributions, or false advertising. Be wary of any email if you are not absolutely sure of the source.

9.25 Cyberstalking

The "virtual community", like any other community, has both good and bad elements. As the use of technology increases, so does its abuse. **Cyberstalking** typically occurs in chat rooms and via E-mail. The lack of face-to-face communication often encourages people to act when they would not otherwise do so. Enforcement of current stalking laws is complicated on the Internet due to jurisdictional issues. For example, a person in Germany who stalks a person in the United States creates a legal jurisdictional issue in terms of extradition treaties and international law. Another problem is identifying cyberstalkers who often use someone else's E-mail account to send messages to their victims. Victims of cyberstalking are encouraged to report incidents to their system administrator. In addition, most of the commercial providers have "kill files" or "Bozo filters", which allow a user to block messages from a particular sender. All incoming messages from the sender's name and address are automatically deleted. Some providers allow a subscriber to change their E-mail address, which would be similar to changing a phone number to avoid obscene calls.

Spamming is unsolicited commercial e-mail. Because of the very low cost of sending e-mail, spammers can send hundreds of millions of e-mail messages each day over an inexpensive Internet connection. Hundreds of active spammers sending this volume of mail results in information overload for many computer users who receive voluminous unsolicited email each day.

The *Children's Online Privacy Protection Act* (COPPA) became effective April 21, 2000. It applies to the online collection of personal information from children under 13 years of age. The new rules spell out what a web site operator must include in a privacy policy, when and how to seek verifiable consent from a parent, and what responsibilities an operator has to protect children's privacy and safety online. The Federal Trade Commission is the enforcement authority for COPPA.

9.26 Protection from Offensive Material

Schools and parents can help to remove temptation and opportunity for inappropriate Internet access and also protect children from cyberstalkers through the use of **blocking** or **filtering software**. Filtering software works on several levels. Generally, they include a list of web sites that have been deemed objectionable. Many of these programs also allow users to screen all Internet materials for certain key words such as SEX, NUDE, SATAN WORSHIP. Many programs also allow users to specify which type of material that they wish to block by categories such as Sex, Nudity, Language, or Violence. The filtering process may be set and changed only by use of a password. When young users attempt to access an objectionable site, the access is denied.

Filtering can be installed on the server side or the user side. If filtering is done by the ISP, nothing needs to be done by the user after initial subscription and set up of the software. The ISP updates its database of objectionable sites regularly. Of course, subscription to the ISP involves a monthly fee, and specific filtering options are controlled by the ISP, not individual users. ISPs can provide subscribers the option of allowing individual subscribers the option to block specific web sites by anyone using their account. A variation on this approach is to allow access only to specified sites, effectively blocking any sites that are not on the approved list. This system is the most severe form of web censorship available.

America On-Line (AOL) offers a blocking feature in their proprietary interface that allows users to block access to chat rooms that may contain objectionable material and discussion groups that are named with keywords you might wish to keep from a child. There is no additional cost for this service, and like other control features of AOL, may be turned on and off only with a password. The other most popular ISPs, *The Microsoft Network (MSN)*, *CompuServe*, and *Prodigy* also have filtering options available. The effectiveness of these systems is not completely reliable as demonstrated by the following article excerpt:

Porn Sneaks Past Search Filters

By Paul Festa

Staff Writer, CNET News.com

July 2, 2008, 4:00 p.m. PT

Search companies are increasingly turning to censorware to court G-rated customers such as corporations, schools, and parents, but they're still showing too much skin.

The shortcomings of porn filters were on display last week when Google launched a version of a search engine for images with an optional filter for what it terms "inappropriate adult content. Even with the filter turned on, Google is serving a healthy dose of pornographic images, often for keywords with primarily nonsexual meanings.

If a filtering program is added to your browser, the user purchases the program and there are no continuing expenses. This approach provides more flexibility in setting the filtering options and leaves changes and updates up to the user. A brief review of some of the most popular filtering programs follows.

9.27 Browser-Based Filtering Software

Net Nanny. This program screens Web sites, news groups, and incoming and outgoing text messages for certain phrases, such as sexual phrases or requests for personal information. If objectionable material is found, the computer shuts down. The program also keeps a log of all activity for later review. Information on *Net Nanny* is available on the World Wide Web at www.netnanny.com.

CyberSitter. This program, by Solid Oak Software, blocks access or alerts you when a user attempts to access adult-oriented Web pages, FTP sites, and news groups. In addition, you can program *CyberSitter* to alert you when users access specific files, programs, or graphic images. For information on *CyberSitter*, go to www.cybersitter.com.

Cyber Patrol. This program blocks access to major Internet resources using a subscription database that groups sites into categories, such as nudity, violence, profanity, racist, ethnic, etc. It also lets you restrict Internet access to certain times of day or to a set number of hours per day or per week. For information from the Web, go to www.cyberpatrol.com.

9.28 Selecting Filtering Software

The first decision concerning filtering is deciding whether you need it. If unrestricted free access to information is desired, then it is likely that you will decide not to use filtering at all. Typically, parents and school systems usually desire to restrict Internet access for children. In some cases, blocking access to many types of objectionable material is a legal or regulatory requirement. This requirement does not exist for most institutions of higher education or training environments. However, the governing body or management may wish to restrict access in order to reduce the time wasted by employees or students on frivolous Web activities, to limit their own liability in "worst-case scenarios," or to protect their users from objectionable material. If a decision is made to purchase and install filtering software, consider these general features in making a decision concerning which one best suits your needs:

- Can standard browsers and other Internet applications be used in combination with the filtering software or is specially modified or proprietary software required?
- Exactly what type of Internet material is blocked? Does it prevent students from giving out last names, phone numbers, addresses, and passwords? Does it filter incoming text, outgoing text, a list of web sites, downloads, etc? Is the list modifiable by the user?
- What criteria were used by the software provider to determine what constitutes objectionable material? Does it block the material that you wish to block and provide free access to other material?
- What is the cost to receive updates? Are updates free or is there a fee?
- Does the software provide additional management features such as the ability to set up profiles for different users, tracking the sites that have been visited, limiting the amount of time that can be spent on the Internet, or setting the filtering to certain times of the day?
- Does access control apply to all Internet applications (e.g. chat rooms, email, downloads) or just to the web?
- What is the cost of the software license to your site?
- How often is the objectionable website's database updated? New websites are added every day and you will want your database to remain current.
- How much direct control over the information in the database does the software provide and how difficult is it to make changes? Most filtering software is modifiable, but exactly which options are supported and how easy is it to use?

The first step in selecting specific software is to decide exactly what features are desired in the product to best fit your situation. Then, you can review specific software titles to locate the one that best suits your needs.

9.29 Privacy on the Internet

The Internet has seriously eroded our privacy. In general, anything you do on the Internet can potentially be monitored. You are probably listed in the Internet *White Pages* or the *InfoSpace* Directory. With this information, anyone can find your location with *MapQuest* or *Yahoo Maps*.

Also keep in mind that system administrators and Internet postmasters at your ISP have the ability and right to monitor your E-mail. Law enforcement authorities can monitor your e-mail under certain circumstances, and courts can require you to produce E-mail in court cases. Therefore, do not say anything in E-mail that you would not say in public.

Those concerned about Internet privacy often cite a number of privacy risks—events that can compromise privacy—which one may encounter through Internet use. Given the complexity of Internet privacy, many people do not understand the real risks and perceive risks that do not really exist. Therefore this section covers not only "real" privacy risks but also perceived risks.

Cookies. Cookies have become perhaps the most widely-recognized privacy risk. Although HTML-writers most commonly use cookies for legitimate purposes, cases of abuse can and do occur. A HTTP cookie consists of a piece of information stored on a user's computer by a visited site. Computer systems do not generally make the user aware of the storing of a cookie. The original developers of cookies intended that only the website that originally sent them would be able to retrieve them, therefore giving back only data already possessed by the website. However, in actual practice programmers can circumvent this intended restriction. Possible consequences include:

- the possible placing of a personally identifiable tag in a web browser to facilitate web profiling or,
- possible use in some circumstances of cross-site scripting techniques to steal information from a user's cookies.

Many users choose to disable cookies in their web browsers. This eliminates the potential privacy risks, but may limit or prevent the functionality of many websites. All web browsers have the ability to disable cookies. As an alternative, users may frequently delete any stored cookies manually. Some browsers have an option to have the system clear cookies automatically whenever the user closes the browser. A software program called *Secrets Guard* offers users the ability to store sensitive *Internet Explorer* data in an encrypted and password-protected file.

Browsing profiles. The process of **profiling** (also known as tracking) assembles and analyses patterns of Internet activity. Capturing data about people's web browsing helps companies gain information that they can use in marketing. Some web-oriented marketing-research organizations may use profiling legitimately, for example: in order to construct profiles of 'typical Internet users'. Such profiles, which describe average trends of large groups of Internet users rather than of actual individuals, can then prove useful for market analysis. Though the aggregate data does not constitute a privacy violation, some people believe that the initial profiling does. Profiling becomes a more contentious privacy issue, on the other hand, when the profile of an individual is associated with personally-identifiable information of the individual. This can result in unwanted emails or junk mail or fraudulent scams targeted to users based on their profile. Governments and organizations may also set up **honeypot websites**, featuring controversial topics, for the purpose of attracting and tracking unwary people. This constitutes another potential privacy danger for individuals.

Much of spam is sent to invalid e-mail addresses. ISPs have attempted to recover the cost of spam through lawsuits against spammers, although they have been mostly unsuccessful in collecting damages despite winning in court.

IP addresses. Every device on the Internet (including each online computer) has an **IP address**, which is an identifying numeric code used to route data. The ISP through which the device connects may assign this address semi-permanently (for example, for the duration of the lifetime of an account) or temporarily. Many dial up connections, get assigned new IP addresses each time they connect. Every piece of data moving through the Internet gets tagged with the IP addresses of its source and of its intended destination. The proper working of the Internet depends on such routing information. Any direct connection between two devices on the Internet (such as when a personal computer reads a website) reveals both IP addresses to both parties. An IP address sometimes becomes personally identifiable data and therefore a privacy concern. An IP address identifies its user's ISP, and often identifies its user's nation, region/province/state, and sometimes even city. The amount of information deducible from an IP address depends on the ISP's policies. Any web site can track the movements of users through its pages by their IP addresses.

ISPs. Consumers obtain Internet access through an Internet Service Provider. All Internet data to and from the consumer must pass through the consumer's ISP. Any ISP can observe anything and everything about the consumer's (unencrypted) Internet activities. However, ISPs presumably do not do this (or at least not fully) due to legal, ethical, business, and technical considerations. ISPs do, however, collect at least some information about the consumers using their services. A common belief exists that most ISPs collect more information than they need to provide service, such as aggregate browsing habits or even personally-identifiable URL histories. What information an ISP collects, what it does with that information, and whether it informs its consumers, can pose significant privacy issues. Beyond usages of collected information typical of third parties, ISPs sometimes state that they will make their information available to government authorities upon request. Often, such a request need not involve a warrant.

Data Logging. Many programs and operating systems are set up to perform data logging of usage. This may include recording times when the computer is in use, or which web sites are visited. If a third party, such as your boss, has sufficient access to your computer, legitimately or not, this may be used to lessen the user's privacy. This could be avoided by disabling logging, or clearing logs regularly.

9.30 Conclusion

The Internet can be an excellent resource of information if you possess the correct tools and the knowledge to use it. Unfortunately, the World Wide Web is a community and, like any other community, it has dangers and undesirable elements. It is hoped that this module has enhanced your understanding of the responsibilities and possible risks associated with using the Internet and the World Wide Web.

Assignment 3: Internet Questionnaire

1. Telecommunications refers to____
   ____.

2. Data communications is____
   ____.

3. An example of a technology that uses analog technology is_________________.

4. A modem is used to____
   ____.

5. An example of a LAN is____.

6. An example of a WAN is _______________ ________________________.

7. Hypertext is used to__________________________ ____________________
   ____ __________________.

8. Commercial companies on the Web would probably the______ domain in their web address.

9. E-mail messages that lack correct capitalization, punctu nd grammar indicate____ __________.

10. Netiquette is___________________________________ __________
    ____ ________.

11. A web browser is used to____________________________ _______
    ____ ______.

12. A web editor is used to_______________________________ ______
    ____ ______.

13. Boolean logic uses these 3 operators: __________ , __________ , ______.

Use this page if you need additional space for your answers.

MODULE 10

Productivity Software

Productivity Software

Productivity is about what you can do in a limited amount of time. You have probably discovered that there is a shortage of time to do all of the things that we need to do or want to do. The same scarcity of time is true for the workplace. Managers want more productivity in the same amount of time and more efficient use of the time available. **Productivity or "tool" software** is designed to help us increase our personal productivity. Productivity software can save us time and improve the quality of our work.

Module Objectives

When you have completed this module, you should be able to:

- identify what tool software is and state examples;
- state some practical uses for tool software;
- identify some of the features of quality tool software; and
- use one or more tool software programs.

Materials Needed to Complete this Module

- This book
- *Microsoft Word*
- Productivity software package of your choice

How to Proceed

1. Read this module.
2. Review the *Key Terms* located near the end of this module.
3. Complete the *Module 10 review Questions.*
4. Complete the Module *Application Assignments* to turn in to your instructor.
5. Take the Module 10 Test.

Productivity Software

Productivity or tool software is designed to perform a specific task. There are countless examples of productivity software, and it is beyond the scope of this book to reference all of them. However, several of the more popular and useful types of productivity software are described in this module. Later in the module, you will be given the opportunity to use some of these productivity tools.

Figure 10.1: Working People with Productivity Software

10.1 Types of Productivity Software

Word processors, electronic spreadsheets, and database management programs are all types of productivity software that you have learned about in previous modules. There are many types of productivity software, and the following is a list of the most common types:

Word Processors. Whether answering thought-provoking questions, taking tests, making notes, or composing papers, writing is a universal task. Word processing software provides an efficient way of writing. It is a more flexible tool than the pen or the typewriter, and a document can be adapted and modified over and over. Computers also have the advantage of being able to store letters, tests, journals, and books, that is, any type of written document that might be beneficial for future use.

Electronic Spreadsheets. In an earlier module you learned that electronic spreadsheets are used to create an environment for the collection and manipulation of numerical data. Once the data are recorded, the user can take advantage of built-in features of the software to make critical comparisons based on the information known.

Database Software. A database is simply an organized collection of information. An address book, a telephone book, and a catalog are examples of databases. Before computers became widely used, databases were often stored in filing cabinets, but now most of them are computerized and stored on disks for easy access and modification.

Graphics Software. A class studying art or electronic media could use graphics software to create many versions of an artistic image. Small changes in color or surface texture can be easily accomplished and compared for different effects. In this way, an artist or designer could experiment with many ideas easily, and then quickly decide which is the most desirable. You can also use a scanner to scan pictures and illustrations that can then be stored in your computer for future use with graphics applications. Graphics software is one of the fastest growing segments of the software market. Magazine layouts, advertisements, commercial designs, web graphics, and banners can be created with graphic software.

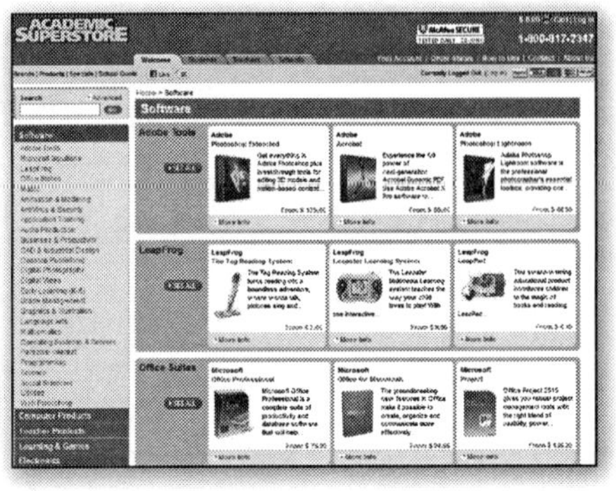

Online Software Store

Presentation Software. This type of software application, also known as presentation graphics, uses a sequence of words, pictures, video, and sound to tell a story or make a presentation to support a speech or report. Presentation software is easy to learn and often includes pre-formatted graphics, video and sound clips. Examples of presentation software include *Microsoft PowerPoint* and *Apple Keynote.*

Desktop Publishing. Desktop publishing software is useful for producing newsletters, announcements, magazines and books, or print products that require a combination of graphics and text. Desktop publishing software is also useful for producing large books that have a large number of tables, charts, graphics, and columns. This book was produced using the desktop publishing program *Adobe InDesign.*

Communications Software. Communications software is designed to help you communicate on-line. Information is a valuable commodity in the information age. Communication packages are used to send and receive graphics and artwork via FTP and E-mail. Communications software is important for delivering graphics to a Web server, as well as displaying the Web page when accessed by the user.

Authoring Software. Authoring software is designed for people who want to create custom software. It is used to create **computer-assisted instruction (CAI)** applications, multimedia applications, and Web-based applications. Some examples of authoring software are products such as *Adobe Flash, Articulate, and Lectora.* Each of these software packages can be used to present information combining many forms of media such as text, graphics, sound, and video into one cohesive package.

Personal Information Managers (PIMs). This kind of software is similar to a paper-based planner that contains your schedule, address book, and business cards. PIMs let you manage your schedule, address book, notes, and E-mail all in one package. You can also convert the information you store in a PIM to a more portable personal digital assistant (PDA) or smartphone. Commercially available PIMs are *Microsoft Outlook, Palm Desktop, and Chandler.*

10.2 Examples of Productivity Software

The purpose of this section is to give you an overview of some representative productivity software programs. Computer software is often designed for only one type of computer, such as a PC or *Macintosh* computer. However, it is becoming common for software companies to produce programs in versions compatible with many types of computers.

Wikipedia is the most popular web-based encyclopedia available today. It is a free, collaborative encyclopedia project supported by the non-profit Wikimedia Foundation. Its articles are not as long and thorough as a set of shelf encyclopedias, but it does provide plenty of sounds, pictures, and movies. Of course, it features hypertext, so you can click on words to be taken to related articles.

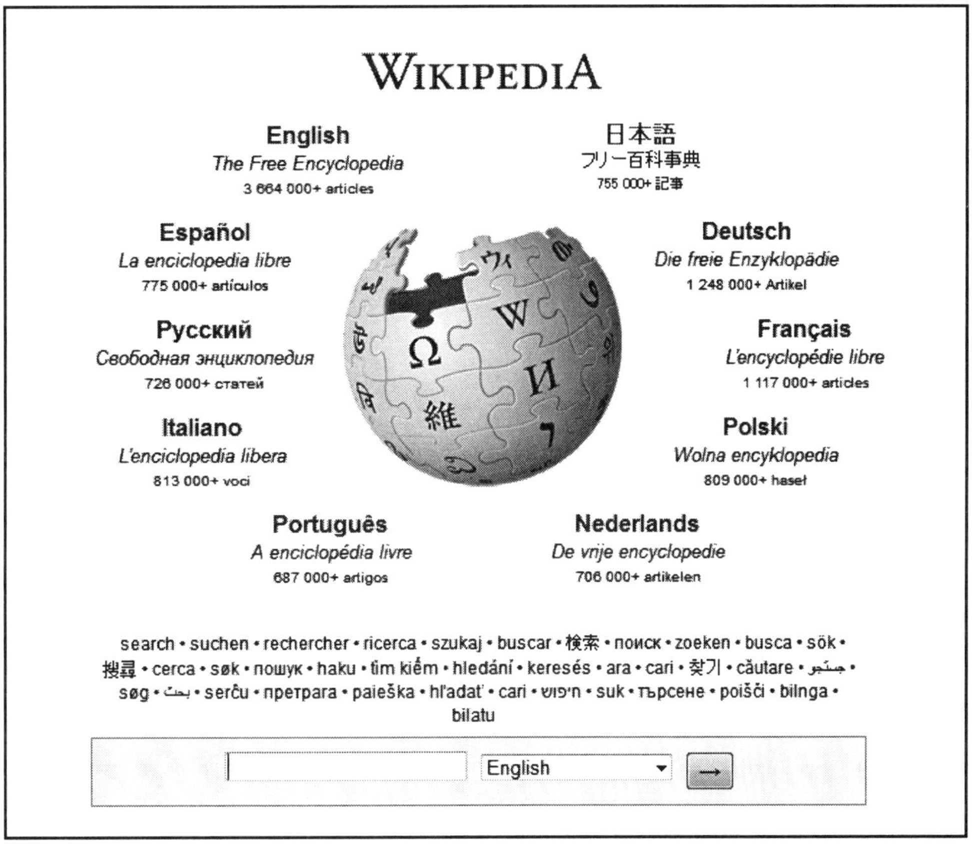

Figure 10.2: Wikipedia

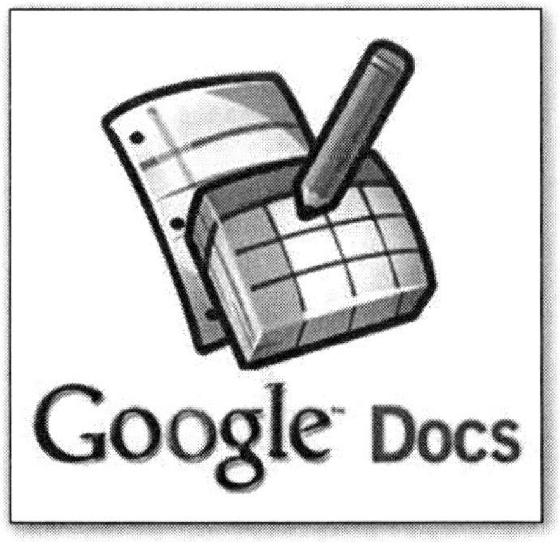

Google Docs is a simple online wordprocessing, spreadsheet and presentation tool that allows you to create, edit, and share documents in real time. You can create documents from scratch or upload existing documents. There is no software to download and all of your documents are available online from any computer with an Internet connection. One of the advantages of Google docs is the ability to collaborate with colleagues on the creation of documents in real time. You can access Google docs for free by signing up for a Google Account at <www.google.com/accounts>.

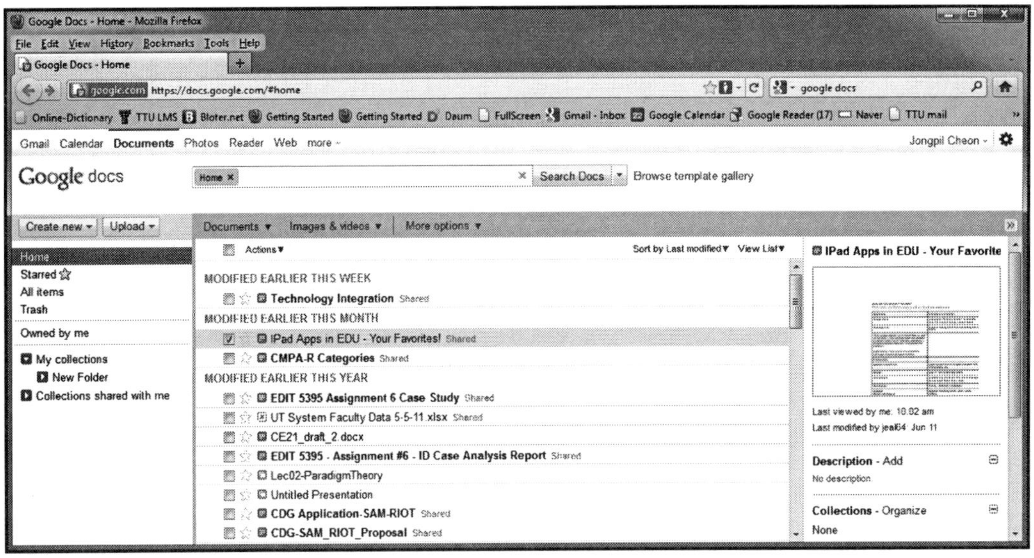

Figure 10.3: Google Docs Page

Google Calendar is a free time-management web application offered by Google. To use the software you must have a Google account. The interface is similar to other desktop calendar applications such as Microsoft Outlook, however, the interface enables users to drag-and-drop events from one date to another without reloading the page. Google Calendar uses Google Sync to synchronize the calendar with several other devices (e.g., smart phone, PC) allowing you to access your calendar from multiple devices while you're out of the office or traveling. You can also share your calendar with others and set privileges to enable them to just view or to edit your calendar. Google calendar is also integrated with Gmail (Google's webmail service) so that when certain key words (such as meeting) are contained within an email message an "add to calendar" button is automatically displayed.

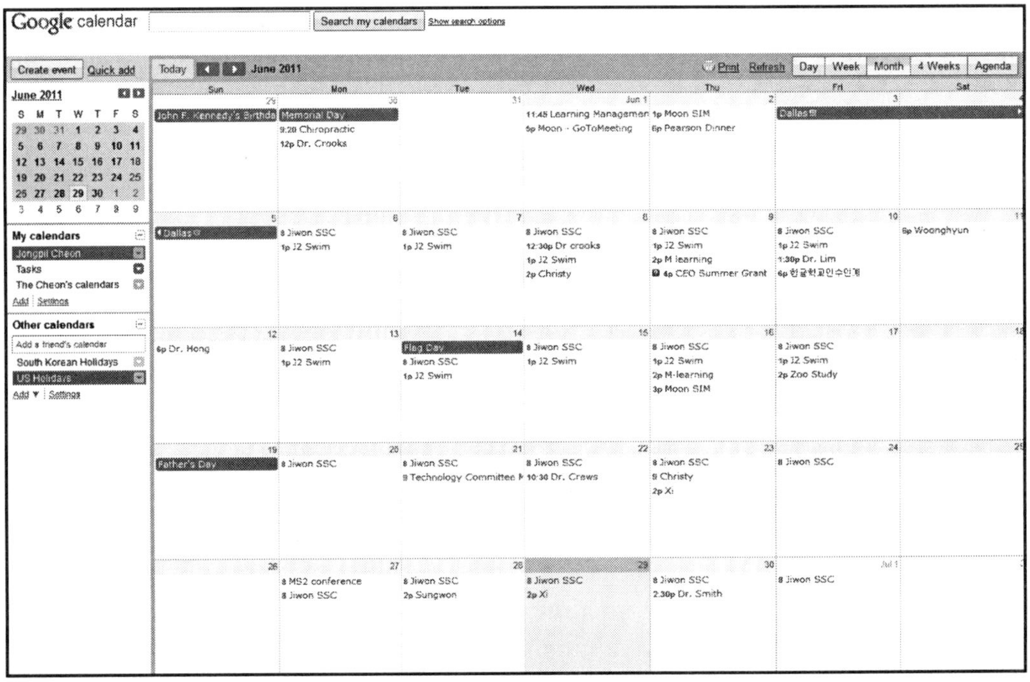

Figure 10.4: Google Calendar

Google Picasa is a free software program that enables you to view, organize, share, and edit digital photos. Picasa uses tags and facial recognition to organize photos. You can also search for photos by filename, captions, tages, and folder names. Picasa also has basic editing features that enable color enhancement, red eye reduction, and cropping. Picasa also supports printing, image timelines, and slide shows. A particularly innovative feature offered by Picasa is geotagging which adds geographical information (i.e., latitude and longitude coordinates) to digital photographs so that the location of pictures can be determined.

Figure 10.5: Google Picasa

SurveyMonkey is a software system for building and administering surveys. It is ideal for individuals, educational institutions, and organizations that need to quickly create and conduct surveys over the Web. It provides point-and-click features that make collecting and reviewing results quick and easy. A spell checker is built in, and the software is simple to learn and use. Users can export data to *Excel*, *SPSS*, and other formats, and publish formal reports via *PDF*. Perhaps the most useful feature of this program is the ability to create Web forms. You can receive answers via e-mail or record them to download later. Anyone who needs to conduct surveys, especially academic and business users, can benefit from this tool.

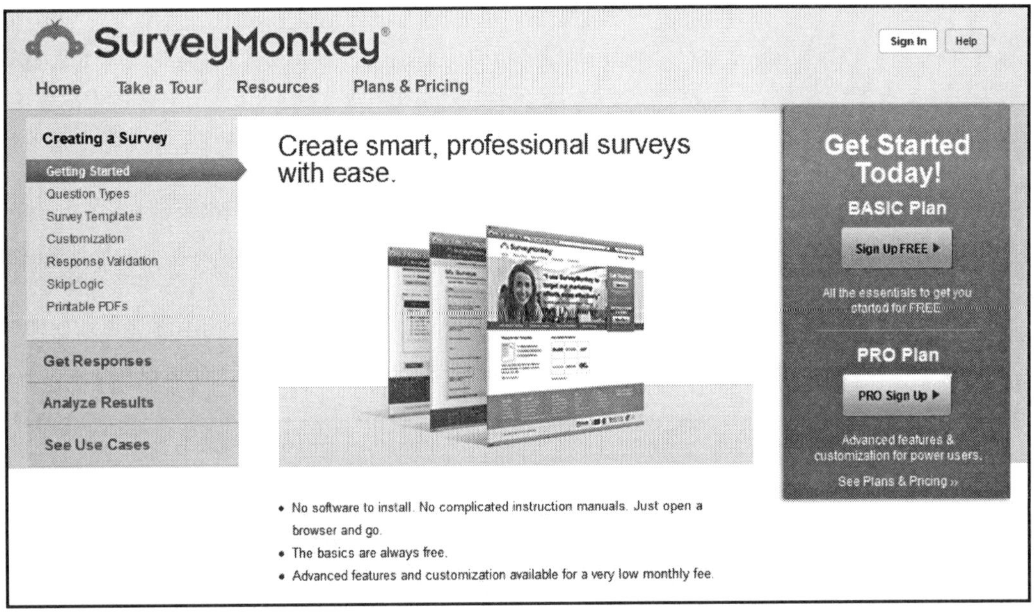

Figure 10.6: Survey Monkey

Skype is a software program, acquired my Microsoft in 2011, that allows users to make voice calls over the Internet. Skpye to Skype calls are free, but calls to land lines and mobile phones require a small fee. Skpye also enables instant messaging, file transfer, and video conferencing. Because Skype is partially free it is illegal in some countries. In addition, some network administrators have banned Skype on corporate, government, and other networks because of concerns related to inappropriate usage of resources, bandwidth, and security.

Figure 10.7: Skype

exPressit is software that can be used to design, create, and print your own custom labels for disks (e.g., DVD), tapes (VHS), and other devices (e.g., media storage cases and iPods). The software's Label Wizard feature contains several templates that make label creation easy. The software also includes a print calibration tool that assists in the print positioning of the tool.

Figure 10.8: exPressit

The Apple ***App Store*** is an application distribution platform developed for iOS (Apple's mobile operating system). The App Store enables users to browse, search, and download applications from the iTunes Store. Many quality applications can be downloaded for a minimal free, and many are free of charge. Applications can be downloaded directly into the target device (e.g., iPhone) or to a PC or Mac through the iTunes store. As of June 6, 2011, there were over 425,000 apps officially available in the App Store. As of January 19, 2011 there were almost 10 billion apps downloaded from the App Store.

Figure 10.9: Apple App Store in iTuens

The ***Android Market*** is an application distribution platform developed by Google (similar in function to the Apple App Store) for devices running their Android operating system (e.g., smart phones, tablets). An app called "Market" is preinstalled on most Android devices that enables uses to browse, search, and download android apps developed by third-party developers. In May 2011, Google announced that the Android market reached the 200,000 app mark.

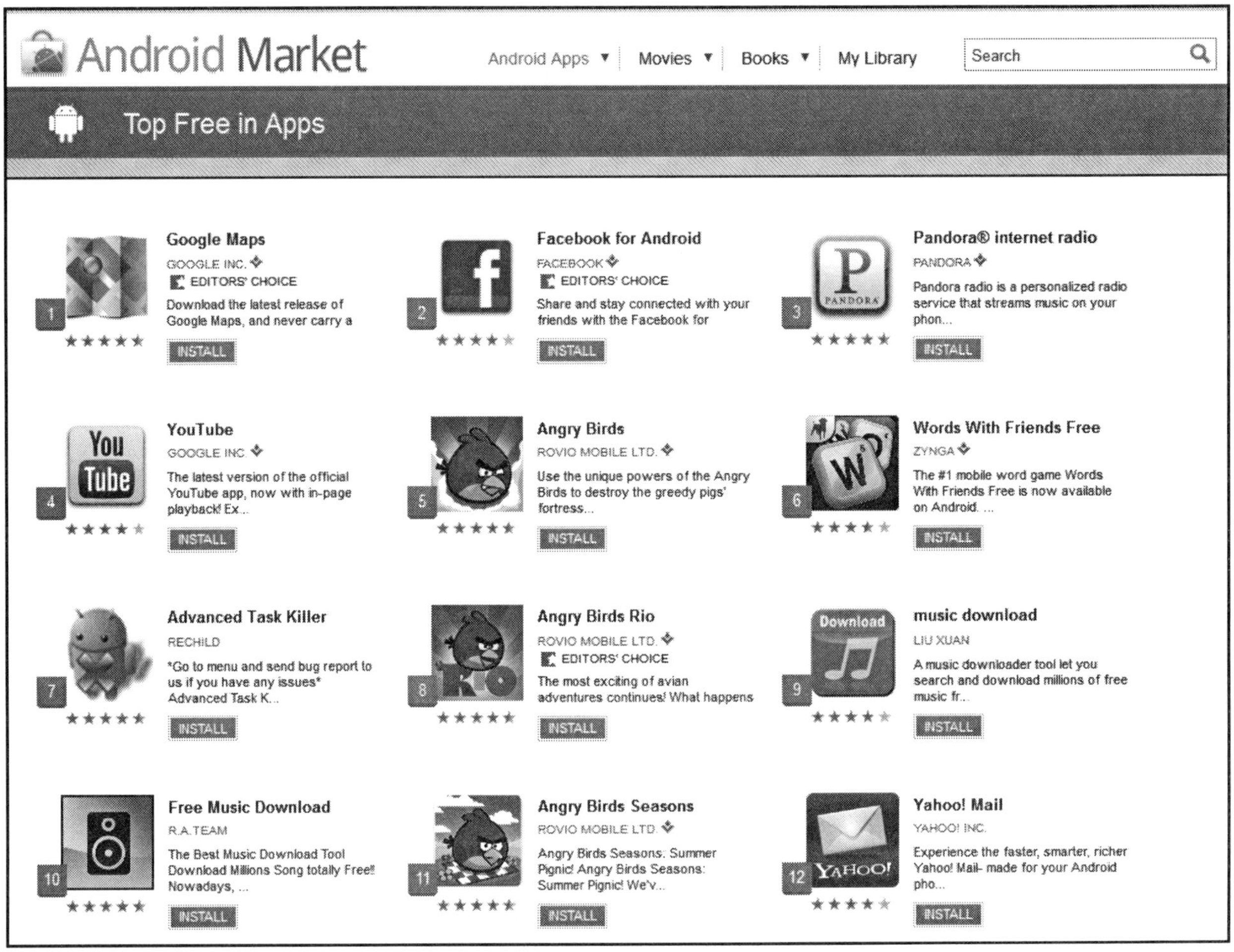

Figure 10.10: Android Market

10.3 Getting Help When Using Productivity Software

Productivity software can be purchased from a variety of locations. Most programs can be downloaded on the Internet. **Download.com** is a good source for many programs. Software is also sold by **Amazon.com.** The publisher of the software will also sell directly to the public. If you need a source for a program, simply type the full name of the program or a general category of software into the search box of your web browser.

Booklets or manuals are commonly published to explain how to use software programs. Such booklets or manuals are called **user guides**. Sometimes the booklets or manuals in the package are short and simple to understand. In other cases, manuals can be extensive and detailed.

Many programs today do not use printed user guides, but instead provide documentation and user assistance from within the actual program. Most current software allows the user to access a *help menu*, and then perform a word search to quickly locate needed information. The information can be read from the computer screen or printed.

The use of on-line tutorials that incorporate graphics, animation, and sound can also serve as an excellent source for information and guidance.

> Shareware has also been known as "try before you buy". A shareware program is accompanied by a request for payment, and the software's distribution license often requires such a payment.

10.4 Shareware

Sometimes individuals and small companies create programs for their own use and are willing to share their work for a small fee. This type of software is frequently distributed by a method called **shareware.** It is called shareware because the author allows individuals to download or copy the program free of charge. However, if the user finds the program useful, the user is asked to send the author a small fee. Programs are shared in this way. The author relies on the integrity of users to compensate him or her. Shareware is copyrighted, but payment is voluntary, and sharing the program is legal and convenient. **Shareware.com** is a good source of shareware. Their Web site lists shareware by the following categories: screen savers, games, antivirus programs, arcade games, fax, and zip programs.

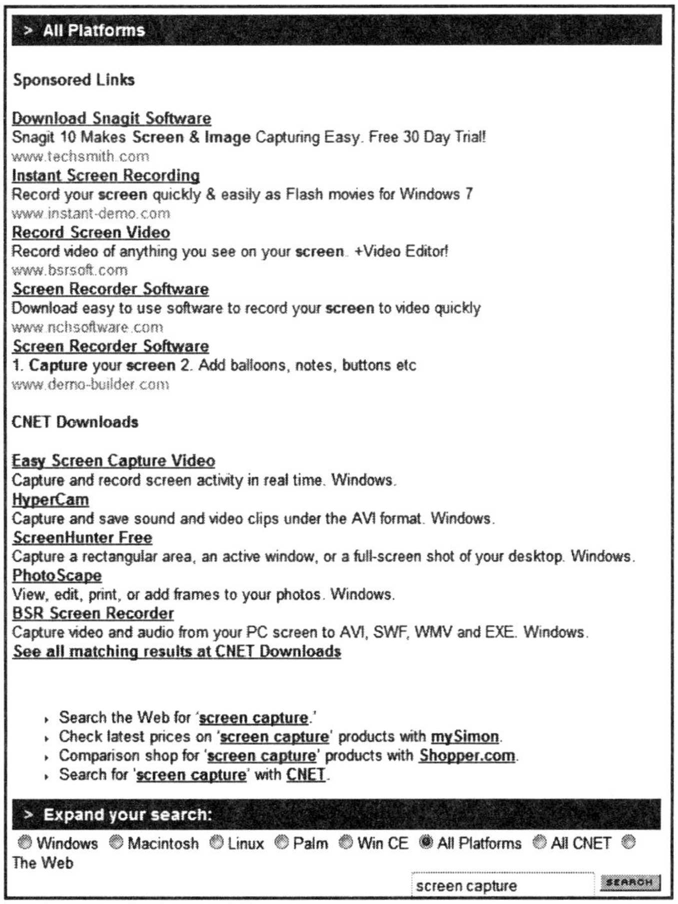

Figure 10.11: A Listing of Screen Capture Software from shareware.com

10.5 Evaluating the Quality of a Software Package

The value of any software package has to be measured against the following question: How does this software help you to do your work better or faster? Remember the saying, "All that glitters is not gold?" To assume that all software has some value is a mistake. Good productivity software makes it possible for a person to do something faster, easier, or more efficiently. It may also make it possible to produce something of a higher quality than could be done without the software.

To determine the value of any software, look at how well the software was designed in terms of making it easy for the intended *user*. The term *user friendly* is used to describe software that is easy to use. Programs that seem difficult to master are not considered user friendly.

Careful planning needs to go into the development of software in order to anticipate problems the user might encounter. As you will discover, all software packages are not equal in terms of user friendliness. Sometimes the user will face a dead end and the computer will not respond to your actions and offers no suggestion on how to escape or continue. Being unable to work with the program can frustrate the user. These are just some examples of poor technical quality that results in unfriendly software.

10.6 Guidelines for Evaluating Software

Here are several useful guidelines to consider when acquiring productivity software:

1. *Compatibility.* When purchasing software, read carefully on the package to determine the system requirements. Is the software compatible with your computer hardware?
2. *Speed of Operation.* The program should operate efficiently without "lags" to complete commands.
3. *Logical Screen Arrangement.* Options and operations should be displayed clearly and logically.
4. *Ease of Use.* Programs should be easy to understand and to use.
5. *User Guide.* The user guide should be written clearly and be arranged logically. It should be written from the user's point of view and should explain clearly how the program operates.
6. *Functionality.* The most important consideration in evaluating any computer program is determining how well it performs a useful task.

10.7 Undesirable Software Features

Some of the most bothersome problems encountered in productivity software are listed below:

1. *Any Sound That Cannot Be Controlled.* Sound can be an effective motivation, but it can also be distracting in an office or computer lab. Constant repetition of the same sound can be extremely annoying.
2. *Technical Problems.* Some software contains flaws. Even expensive software may contain a *bug* that causes it to crash or perform an unexpected operation.
3. *Inadequate Instructions.* Users should not have to guess how a program operates. All necessary instructions should be included either on screen or in the written program documentation.
4. *Errors of Any Kind.* Poor quality control resulting in misspelled words or random errors should be avoided.
5. *Poor Documentation (or No Documentation).* All of the items described should be included along with a set of clear instructions that tell the user what a program is supposed to do and how it does it.

10.8 Conclusion

In this module, you have been introduced to a variety of productivity software programs, and you have learned how to evaluate and select programs that best meet your needs. These skills and concepts should enhance your understanding of how the computer can be used to enhance your personal productivity.

Key Terms

Authoring software
Apple App Store
exPressit
Communications software
Compatibility
Google Calendar
Desktop publishing
Download.com
SurveyMonkey
Skype
Functionality
Google Picasa
Android Market
PIMS
Presentation software
Google Docs
User Friendly
User guides

Computer Application Assignment

Productivity Software Review

Select a productivity software program to review. It can be one of the programs discussed in this module or it can be another program of your choice. Run the program and work through it to produce an appropriate application of your choice such as a greeting card, budget, tax report, or newsletter, depending of the type of program that you have chosen. After producing your application, write a brief report (about 1 page or so) about your experience using the program. Put the title of the program that you used and t he publisher on the first line of your report. Enter your name and the current date on the 2nd line. Your report should include the following elements:

- Program title and publisher
- Your name and the current date
- A brief description of your experience in using the program
- An evaluation of the program based on the criteria given in Section 9.6 of this module

Submit your software review together with the application that you produced with the software either in print form or electronically as directed by your instructor.

MODULE II

Computer Application Skills

Computer Application Skills

This module is different from the other modules. The purpose of this last module is to provide you with an opportunity to review and practice the computer skills that you have learned in previous modules. No new information is presented in this module. References to previous modules are provided, rather than step-by-step directions. Refer to previous modules for how-to-instructions if necessary.

Documents that you prepare for this module should be professional in appearance, so take care to complete the assignments thoroughly and correctly. This module does not have a reading assignment or test component, so your evaluation will be based entirely on the computer application assignments.

Materials Needed to Complete this Module

- This book
- *Microsoft Office*
- *Adobe Photoshop*
- Internet access
- Flash drive or other storage media on which to store your work. (These may be the same disks you used for previous modules.)

How to Proceed

To receive credit for *Module 11* you must successfully complete 4 of the following 5 assignments:

Assignment 1 - Resume with cover letter

Assignment 2 - Spreadsheet & PowerPoint Presentation

Assignment 3 - News Article Research

Assignment 4 - Software Brochure

Assignment 5 - Digital Imaging

11.1 Computer Application Assignments

This module contains 5 Computer Application Assignments. Complete any 4 of the 5 assignments. Each assignment will take time and thought on your part. These assignments are designed to give you practice in real world activities using the knowledge you have gained through this book. Please be sure to allow yourself adequate time to properly complete the 4 assignments in this module. After completing your assignments, use the *Module 11* Checklist to be certain that you have prepared and printed all of the work assigned.

Assignment 1: Create a Resume with an Employer File and Letter

For this assignment, you will create a resume, an employer data source file, and an employment cover letter that will be merged with the employer file. Review Modules 3 and 4 as needed to complete this assignment.

1. First, create a resume. The information that you include in it may be either factual or imaginary. The resume should be at least 1 full page in length. Include your name and information about yourself, your experiences, and your job objectives. See Figure 11.1 for a sample resume.

   Save and print your resume.

2. After you create your resume, create an employer data source file using the *Mail Merge Tool* available in *MS Word* as you did in *Module 4*. This file should include records for 6 potential employers. Records should include the following fields:

- Company Name
- Mailing Address
- City
- State
- ZIP Code
- Name of the Contact Person
- Title of Contact Person
- FAX Number of Contact Person
- E-mail Address of Contact Person
- Phone Number of Contact Person

Employer records can contain either real or fictitious information. See Figure 11.2 for a sample employer data file.

After you create your employer file, save it to your disk.

Print the employer file to turn in to your instructor as part of this assignment.

3. After you have finished both the resume and employer data source file, create a form letter, which will be used as a cover letter to be sent to potential employers. The content of your letter may be anything that is useful to you. However, you should include all of the mail merge fields in your letter. Merge the fields from the employer data source file with the letter. Also, insert the current date into your letter. See Figure 11.3 for a sample letter with merged fields.

- Save your form letter.
- Complete a mail merge.
- Save your work.
- Print the first 2 (only) mail merged letters to be submitted to your instructor.

For this assignment, you will turn in these items:

√ Your resume

√ Employer data source file with 6 employer records

√ Form letter showing mail merge fields

√ 2 mail merged letters

2314 Utica Dr.,
Lubbock, Tx 79602

Phone: 806-788-2314
Fax: 806-789-0098

Carrie Price

Objective — **Secondary English/Journalism Teacher**

Experience

Spring, 2003 — **Student Teacher** — Wolffarth High School

- Taught gifted and talented class in Honors English.
- Tutored students in English 101 in all areas of English.
- Constructed tests and graded assignments for 5 English classes.
- Administered standardized tests.
- Participated in parent – teacher conferences, planning committees, and PTA meetings.

2002-2003 — **Teacher Aide** — Wayside High School

- Tutored students in junior English classes in after school program.
- Assisted teachers in preparing class materials and exams.
- Conducted small group instruction in English classes

2001-2002 — **Volunteer** — Women's Protective Services

- Office assistant for office.
- Assisted battered women and children in finding shelter.
- Contacted and dealt with Police as needed regarding resident cases.

Summers 2000 - 2001 — **Girl Scout Camp Counselor** — Camp Hilldale, TX

- Supervised troup activites.
- Assisted girls with planning and trip activities.
- Conducted field trips and social functions with other counselors.

Education

2000-2003 — **Texas Tech University**

- B.S. in Secondary Education
- Graduated *summa cum laude*.
- Vice President, Future Teachers Association

Interests — Camping, Canoeing, Piano, Photography

Figure 11.1: A Sample Resume

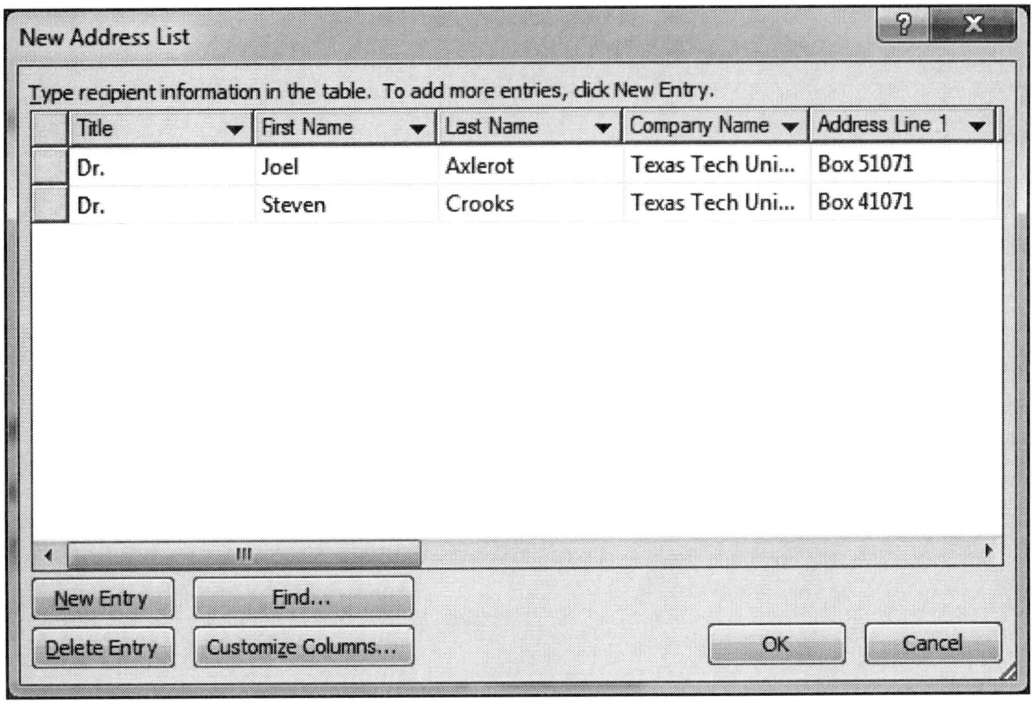

Figure 11.2: Sample Employer Data Entry Showing Fields

John Crooks
2314 Utica Avenue
Lubbock, Tx 79423

Phone: 806-123-4567

6/16/2011

«Contact_Person»
«Company_Name»
«Street Address»
«City», «State», «Zip_Code»

Dear **«Contact_Person»**

I would like to apply for a position as a secondary English teacher with **«Company_Name».** Enclosed is my resume.

Please feel free to contact me at any time. I am available for an interview at your convenience.

Figure 11.3: Partial Cover Letter Showing Fields for Mail Merge

Assignment 2: Create a Spreadsheet Graph and PowerPoint Presentation

For this assignment, you will create a spreadsheet showing income for an organization that includes a column chart. Import the column chart into a *PowerPoint* presentation that you design. Review Modules 5 and 6 as necessary to complete this assignment.

1. First, create a spreadsheet using *MS Excel.*

Assume that you are the treasurer for an organization (fraternity, sorority, PTA, church group, or other group of your choice). Assume that you were in charge of a recent fundraiser and are responsible for reporting the amount of money raised.

Create a spreadsheet in *MS Excel* that includes the amount of money that was collected. Include four or five categories of income and totals in your spreadsheet. Make up the data entries.

Create a column chart that illustrates the monthly totals. The chart/graph will be placed into your *PowerPoint* presentation.

Save your spreadsheet to your disk.

Print a copy showing the spreadheet with the chart to turn in to your instructor.

2. Second, create a 6-slide *PowerPoint* presentation to show the results of your fund raising activity to a meeting of your organization. Use appropriate layout and content planning as discussed in *Module 8.*

The presentation should contain the fundraiser chart that you created in Step 1. You can make up other information concerning the fundraiser to include in your presentation.

Include at least 1 graphic that is appropriate to the content of the presentation.

Save your presentation to your disk or other storage medium.

Print the presentation in a *Handout* format showing 6 slides per page (See Figure 11.4) to turn in to your instructor.

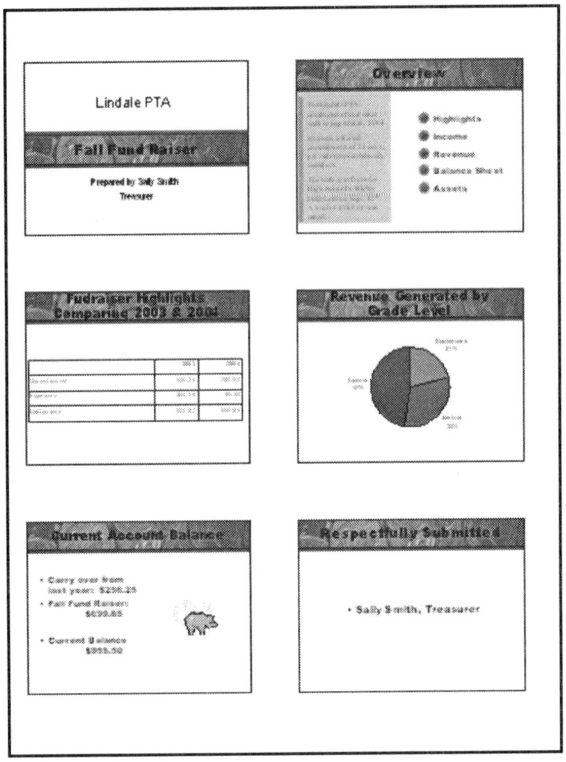

Figure 11.4 Sample Assignment 2
(6 Slide Handout, Including *Excel* Graph)

Assignment 3: Research a News Story

Assume that you have recently been hired at a local newspaper. You have been tasked with researching a current news topic and preparing a brief report (1 or 2 pages) for your editor. You may choose the topic, but it must have been "news" within the past 3 months. You might choose a topic in politics, international affairs, medicine, or entertainment. You will first use the Internet to gather current information about your topic. The second part of this assignment is to find background information on your topic using multimedia CD-ROMs or the Internet. You will be using word processing skills acquired in Modules 3 and 4, the Internet skills acquired in *Module 9*, and the tool software covered in *Module 10*. Refer to these modules as necessary as you complete this assignment. Use *MS Word* to prepare your report.

Open *MS Word* before you begin your searches. Place your name, your topic, and the current date at the top of your report.

First, conduct 2 different Internet searches on your chosen topic. A good place to begin your search would be a news organization. Several web sites are provided on the next page. You can use any search engine such as *Yahoo! or Google.* Both have many links to news organizations and special interest groups.

Some other sources of information are:

www.news.com

www.cnn.com

www.abcnews.com

www.cbsnews.com

www.nbcnews.com

Summarize the information you find in your searches into a report of about 1 page or less. Include the Web site addresses of your sources of information.

Second, conduct an Internet search to find background information related to your topic. Summarize the information that you find to include in your report. Remember to make your report concise, with a length of 1 page or less. You may use the copy and paste function. Include a picture or graphic if one is available.

Save your report to your disk and print it to turn in to your instructor.

Assignment 4: Create a Software Brochure

Assume that you have a summer job working for a local computer store. Your employer wants you to prepare a brochure highlighting some personal productivity applications of computers which can be given out to customers. The brochure would give customers ideas that could motivate them to purchase a computer as well as promote sales of the store software. You will use skills that you learned in desktop publishing from *Module 7* and also some productivity software information which was covered in *Module 10*. Refer to these modules as necessary as you prepare your brochure.

First, review three or four productivity software programs of your choice, and write a brief report on each one using *MS Word*. One paragraph on each program will be adequate. Give the program name and a brief description of it along with some of the highlights of the program.

Second, using *MS Publisher*, create a brochure using one of the brochure templates. Copy and paste your reviews into the brochure. Format your brochure for a professional appearance.

Save your brochure to your flash drive. Print it to turn in to your instructor.

Assignment 5: Digital Imaging

Using *Adobe Photoshop* and a photograph of your choice, edit the image for a better or more functional appearance. Refer to *Module 8* for instructions on using *Photoshop*. You may use one of the sample pictures on your computer or one of your own pictures. Use at least 5 of the editing features listed below in editing your photograph.

1. Add text (such as a title or labels)
2. Adjust the contrast and brightness or color balance
3. Correct perspective distortion
4. Remove an unwanted picture element from the photograph
5. Copy or add new picture elements to the photograph
6. Change the image size or orientation
7. Crop the image

Save your edited photograph and print it to submit to your instructor. Also, write a brief report (about ½ page) listing and describing the changes you made to your picture editing it with *Photoshop*.

11.2 Module 11 Checklist

Before submitting Module 11 to your instructor, review this checklist to be certain that you have completed all 5 of the assignments completely.

Assignment 1 Requirements

- Resume
- Employer data source file
- Form letter showing mail merge fields
- 2 Mail merged cover letters

Assignment 2 Requirements

- *Excel* spreadsheet file showing graph or chart
- *PowerPoint* Presentation in handout format (6 slides per page)

Assignment 3 Requirements

- Report showing summary and background information from 2 web searches

Assignment 4 Requirements

- Software brochure created with *MS Publisher*

Assignment 5 Requirements

- Edited digital Photograph
- Brief report listing and describing the changes made to your photograph in editing

11.3 Conclusion

The material presented in this book was designed to help you become familiar with the world of computers and related technology. You have learned *about* computers, but more importantly, you have learned *how to use computers* to improve your personal productivity through specific skills in using word processing, electronic spreadsheets, desktop publishing, computer graphics, telecommunications, digital imaging, the Internet, presentation graphics, and tool software. The self-guided mastery approach applied in this book was designed for independent learning. By mastering each of the modules, you should have gained the skills and confidence necessary to be comfortable in the use of computers in each of these applications.

While no attempt was made here to cover every aspect and detail of the computer applications that were presented, the most important and most commonly used skills were included. You should now have a good idea of how you can extend your knowledge through use of software help features and resources on the World Wide Web. Use the base of knowledge that you have built to learn more.

Like all skills, the computer skills that you have learned through this book will fade with time if they are not reinforced through continued use. Keep this book as a reference to review these skills as necessary.